ARE YOU MORAL?

Ronald Suter

UNIVERSITY
PRESS OF
AMERICA

LANHAM • NEW YORK • LONDON

University Press of America,™ Inc.

4720 Boston Way
Lanham, MD 20706

3 Henrietta Street
London WC2E 8LU England

ISBN (Perfect): 0-8191-4299-9
ISBN (Cloth): 0-8191-4298-0

All University Press of America books are produced on acid-free
paper which exceeds the minimum standards set by the National
Historical Publications and Records Commission.

For

Sonia and Monica

ACKNOWLEDGMENTS

I have incurred many debts in writing <u>Are You Moral?</u>. In 1982, I used an early draft in a graduate seminar in ethics at Michigan State University, and since then I have used later versions in our introductory ethics course. I was helped by the reactions of both groups. From Thomas Burke, Chris Couch, Jahan Eftekhar, Toby Conley, Phillip Singer, Roy Sorensen, Sonia Suter, Ronald Tiller, Stuart Warner, and Betsy White I received many valuable comments and suggestions. Ronald Tiller and Stuart Warner were especially helpful in their cross-questioning.

My work has benefited from the encouragement and comments of my colleagues as well, several of whom read and criticized all or part of the manuscript: Martin Benjamin, Albert Cafagna, George Ferree, Richard Hall, George Kerner, Donald Koch, Richard Peterson, Craig Staudenbaur, Scott Vaughn, and Winston Wilkinson. I feel particularly fortunate to be able to discuss my ideas with such intelligent, open-minded, and congenial colleagues, each of whom has his own unique approach to philosophy. Among them my heaviest debts are to Martin Benjamin, Donald Koch, and Winston Wilkinson. They each gave me detailed criticisms of the entire manuscript—criticisms that improved it significantly.

There are others I should also like to thank: Professor William Frankena of the University of Michigan for his helpful comments on my account of moral reasons; Steven Holtzman, Ohio's Director of the Thomas Alva Edison Program and former Rhodes Scholar, for his thorough critique of the first three chapters; Professor Sidney Chapman of Richland College for his evaluative comments on my discussion of utilitarianism; Janice Cohen for pointing out certain infelicities in an earlier draft; Mimi Grover for suggesting the title; and Jahan Eftekhar and Stuart Warner for their help with the index. I also wish to thank Betsy White for her assistance with the bibliography; Beth Rigby for unraveling the mysteries of a complex word processor; and Katherine McCracken for her careful and always intelligent editing.

Finally, I am grateful to my wife, Carmen, for her comments and encouragement.

CONTENTS

PART TWO: SOME MAJOR ETHICAL THEORIES

PREFACE

Everyday we are faced with choices and decisions, with competing alternatives. Some choices are easy, others problematic; some are trivial, others important. For most of us, it is usually a minor and easy decision, for example, whether to go to the movies or to buy a record, whether to wear a blue or brown sweater, and so on. It is generally much tougher—and certainly more momentous—to decide whether to put your mother in a home for the aged or to invite her to live in your home, whether to get a job or to go to college. When we choose from the available alternatives, we typically weigh the pros and cons of each, evaluating their relative importance and consequences. This means making value judgments. We cannot avoid making such judgments. For whenever we decide to do any thing, our decision will be based on our conscious or unconscious values and beliefs. I imply that our inmost beliefs and values may be unconscious, because sometimes we are unaware of them, and it is generally hard to say what beliefs and values we hold and how they affect our lives. Yet we can become more aware of them by considering how we live, the moral problems we have, how we reason about moral questions, and how we respond to traditional ethical theories. One of the aims of this book is to help make us more conscious of the values we hold and to see whether, and how far, they are moral ones. Thus it should help each of us to answer the questions "Am I moral? and "If I am, how moral am I?" increasing our self-knowledge.

There is a sense in which no one can make our decisions for us; only we can make them. For even if we follow someone else's advice and values, the decisions or choices to follow that advice, or those values, will itself be ours. In another sense, others can make decisions for us if we let them. And some decisions we shall, and probably should, sometimes even must, let others make for us. For example, we shall probably let the dentist choose which denture adhesive to use to keep in our false teeth, the surgeon decide how to set our broken bones, and maybe the professional wine taster select the wine for dinner. It would also be sensible for most of us to let the defense lawyer decide on what strategy to employ in defending us against a charge of bribery or conspiracy, since lawyers understand better than we the problems that arise in the prosecution of such cases. In all of these matters we defer to the expertise of others. I shall argue that moral decisions, in contrast, we cannot let others make for us, for here there is no such thing as expertise.

I am assuming that not all of the choices and problems we confront are moral. For example, it is not generally a moral question whether I should eat peas with a knife or a fork, whether I hang an etching by Picasso or by Rembrandt in the living room, whether I buy stocks or invest in the money market, or put six rather than five inches of insulation in the attic. These are questions of etiquette, aesthetics, economics, and technology. Of course, such questions may also become moral questions in certain contexts. So we should not assume that because a problem is, say, an economic problem, it cannot also be a moral problem. Indeed, probably most major economic problems--the unemployment problem, the problem of inflation--are also in part moral problems. They are also moral problems because they involve moral considerations. Thus, while there are questions that are not generally moral questions, there are others that are mixed or have a moral dimension. Finally, there are choices and problems that are simply moral. Strange as it may seem, books on ethics sometimes fail to mention any genuine ethical or moral problem. I do not want to be guilty of this omission. So I shall begin by describing briefly several moral problems and disputes drawn from both literature and life. These concrete issues should keep us from losing touch with basic moral realities. I also shall attempt to derive from them an account of moral problems, moral disagreements, and moral reasoning. We shall then see how such reasoning differs from mathematical, scientific, and technical reasoning, and why there cannot be any moral experts. These will constitute the major topics of the first part of this book.

In Part Two, we shall look at some important normative proposals--so-called ethical theories. First, at approbative theories--such as subjectivism, conventionalism, divine-command theory, the golden rule. Then, at objectivist theories--ethical egoism, utilitarianism, two formulations of Kant's ethics, the appeal to nature for moral guidance, and agapism or the ethics of love. Philosophers have put forward these different views to enable us to solve our moral problems and to settle our moral disagreements. We shall examine each of these to see how helpful it is in dealing with these problems and disputes and see what can be said both for and against the proposal. We shall find that there is no single basis or formula for deciding moral questions that all morally competent and rational people must or can accept. I shall try to show that the sole surviving normative position will be a certain intuitionist form of moderate deontological objectivism.

The book has a glossary of relevant philosophical terms to help the reader new to philosophy and a lengthy bibliography to help him or her go more deeply into the subjects covered here. The bibliography also includes other subjects not dealt with but directly relevant--for example, the moral virtues and vices. Occasional comments are made on these works where it is thought they may be useful.

PART ONE

MORAL PROBLEMS, DISAGREEMENTS, AND REASONING

CHAPTER I

EXAMPLES OF MORAL PROBLEMS AND

MORAL DISAGREEMENTS

First moral problem: whether a young Frenchman should stay with his dependent mother or go off to fight with the Free French. This example of a genuine moral problem comes from Sartre (1905-1980), the famous French philosopher. Here is how Sartre describes the dilemma faced by his student, whom I am calling Francois:

> [Francois's] father was on bad terms with his mother, and, moreover, was inclined to be a collaborationist; his older brother had been killed in the German offensive of 1940, and the young man . . . wanted to avenge him. His mother lived alone with him, very much upset by the half-treason of her husband and the death of her older son; the boy was her only consolation.
>
> The boy was faced with the choice of leaving for England and joining the Free French Forces—that is, leaving his mother behind—or remaining with his mother and helping her to carry on. He was fully aware that the woman lived only for him and that his going off—and perhaps his death—would plunge her into despair. He was also aware that every act that he did for his mother's sake was a sure thing, in the sense that it was helping her to carry on, whereas every effort he made toward going off and fighting was an uncertain move which might run aground and prove completely useless; for example, on his way to England, he might, while passing through Spain, be detained indefinitely in a Spanish camp; he might reach England or Algiers and be stuck in an office at a desk job.[1]

In short, Francois is torn between two courses of action that seem to exclude each other. His loyalty to his mother and his loyalty to his country and his brother's memory tug him in opposite directions. I

----

1. Jean-Paul Sartre Existentialism and Human Emotion, tr. Bernard Frechtman (New York: Philosophical Library, 1957), pp 24-25.

owe so much to both, he thinks. Yet if I fight for my country, how can I be the anchor of my mother's life that she now needs? But if I stay with her, I let down my country and my brother. Francois's problem is to choose between these two courses of action, to decide which one he ought to follow.

A second moral problem: whether Gauguin should leave his wife and family or abandon his art. I use the name 'Gauguin' here because Paul Gauguin, the nineteenth-century French painter, apparently felt a conflict between familial responsibilities and his work. He eventually left his wife and children and a successful business as a stockbroker to become a "real painter." "Art is a jealous mistress," observes Emerson;[2] she demands lavish homage. So what is a man to do who comes to the conclusion that he must either leave his wife and family, whom he loves deeply, or abandon his art, which is his life? Should home responsibilities and rearing your children always be put first? Or can it be morally acceptable to desert your family in this rather special case? We can well imagine such a person feeling like saying, "I wish to God I knew what I ought to do."

A third, closely related moral problem: whether Emily, in her early twenties should leave her loving but possessive and emotionally and financially dependent father to accept a challenging job in another state.[3] Her father opposes the move. He is now a widower and has no other children and few friends. He reminds Emily of all the sacrifices he has made for her, working long hours to give her a much better education than he had. Emily does not want to be ungrateful or unkind, and she feels a protective anxiety for her father. She is afraid that her father may become depressed and perhaps even commit suicide if she leaves. She would like to loosen the bonds, which often seem like chains to her, and to accept the challenge of the new job, yet she is concerned that her father may go to pieces and suffer financial hardship should she leave. Could she live with that awareness? What is she to do?

---

2. Ralph Waldo Emerson, his essay "Wealth" in the Conduct of Life, The Complete writings of Ralph Waldo Emerson, vol. 1 (New York: William H. Wise & Co., 1929), p.554.

3. In Robert Anderson's broadway play and movie, I Never Sang for My Father (1968), the main character, Gene, has a similar problem with his demanding eighty year old father, Tom. Gene struggles to determine the limits of his obligation to himself versus his duty to his ailing father. This conflict between personal freedom and self-fulfillment, on the one hand, and commitment to another person and family, on the other hand, is a frequent theme in literature and a common occurrence in life.

A _fourth moral problem_: whether Tex, father of three young children, aged three, five, and eight, should ask for a separation from Felice, whom he loves. For several years Felice has been having an affair with another woman. She thinks the world of her husband and her female lover and it would distress her to give up either. On the one hand, Tex says he has a good intellectual and physical relationship with his wife, whom he sees as a wonderful mother to their children. He says he wants to respect Felice's honest needs and desires and not treat her as his property. On the other hand, he is pained and humiliated by the affair and strongly resents Felice on account of it. Should he ask for a separation or try to accept the situation with good humor? And would it make a difference to the case if Felice's affair were heterosexual?

A _fifth moral problem_: whether Jeannie should report her class-mate for cheating on a couple of important examinations. Suppose her school uses the honor system and the exams are graded on a curve. Not reporting him would mean that some of the abler students would get lower grades and perhaps not be admitted into professional or graduate school. That would not be fair. Yet reporting the cheater would probably mean destroying a talented person's career, which does not seem to Jeannie to make much sense or to be very humane. Thus humanity and justice seem to tell her to do different things. She wonders whether there are not times when cheating is excusable or forgivable and whether this is one of them. She agonizes: "Should I be a narc?"

A _sixth moral problem_: whether Carmen should tell her father that he has incurable cancer. Suppose earlier she promised she would tell him when he was dying. She thinks that he may feel betrayed if he learns that he has been misled. Another part of her worries about the harm she may do to her own integrity if she keeps him in the dark. But she is also convinced that the knowledge that he is dying will increase his suffering and perhaps even hasten his end. Part of her inclines to the line from Shakespeare that goes, "Though it be honest, it is never good to bring bad news" (_Anthony and Cleopatra_, II, v. 85). Ought she to deceive her father about the truth of his condition?

A _seventh moral problem_: whether Isabella, of Shakespeare's _Measure for Measure_, should sleep with Angelo. Angelo is the Duke's deputy and a hard-hearted and corrupt man who has sentenced Isabella's brother, Claudio, to die for having had sexual intercourse with his fiancee. The law in that time and place was that a sexual relationship between unmarried people—even those who are engaged—is punishable by death, but no one had been condemned to die for the offense before. Isabella, who intends to become a nun, pleads with Angelo to spare her brother. He agrees to do so but only if—as he quaintly puts it—she lays "down the treasures of [her] body" for him. (We can easily think up variations of Isabella's problem if we consider twentieth-century rapists and the less poetically worded threats they

-5-

level at their victims.) Isabella is, of course, horrified. She sees this as a "foul redemption," as an "abhorr'd pollution," as utterly shameful (Measure for Measure, II, iv). Yet she wants to save her brother. How should Isabella deal with her dilemma? Would it make a difference if she did not intend to become a nun and she had been very promiscuous?

The eighth and final moral problem: whether Mack should kill the rapist-murderer who raped and murdered his wife and four other innocent women. Suppose that through skillful plea-bargaining the murderer, a clever ex-criminal-justice major, has succeeded in making a mockery of justice and as a result will be back on the streets in only ten years. Suppose, further, that psychologists estimate that the chances of his murdering again are about twenty-five percent. Should Mack take the law into his own hands and avenge those this woman-hater killed? He believes he has the courage to risk his life doing this. But he hesitates. He remembers John Locke's remark, "Wherever Law ends, Tyranny begins. . . ." (Concerning Civil Government, Second Essay, sec. 202). It strikes him as an awesome thing to take the life of another human being, however vicious. Besides, he wonders whether the fellow may not have come to terms with himself after so many years, whether he may not be a reformed person. Perhaps, after all, he is not irredeemably bad. Mack fears that he may be diminished morally if he either murders or does not murder this man. He is not at all sure what he should do.

You might, at this point, become a little frustrated, since it has not been made clear what any of the solutions are to the eight problems. My aim has not been to find solutions for them that we can all agree on, but initially only to give illustrations of moral problems that people have. I shall offer next examples of what I hope are equally genuine moral disagreements. Our first major aim after we consider these examples will be to discover the nature of a moral problem and the nature of a moral disagreement.

First moral disagreement: Isabella versus her brother. It is not hard to understand how Isabella's problem (the seventh moral problem) can lead to a moral disagreement. Remember, Angelo tells Isabella that if she does not sleep with him, her brother dies. In the end, she decides that her main obligation is to keep her vows and to preserve her chastity, resolving:

> Then, Isabel, live chaste, and brother, die:
> More than our brother is our chastity.

> [Measure for Measure, II, iv]

Not surprisingly, her brother takes a different view of the matter. When he hears her decision, he pleads:

-6-

Sweet Sister, let me live:
What sin you do to save a brother's life,
Nature dispenses with the deed so far
That it becomes a virtue.

She replies harshly:

O you beast!
O faithless coward! O dishonest wretch!
Wilt thou be made a man out of my vice?
Is't not a kind of incest, to take life
From thine own sister's shame?

[III, i]

Here we have a genuine moral conflict. (And we could easily develop a similar one between a twentieth-century brother and sister who have both been kidnaped by a rapist.) Try to put yourself into the position of the two disputants. Which one seems to you to be right? Why? And how would you propose resolving the disagreement?

A second moral disagreement over birth control. A Roman Catholic housewife—let us call her Patricia—constantly praises large families, remarking that they are a blessing and that it is unnatural to try to limit family size by contraception—that is, by coitus interruptus, by using the pill, a diaphragm, a cervical cap, a condom, or the like. These devices falsify and demean the sexual act that should be treated as a sacrament. In fact, they destroy the very meaning of coitus. After all, Patricia argues, one of the primary purposes of marriage and intercourse is procreation, which contraception is designed to prevent. Contraception thus goes against nature. And is also goes against God's law. So it is a sin against both divine and natural law.

Jan, her neighbor, disputes this, asking, first, whether we can know God's will concerning the purpose of coitus. (The question of knowing God's will is relevant to the divine-command theory, which is discussed in Chapter V.) Maybe God want us to do it for fun. Jan claims that we have no good basis for thinking that our using contraceptive devices should be offensive to God. And as for the second point, that contraception goes against nature, she says it no more does so than it goes against nature for men to shave their faces, women their armpits and legs, people to have cancers removed by surgery, or communities to build aqueducts for irrigation purposes. Surely we do not wish to issue a blanket condemnation of these activities. Quite the contrary. Hence she concludes that we can reject the contention that birth control violates either natural or divine law. Finally, Jan argues that using contraceptives is not only morally permissible but often obligatory as well. For in the absence of contraception, sexual activity on the part of married and unmarried couples will often result in the birth of a child as often as every year. But having so many children will harm everyone involved—the mother, the father, the children already born, the community, and future generations. It will be much harder—and after a while impossible—to feed, to clothe, and to educate so many people. Moreover, if couples are forced to abstinence as the only accepted way of regulating their offspring, this may eventually endanger heterosexual love.

Who is right, Patricia or Jan? What stand do you take on this controversial issue? Finally, how would you argue for the correctness of your position?

A third moral disagreement: whether there should be capital punishment for convicted first-degree murderers. Joe argues for imposing the death penalty on murderers, not only because it serves as a deterrent, but, more important, because it is a way of establishing our respect for human life and the moral order. If we really care about people, we shall not take their murder lightly. Indeed, we shall make those who deliberately deprive them of life themselves pay the supreme penalty. This is just and also guarantees that they will never again kill another human being.

Tarron counters that nothing can justify such a cruel punishment. He has witnessed an execution and was appalled by the mental anguish and human suffering and says nothing can justify our imposing such a dreadful punishment on anyone. If we really want to show respect for human life, we shall ourselves never deliberately take it. He contends that Joe's argument makes the elementary mistake of assuming that two wrongs can make a right.

Which is the correct view, Joe's or Tarron's?

A fourth moral disagreement between a Jehovah's Witness and a doctor. Suppose that a nearly adult, seventeen-year-old Jehovah's Witness named Barbara has been seriously hurt in an automobile accident. It is clear from a medical point of view that the girl needs a blood transfusion. Indeed, the doctor who is present points out that she might die without such treatment. Barbara agrees—she is a premed student and understands the condition she is in. Yet she protests. She will not have a transfusion administered. She contends that transfusions are prohibited by her religion and by the Bible. She quotes Leviticus 17:10: "Whatsoever man . . . eateth any manner of blood; I will . . . cut him off from among his people." And she quotes from Acts: "Abstain from . . . things strangled, and from blood." Her attitude is: if it is God's will that I die now, so be it. For, as is stated in Psalms 19:9, "the judicial decisions of Jehovah are true; they have proved altogether righteous." It is not that Barbara wants to die. Far from it. But she is courageously willing to take that risk rather than violate what she believes to be Jehovah's commandment. And she is convinced that she will, in some sense, have an everlasting life even if she does die now.

Is there any hope that Barbara and the doctor can rationally resolve their dispute? How?

A fifth moral disagreement over turning in a drug pusher to the law. Officer Tracy, from the narcotics squad, asks Leary, a high school student, to help combat the serious drug problem in the grade schools. Leary once was himself a heavy user of illegal drugs, but is now clean. Since he knows all the local pushers of narcotics, he is asked to report their names to the police. Leary thinks that would be a mean and sneaky thing to do. He does not want to rat on his friends. "What kind of a friend would I be if I did that?" he asks. "These guys trust me!" "But they are ruining many innocent children's lives," the officer replies. "They are getting them hooked on a filthy habit, undermining their health, their intellectual capacities, and teaching them not to face up to life's problems. How can you not help us when you know the harm these pushers are causing these vulnerable, naive kids. You could procure far more good for many more people if you cooperated with us."

Is there any way our disputants can come to an agreement?

A sixth moral disagreement between a sixteenth-century Christian missionary and an Aztec cannibal who wants to eat the heart of a conquistador killed in battle. Suppose that the Aztec regards his cannibalistic act as a way of showing respect for the courageous warrior killed in battle. We may imagine that the missionary has an equally high regard for courage and that he also wants to show respect for the fallen warrior. He will nevertheless vehemently oppose the proposed action of the cannibal. Or, for a related twentieth-century case, consider the disagreement among passengers in the Andes plane crash in 1972 who argued that they should eat the dead bodies of their friends to survive and those who were horrified by the thought. There was no disagreement among them that eating human flesh would increase their chances of survival. It was their only source of food after the chocolate, wine, jam, and canned fish were finished. As one of the more religious among them said, "It is meat. That's all it is. The souls have left their bodies and are in heaven with God. All that is left here are the carcasses, which are no more human beings than the dead flesh of the cattle we eat at home.[4] Several of the people argued that they ought to eat the bodies of their dead companions, otherwise they would die; and it was their duty to live, both for their own sake and for the sake of their families. A minority said they could not do it. It was too revolting, too horrible.

---

4. Quoted in Piers Paul Read's Alive: The Story of the Andes Survivors (New York: J.B. Lippincott Co., 1974), p.83.

Who is right, if anyone? Must the resolutions of the cases go hand in hand? Apparently the Roman Catholic Church does not think so. For the New York City Roman Catholic Archdiocese said on December 27, 1972, that the survivors of the plane crash in the Andes "acted justifiably" when they ate parts of the bodies of their dead companions to keep from starving to death (New York Times, 28 December 1982). It is unlikely that the Church would say the same of the Aztec's contemplated act.

A seventh moral disagreement: a well-off business woman, eager to make more money, plans to expand her chain of fast-food restaurants. She anticipates an eleven to fifteen percent sales gain. Unfortunately, a likely consequence will be that her sister will no longer be able to run her small chicken place at a profit. She will not be able to compete, since her richer sister can buy much more cheaply at greater volume; hence the poorer sister will probably be forced out of business. She pleads with the entrepreneur to cancel her expansion plans. "Have some feelings of loyalty!" she demands. The more prosperous sister assures her that she does, but that business is business. She says what she plans on doing is perfectly legal and that she will be making more money by fair means. "But not innocently," her sister melodramatically counters. "It will be blood money!"

Who is right? Would it be wrong for the woman to go forward with her business expansion?

Eighth and final moral disagreement: whether a cattleman should not stop cooping up and force-feeding his steers to raise his meat yield and hence his profit. Replying to his critics from the Humane Society, he says he would not do it if they were cows. "Cows bruise more easily and their being too confined might affect the milk yield." "That's not the point," says the defender of animals. "You're causing the steers discomfort and probably needless suffering as well." The cattleman replies that he treats all his animals as business objects. "Don't you remember God's very first commandment to mankind in the book of Genesis? It was that we were to have dominion over the fish of the sea and over the birds of the air and over everything that moves upon the earth." The critic answers: "But that doesn't mean we can do whatever we like with them. We have a moral responsibility to treat them well and with care and to avoid cruelty to animals. 'Dominion' does not mean 'unrestrained maltreatment and exploitation'. It means we are to serve as steward and protector of all God's creatures."

Which position, if either, is correct in your view?

This brief sampling by no means exhausts the range of moral problems and moral disagreements people confront. I hope, however, that my examples are not too one-sided and that they are representative enough. The point of considering a number of variants is to enable us to check whether the characterization of moral problems and of moral disagreements that will be developed in the next chapter is accurate and sufficiently broad in scope.

CHAPTER II

THE NATURE OF A MORAL PROBLEM AND

OF A MORAL DISAGREEMENT

Eleven Characteristics of Moral
Problems and of Moral Disagreements

1. One characteristic of a moral problem is that (a) it is something had by at least one person, and that (b) it exists only if whoever has it perceives it as a problem. In these respects, as well as some others, moral problems resemble headaches: there are neither headaches nor moral problems without someone who feels them. (Not that they are literally headaches.) (b) implies that we cannot say somebody has a moral problem but is not bothered by it. It does allow us to say, however, that somebody should see something as a moral problem that he or she does not in fact see as a moral problem. Notice that on this account, members of a community or a family might have one and the same moral problem. A moral disagreement, in contrast, (a) requires at least two people; hence it may be compared to a telephone conversation or a tango. As it takes two to tango, so it takes at least two to have a moral disagreement. One or more persons take one side; one or more, the other. It is true that we sometimes speak of a person as being in disagreement with himself, which suggests that they do not require at least two people. But I think that such remarks are not meant to be taken literally. They are comparable to someone's being "all broken up," which seems to imply that he is in pieces. Yet someone may truly say, " I am all broken up," even when physically quite intact, since it is clearly meant metaphorically. A moral disagreement also differs from a moral problem in that (b) it can exist without those involved perceiving it as a disagreement. Thus we can speak of two people as being in disagreement about abortion, say, even if they themselves are not aware that they disagree on this issue.

2. While a person with a moral problem must be personally perplexed, or in a state of bewilderment, this is not necessary for moral disputants. The latter, in fact, are often, if not always, quite sure of the soundness of their positions. Think, for example, of the Jehovah's Witness and the doctor, in disagreement number four.

3. People with a moral problem are perplexed in a special way. They see themselves as facing a dilemma, as needing to choose between two or more unacceptable, or acceptable but mutually

incompatible, alternatives. The alternatives themselves may seem roughly equally attractive—you may feel that you ought to do both—yet that if either is done, you cannot do the other. Thus Jeannie in the fifth moral problem thought she should report the cheater and also that she should not. Her dilemma was that she could not do both—each ruled out (logically) the other. This characteristic, of facing a dilemma, need not apply individually to the people who disagree with one another morally.

4. Merely to confront a dilemma, however, is not yet to have a moral problem. The dilemma must be a moral one. That is to say, the person must have moral objections to at least one of the alternatives either in itself or because it rules out another morally compelling alternative. People with moral problems experience within themselves a conflict of rights or obligations, of values or reasons, some or all of which are moral. (I equate here moral reasons with moral values. The next chapter will give an account of moral reasons.) For example, Isabella (in the seventh problem) felt it a moral and religious obligation to preserve her chastity, to uphold her vows, and also to save her brother's life. It was these conflicting moral values that she had, or conflicting moral considerations, which pulled her in opposite directions, creating her nightmare. This is an example of what may be called a pure moral problem, since moral considerations tug her in both directions. Gauguin in the second moral problem (not necessarily the historical Gauguin) provides us with an example of an impure or mixed moral problem—specifically, a moral-aesthetic problem—because here a nonmoral value (the love of painting) competes with a moral one (concern to prevent the suffering of his wife and children). If he finally acts on the basis of the nonmoral considerations, his action will not be a moral one, in one sense of the word 'moral'. Instead, it will be a nonmoral action. This does not imply that it is morally wrong or that it is morally right, though it may be one or the other. That is, it may either be, or fail to be, moral in a second sense of the word as well. For the same reason, something cannot be a moral (as opposed to a nonmoral) judgment unless it is supported by one or more moral reasons. On the other hand, if Gauguin's moral values prevail—that is, carry greater weight with him—his action will be a moral one in this same sense of 'moral' in which 'moral' is contrasted with 'nonmoral'. Again, this will still leave it open whether his action is moral in the additional sense in which 'moral' means 'morally right'. There may or may not in fact be more powerful moral reasons for choosing a different course of action. A moral action in one sense of 'moral', then, is not necessarily moral in the other sense, though it may be.

Contrast next these moral dilemmas with a simple nonmoral dilemma. The city planners of East Lansing want to make it possible for cars to go faster down Grand River Avenue; they also want to make it easier for pedestrians to cross Grand River Avenue. If the pedestrians are given special privileges, traffic will be slowed; yet if the drivers reign supreme, it will get harder and harder to cross the

-14-

street. The dilemma is not a moral one as long as the only values or reasons involved are those of efficiency and convenience, because these are not moral considerations.

Let us return now to moral disagreements. Since people in moral disagreements need not be perplexed (point number 2, p. 13), they need not be perplexed in the special way of confronting a moral dilemma. But it is necessary that they be in opposition (whether they realize it or not) to someone else, if not with themselves; and this too is a conflict of obligations and values or reasons, some or all of which are moral. Thus, while the cattleman in the eighth moral disagreement defends his right to coop up and to force-feed his steers, his critic maintains that there are compelling moral reasons—it causes the animals discomfort and perhaps even needless suffering—why he should discontinue this practice. In this case the two disputants either have different values, or different ordering of priorities, and/or they assign different importance to their values. If both disputants support their positions with moral reasons, the disagreement may be called a pure moral disagreement. If only one does—for example, the cattleman merely gives the nonmoral arguments that it is to his advantage, that he makes more money this way—the dispute is an impure or mixed moral disagreement.

The next three points are corollaries that follow from the first four.

5. In a moral problem the conflict or split is in yourself. It is internal or intrapersonal. It is as though you had two or more inner voices urging you in conflicting directions. Thus Jeannie, in the fifth moral problem, told herself to report the cheater—it was the only just thing to do. Yet another voice in her replied that she should not do that, because it would probably mean destroying a talented person's career. In a moral disagreement, in contrast, the conflict or opposition is between or among people and not within a person: it is external or interpersonal. Here we literally find different people speaking, or being disposed to speak, on behalf of conflicting courses of action. For example, in the second moral disagreement, Patricia argues against the morality of contraception, while Jan defends it.

6. Typically the person who has a moral problem is unsure what to do, is torn between two or more alternative actions: this is what is under consideration. For example, Emily, in the third moral problem, does not know whether she should leave her father and take the challenging job in another state, and Gauguin, in the second moral problem, does not know whether he should leave his wife and family or abandon his art. If it were obvious to them what to do—for example, that they should stay at home—they would not have their moral problems. Notice that we might then say: "They should have a moral problem," either because their own professed values should produce a conflict in them, or because they would be better people if they had some additional values that would make them see their

-15-

situations as morally problematic. One qualification: most of the actions mentioned are purely "personal," involving only two or three individuals. But this is not essential. The actions may involve many people and future generations—as in the cases of using the atomic bomb and passing effective pollution legislation.

The same point holds for moral disagreements. Generally, the alternatives argued about in them are also actions, which may or may not be socially significant: whether capital punishment is ever moral (the third moral disagreement); whether Barbara should or should not be given a blood transfusion after the accident (the fourth disagreement); and so on. If the people discussing these questions were in agreement about whether the action ought to be performed or whether it is morally permissible, they would not have a moral disagreement about it.

However, one important qualification of the point must be mentioned here. People may have moral disagreements and moral problems about beliefs and attitudes as well as about actions. For example, Jones may think Smith should believe in Tom's honesty; Smith, that Jones should not have such a contemptuous attitude towards Sally. Similarly, a racist brought up to believe in individual rights may come to have a moral problem about whether he has the right attitude towards people of different races. He may come to be troubled about this and debate with himself the reasons both pro and con why his attitude towards them is morally right or wrong. In the discussion that follows I shall not focus on these sorts of moral problems and disagreements, since they are not the most common kind. Instead, I shall concentrate on the more typical kind—the kind that is concerned either with particular actions (for example, all the eight moral problems and most of the moral disagreements) or with kinds of actions (the second and third moral disagreements).

7. Still another corollary: moral problems and moral disagreements depend on our values and upon our beliefs about matters of fact. Change a person's moral and other values or beliefs in any way, and you change a person's moral problems and moral disagreements. That is why what is a moral problem for one person may not be for another or may be a quite different moral problem. Here is a joke that illustrates both points:

> A father was explaining ethics to his son who was
> about to go into business. "Supposing a woman comes
> in and orders $100 worth of material. You wrap it
> up and give it to her. She pays you with a $100 bill.
> As she goes out the door, you realize she has given
> you two $100 bills. Here's where the ethics comes

-16-

in. Should you or shouldn't you tell your partner?"[1].

A more typical father might ask instead: "Shouldn't you run after the woman and return the extra $100 bill?" Still a third might say: "Frankly, I understand the situation, but I fail to see the problem. I'd pocket the extra $100. There's plenty I can spend it on." Finally, a fourth might agree that it is absolutely clear what he is to do—what he has to do is to return the money to the customer.

Here are some more illustrations of how a change in beliefs or values can make for a change in moral problems. Imagine that Isabella (in the seventh moral problem) were a different woman, one who was in fact fascinated by Angelo. Suppose she had a secret crush on him. She might then plead, echoing St. Augustine: "Give me chastity and continence, only not yet" (Confessions, VIII, 7). The point is that a person may either (a) not attach any importance to the alternatives being considered or may (b) see one as being of much greater importance or appeal than the others. It is only if you care almost equally strongly about both or all of them that you have a moral problem. Thus it is only because Francois (in the first moral problem) loves both his country and his mother and thinks he should stand by one as he would stand by the other that he has the moral problem he has. Another Frenchman's problem might be whether he would derive more profit from collaborating with the Nazis or by smuggling cigarettes into Spain. That would be a totally different problem—and not even a moral one, since this Frenchman of ours would not be motivated by any moral considerations. And he would be a very different but no less believable person. Finally, Emily's problem would vanish should her beliefs change and she become convinced that her father would remarry and be much happier if his daughter only left town.

Changes in your factual beliefs or values, including your ordering of priorities and the importance you assign to your values, as well as your understanding of them (of what it is to show respect, be just, and the like), play a decisive role in moral disagreements as well. Leary, for example, will probably cease to disagree with officer Tracy about the advisability of reporting the local drug pushers (see the fifth moral disagreement) if his main concern becomes the protection of the well-being of young school children. And the officer might drop the whole issue if he came to believe through a religous conversion that the drugs the school children were getting were in a strange way beneficial to their health. Point number 7 thus shows that there is a close relationship between the beliefs of people and their character and the moral problems and moral disagreements they are likely to have.

---

1. The Best of Henny Youngman, vol I, (New York: Gramercy Publishing Co.), 1978, p. 16

8. Let us say that people solve their moral problem when they decide to do one of the things that is unacceptable to them. Or when they decide to do something acceptable to them but incompatible with some other thing they approve of. And they decide this on the basis of moral or other deeply cherished values and beliefs, and thus go against at least one of their own values. So, if Carmen in the sixth moral problem decides, on the basis of a moral reason, not to tell her father that he is dying of cancer, that is her solution to her problem. She would then have come to see that on this occasion one or more considerations—for example, preventing further suffering on his part—is more important than another one—say, keeping her promise to him. This does not mean that she must, if she is consistent, now always count promise-keeping as less important than preventing suffering. For the next situation in which these two considerations come into conflict may, in her judgment, be quite different in all sorts of morally relevant respects. Besides a solution, another possibility is a dissolution of a moral problem. This, like the topic of moral reasons or moral values, remains to be examined. Dissolutions will be discussed under point number 11 below.

We may now parallel the use of 'the resolution of a moral disagreement' with that of 'the solution of a moral problem'. Accordingly, let us say that the resolution of a moral disagreement is the parties' arriving at an agreement in judgment about the action in question, on the basis of their moral or other deeply cherished values and beliefs. Thus Angel Clare (of Thomas Hardy's novel Tess of the D'Urbervilles) came to agree with his traveling companion in Brazil that he should return to Tess in spite of her not having been a virgin when they married, because, among other things, he now put more importance on people's aims and impulses than on their actions. He reminded himself that her "illegal surrender" was, after all, due to the treachery of another person. Should two parties have the same values and the same ordering of priorities, assign the same importance to them, understand them in the same way, and nevertheless disagree with each other, then their disagreement would be a purely factual and not an ethical disagreement. Hence the resolution of such a disagreement—a resolution resulting from the parties' ceasing to have different factual beliefs—would not be the resolution of a moral disagreement. But the resolution of moral disagreements may, and often does, also include the parties' coming to agree on certain factual matters.

One other point of clarification. When I say the parties come to an agreement in judgment about the action in question on the basis of certain sorts of considerations, this does not imply that they arrive at a total harmony of outlook about the action. For instance, the Congress recently debated the question whether to adopt the largest defense budget ever. Imagine representative A, B, and C agreed in their opposition to the budget. Suppose Congressman A argued against it on the grounds that it will mean reducing almost everything else in the budget, especially aid to the world's poor and sick, since we have

-18-

only so many real resources to spend. Congressman B opposed the budget because he is a pacifist who wants to stop the arms race by the United States and the Soviet Union. Congresswoman C argued against it because she thinks the only just state is the minimal state which confines itself to protecting individuals from theft, fraud, or breach of contract. Here we have a moral agreement on what action to perform—whether to vote against the defense budget—yet the three imaginary representatives clearly disagreed on some fundamental matters. So moral agreement whether to perform an action can mask considerable disagreement in values.

9. It follows from point number 8 that, while there is certainly one sense in which moral problems are soluble, they are soluble in this sense only by the person who has the problem. Nobody can solve other people's moral problems for them, since the decision has to come from the one who has the problem. This may seem surprising: yet there are many things you cannot, by the nature of the case, do for others. For example, you cannot have a good time for me, eat for me, or do my kissing for me. Nor can I do these things for you; it would be absurd to try. Similarly, it would be absurd for a wealthy man to try to cooperate with the President's Council on Physical Fitness by sending his butler for him on a fifty-mile hike. A Worry Service that you could pay to do your worrying for you about grades, money, marriage, or the future would be no less absurd. For another person cannot do your hiking, exercising, or worrying for you.

No third party can resolve a moral disagreement for two disputants either, in the above-mentioned sense. What is required is that they come to an agreement in their judgments about the action. Until that happens, the disagreement is not resolved.

Of course, in another sense, a solution to a moral problem, or a resolution of a moral disagreement, may be provided by someone else by that person's convincing the parties involved which is the morally best course of action to take. Moreover, we shall see under point number 11 how others can sometimes help us dissolve our moral problems and disputes by correcting our beliefs and making us aware of other courses of action.

10. People suffer heartache, despair, or anguish—perhaps sometimes even remorse or guilt—and certainly regret, when they solve (not to be confused with dissolve) their moral problems. Generally people do not feel any of these negative emotions, however, when they settle a moral disagreement. On the contrary, they are likely to feel rather pleased or at least relieved. Not that I am denying that people may also feel a degree of relief, along with these negative feelings, when solving their moral problems. For it may bring some relief finally to arrive at a difficult decision.

But why the negative emotions? Because it is in the very nature of the case that solving a moral problem means going against

-19-

some of your own values. Suppose we succeed in choosing the lesser or the least of the evils. We are still choosing something that we ourselves regard as evil, bad, or as morally wrong; hence the feeling of heartache, the rending of conscience, and perhaps remorse, and at least regret. Small wonder that we have a heavy heart when we solve our moral problem! We would feel equally bad if we were forced to go against one friend in order to be loyal to another friend.

These negative feelings, then, are not neurotic or gratuitous in the sense of not being grounded in anything. Neurotic guilt may be characterized as guilt that you feel no matter what you do. Such an emotion is irrational, unlike the feelings I am talking about. Moreover, the anguish or regret I am discussing is to be distinguished from the anguish or regret you sometimes feel when you come to be convinced that you did not after all choose the best or the least harmful course of action or the least of the evils available to you at the time; you then wish you had chosen otherwise. Gauguin, for example (the second moral problem), will feel despair or anguish when he abandons his wife and family for painting since it means going against some of his own moral values. But if he later comes to believe that he has more talent for the stock market than for painting, he will no doubt feel an additional regret. He will then probably wish that he had never decided to become a "real painter." The first feeling, however, does not depend on having the second. For even if Gauguin does not later regret his decision to become a painter, he will still feel heartache or regret when he first makes the decision since we have noted this involves going against some of his own moral values. Putting it another way: although there may be "no-fault" car insurance and "no-fault" divorce, there may be no "no-fault," no anguish-free solutions to moral problems.

This point may be restated and clarified in terms of the doctrine of original sin. There is at least one sense of that doctrine I want to endorse, and that is that our human condition is such that moral evil is inescapable for us, judged by our own standards. By that I do not mean to say that people are especially wicked--that the human heart is full of evil, pride, and conceit or that we are too self-centered and unloving--though human beings are often flawed in these and other ways and surely will never be perfect. Nor do I wish to affirm that the wrongdoing of one generation lives into the successive ones, although there is probably a sense in which that is true, too. My point is rather that it is part of our nature to have values, some of which are normally moral ones. It is these values, and not primarily our wickedness, that gives rise to our moral problems, and hence to the confrontation of choices in which we sometimes cannot act without doing something wrong (something unfair, unkind, and the like), judged in terms of our own values. The curious fact is that if we had fewer, or no, moral values, we would probably have fewer, or even no, moral problems, in which case we would less often—or never—go against such values. Paradoxically, then, it is only the perfectly amoral or nonmoral person who escapes the sin I am speaking of here—namely, of going against your own moral values. Since all who are not amoral may be said to have eaten "of the trees of the knowledge of good and evil" (Genesis 2:17), the rest of us cannot escape such moral evil. (I give examples of amoral people in the next chapter, pp.37-40.)

In brief, when we learn moral values, we acquire moral problems, which in turn means we shall sometimes go against some of our values and consequently feel anguish or despair or some similar negative emotion. I once read an article in a popular magazine entitled "Teach Values, Not Guilt." It should be apparent now why this is both a simplistic and maybe even an incoherent proposal if the values taught are moral ones. For given moral values, we cannot judge our own lives to be totally free of moral evil. Only the perfectly amoral person can completely avoid the feelings of anguish, despair, heartache, and perhaps even remorse or guilt.

11. Sometimes, however, we can dissolve our moral problems and thus prevent these negative feelings. I wish to contrast what I call dissolving a moral problem with solving it, though the two actions have similarities. Remember, that a moral problem is always a dilemma involving conflicting values, at least one of which is moral. When a moral problem is solved, you choose one of the alternative actions, A, B, C, on the basis of moral or other deeply cherished values and beliefs, thus going against one of your own values. In contrast, when a problem is dissolved, it is shown not to be a real problem; so, the dilemma vanishes, and you do not have to solve it by going against your moral or other deeply cherished values.

Before I illustrate dissolutions of moral problems and moral disagreements, I would like to consider a possible dissolution of the nonmoral dilemma mentioned above in point number 4. The problem was to speed traffic down Grand River Avenue, but at the same time not to make it harder for pedestrians to cross the street. The conflict between people and cars seemed irreconcilable. But then a clever artist-designer pointed out that the problem was not really one at all if you took a three-dimensional instead of a two-dimensional approach to it. He suggested a park-like overpass for pedestrians above a depressed highway: this would speed car traffic and at the same time make it easier for people to cross Grand River Avenue. There may, of course, be a hard practical problem of getting the money to build such a complex roadway and overpass.

Dissolutions of moral problems are similar. There seem to be three ways, not necessarily mutually exclusive nor exhaustive, to dissolve moral problems. First, you may discover an alternative course of action that does not conflict with your values. For example, Jeannie (see the fifth moral problem) might talk the cheater into confessing. Mack (the eighth problem) might take the murder case to court again and try to get a stiffer sentence. If he succeeded, his problem would be postponed or perhaps no longer arise or be an altogether different one when the murderer was released from jail. Isabella might help her brother escape from prison. Once his life stopped being threatened by the deputy, her problem would disappear. (In the actual play, Measure for Measure, the Duke, Isabella, and others together dissolved her problem in a rather more complicated way, which is explained briefly below, p. 24.) Secondly, outside forces or new developments may change the situation in such a way that the problem ceases to pose itself. Emily, for instance, might get a better job offer in her hometown or within commuting distance. Or Tex's wife might leave him, in which case he might have a new problem but no longer the problem of whether to leave her. Again, should Mack's murderer-rapist die from cirrhosis of the liver, caused by his excessive drinking, or the Second World War end suddenly in the defeat of the Nazis, the problems of both Mack and Francois would vanish. Finally, if people either changed (a) their factual beliefs, (b) their values, and/or (c) their understanding of those values, they would cease to have certain moral problems. For example, were Carmen (see the sixth problem) to become convinced—perhaps from her reading of Kant—that lies are always wrong, her situation would lose its problematic aspect; this would represent a change in values. And if Gauguin concluded, maybe after reading the lives of famous artists and corresponding with someone like Ann Landers about his problem, that being a family man does not rule out his being a real painter, his problem would also be dissolved with his changed beliefs.

Notice that in all of the three ways mentioned in which a moral problem may be dissolved—through the discovery of alternative actions, the alteration of the situation, a change in your beliefs and/or in your values or understanding of your values—there are changes of beliefs, but there is no need for the parties involved to go against any of their own moral values. This is why individuals generally prefer what I call dissolutions to solutions or moral problems. But the dissolutions are not always preferable, from another person's perspective, since some changes in an individual's values may result in the disappearance of a moral problem we may think it is to the individual's credit to have. Francois, for example, would be a lesser man, morally speaking, in our opinion, if his problem was dissolved by his becoming a sadist who no longer cared for his mother and who stayed at home only to taunt her and to brutalize his neighbors. Should he dissolve his problem in another way, however, we might of course think even more highly of him, morally speaking.

Let us turn now to moral disagreements and see how they, too, may sometimes be dissolved. Suppose two people disagree about whether to do A or B, two incompatible actions. They resolve or settle their disagreement if they come to agree about which of these two things they should do, on the basis of their moral or other deeply cherished values and beliefs. In contrast, their disagreement is dissolved if it vanishes, but not by either or both of the parties' agreeing to do either A or B. This may happen in at least two ways. First, they may find an alternative course of action, C. that does not conflict with the values of either person. For example, the Jehovah's Witness and the doctor may dissolve their moral dispute by using artificial instead of real blood. The first known case of the use of such "blood" in a human being in the United States was reported in November of 1979. Interestingly enough, the transfusion was done on a sixty-seven-year old Jehovah's Witness (New York Times, 25 November 1979). Still another example: the well-off business woman who wants to expand her chain of fast-food restaurants (see the seventh disagreement) might dissolve her dispute with her less prosperous sister by proposing to make her a partner or a manager of one or more of the new restaurants. Of course, there is no certainty that such a proposal would be willingly and happily accepted by her sister, but it might be. Secondly, just as in the case of moral problems, moral disagreements can sometimes be dissolved by a change in the situation or circumstances. For instance, if either disputant died, obviously the dead one would cease to be party to a dispute with the survivor.[2] It should not be thought, however, that the passage of time always helps to ease or to dissolve moral disagreements: sometimes it makes them much worse. For example, the moral disagreement over apartheid in the Union of South Africa seems gradually to be developing into an ever more acute and dangerous dispute.

Now that we have seem what it is to dissolve a moral problem or a moral disagreement and the ways in which dissolutions are to be preferred, at least in the case of moral problems, to solutions, we understand how important it is to check our empirical beliefs and to come up with alternative actions compatible with the agent's or the disputants' values. So, in looking for possible breakthroughs or reconciliations of values that at first seem irreconcilable, it is advisable to search for, and to develop, a list of alternative courses of action. Nor should you worry if at first some of your ideas seem foolish or weird: the bad ones can always be modified or discarded. Of course, it can be that all of the ideas you come up with will seem—and may be—quite worthless. Tex, for example, who is considering whether he should get a separation from his wife who is having an affair with another woman, may only think of the following: either to snap his wife's female lover's umbrella in two while remarking that he hopes it rains; to ask the Reverend Jim Jones to give the three of them sex therapy; to try to get his wife to repeat after him "I will not commit adultery again!"; to develop a witty

---

2. A third possibility is that the disputants might settle their differences by mutual concessions, that is, by making a compromise. This notion of a compromise is not examined here, except to note that it differs from the notions of resolving and dissolving a moral disagreement. It is, however, the main subject of a book originating in a conference on the topic: NOMOS XXI: Compromise in Ethics, Law and Politics, eds. J. Roland Pennock and John W. Chapman (New York: New York University Press, 1979).

polemic satirizing the claim that women love women best; to subject his wife to group criticism, the way they do in Communist China; to start cheating on her with her female lover; or to follow the example of the character in Woody Allen's movie <u>Manhattan</u> whose wife left him for another woman—try to run over his wife's lover with the car. In contrast, Isabella's brainstorming may produce a mixed bag of new alternatives, some of which have acceptable consequences and accord with her values and some of which do not. For example, she may consider subduing the deputy with a karate chop; shooting or knifing him; offering him ransom money rather than her body; enrolling him in therapy; getting him drunk and arranging for her unchaste but look-alike roommate to sleep with him; or of pretending assent herself and then letting her place be taken by Mariana, who was once his intended bride. (The last alternative is what she in fact chose to do in the play.) The point I want to stress, however, is that striving to think of alternative actions and to have correct factual beliefs can sometimes help you to see that your problem or disagreement is not as black and white or simple as it at first appeared to be. It may not be merely a choice between A and B, but between A, B, C, D, E, F, and so forth. Recognizing this richness of alternatives will sometimes lead to a dissolution of the problem or dispute.

But suppose that the moral problem or moral disagreement remains undissolved in spite of your best efforts to think up alternative actions that will dissolve it. Then what? Then you have to weigh the values and actions that are in conflict and see which values in your judgment outweigh the others or which considerations are weightier. Our aim must be to think as deeply as we can think about the alternative actions, exploring their character and consequences. Here dialogue can be very useful, especially in getting correct descriptions of the actions. Eventually you may reach a solution or resolution (as opposed to a dissolution) of the conflict. Others may or may not agree and give moral reasons for or against doing such things. In the next chapter, I shall examine the topic of moral reasons. We shall find that there are indeed such reasons, and hence philosophers who deny this are mistaken (for example, H. A. Prichard and A. J. Ayer). Modifying what I judge to be the incorrect accounts of moral reasons of Charles L. Stevenson and R. M. Hare, I shall try to give an acceptable characterization of moral reasons. Finally, we shall see how moral reasoning differs from mathematical and scientific and technical reasoning, and why there cannot be any moral experts.

CHAPTER III

MORAL REASONS AND MORAL REASONING

Examples That Are And Are Not Moral Reasons

We have seen (point number four, pp. 14-15) how the characterization of moral problems and moral disagreements depends on there being moral reasons and hence on its being possible for people to have moral values. Some philosophers maintain that there are no such reasons or values. In "Does Moral Philosophy Rest on a Mistake?" (Mind, 1912), the intuitionist H. A. Prichard (1871-1947) maintains that you cannot give justificatory reasons why a person is morally obligated to do something. You just know—if you know—immediately, by intuition, what your obligations are and what actions are morally right. It is only the irksomeness of carrying out these actions that makes us ask for justificatory reasons. He acknowledges that it is sometimes possible to give psychological incentives ("It's to your advantage," "You'll enjoy it"), or reasons that motivate people to do what they know they ought to do, but these are not reasons that justify saying that the actions are obligatory. The best we can do by way of justification is to assert that they are obligatory because they are, which of course is not to give any moral reason why they are obligatory. Surprisingly enough, in Language, Truth and Logic (1936), A. J. Ayer (b. 1910), who takes a radically different approach to ethics, agrees that, strictly speaking, there cannot be any moral reasons in support of moral judgments. In his view, which is known as a noncognitive and emotive theory of ethics, moral judgments lack both cognitive meaning or significance and truth-value (they are noncognitive); that is, they cannot be used to express a thought or to say something true or false. Instead, moral judgments function merely to express or to evince the speaker's feeling about some object or action and to excite or to evoke similar feelings towards it in others (their function is purely emotive). So, unlike Prichard, Ayer denies that it is even theoretically possible to have knowledge of what is morally right or wrong, good or bad.

To demonstrate how mistaken these philosophers are on there being no moral reasons I shall give examples that show that in general we have no trouble sorting out moral from nonmoral reasons, and that there are clear instances of the former as well as of the latter. We shall then turn to the analysis of moral reasons.

Let us begin with examples that we, who are after all generally competent and fluent speakers of the language (here English), recognize not to be moral reasons, using the sixth moral disagreement about eating human flesh as a focal point. Suppose we ask the Aztec cannibal, the missionary, and the survivors of the Andean airplane crash why, morally, you should or should not cannibalize a human corpse. The following replies would surely surprise us. "It tastes like good veal." "Potted baby is simply delicious." "The principle or maxim of the action is coherent and can be universalized without contradiction." "The Ouija board said I should (shouldn't)." "My neighbor said I should." "The human adult may serve as many as sixty, if properly butchered." "We just ran out of bread." "He'll meet (or fail to provide) our daily protein requirements." "He was a poor (a rich) man." "Human flesh is low (high) in cholesterol." "He cut me once—now it's my turn!" "I'll give you $100 if you do (don't)." "Look at the tasteless socks he's wearing!" "I've always wanted to convert him into a stew, a nice little, white little, missionary stew!" (T.S. Eliot, <u>Sweeney Agonistes</u>). "Just about everybody does it." "He's black (white, yellow; old, young)." "He might be infected and transmit a serious viral infection." "I'm on a low-protein diet." "We could get caught." "It's legal (illegal)." "It's to my advantage." "When marinated, it's really quite good." "I swear if you try it, next time you fly, you'll ask for the passenger list instead of the menu!"

I think we would all agree that some of these responses may be reasons—several of them even reasons for or against eating a dead human being in certain contexts—but that none of them could be moral reasons for doing so.

Contrast now a reason that is a paradigm or a typical example of a moral reason. Imagine that the Aztec gave the following more natural reply to our question: "Brave warriors inspire us with respect. After they die in battle we eat them to show our respect for them." We may disapprove or find the reason unconvincing, but we recognize that we have just been given a moral reason for eating a human corpse. The missionary is also likely to emphasize respect for the dead, except that he will think this means the dead should have a proper funeral and then be buried. He will reject the cannibal's way of showing respect, contending that since the body is the temple of the soul, we violate its dignity when we dismember a human corpse. The cannibal may scoff that letting the worms dine on a courageous warrior is what cheapens and demeans his dignity. It is interesting that both disputants appeal here to the same moral value—respect for the dead person—but disagree on what is the proper way to show respect: they have a different understanding of what this consists in. Many moral disputes are of this nature. Mrs. Post, the First Lady of Etiquette, for example, thinks it is a flagrant violation of good manners and shows lack of respect for parents for children to call them by their first names. Some children believe it is actually a compliment and shows respect for parents. We have seen in the third moral disagreement how respect for human life was appealed to both

-26-

to argue for and against capital punishment. Still another illustration: some feminists maintain it is sexist and disrespectful to describe a woman as cute or attractive, while others heartily disagree. Russell Baker mentions a similar example when he recounts the story of how offended Pietro was when Tess presented him to her parents, saying, "Mommy and Daddy, this is my lover Pietro." Pietro said it made him "sound like a sex object [and he accused Tess] of not respecting him as a person who had a fine mind and was a first-rate stockbroker." Tess assured him that next time she would introduce him as her stockbroker (The New York Times Magazine, 7 January 1979).

Admittedly, respect for persons and for human life--though terribly important--are not the only moral considerations. A reformed cannibal might morally defend his not partaking of his fellow passengers on the Andean crash because he promised he would never again do such things. And should other survivors argue in favor of eating the dead passengers on the grounds that it would prevent human death, injury, great suffering and hunger, we would recognize that we were being presented with moral arguments, whether or not we found them persuasive.

In short, whenever considerations or courage, respect for persons, for human life, concern for suffering, and promise-keeping enter a discussion, we know we are up against moral reasons for or against doing something. All of these concerns enter our eight moral problems, as well as the considerations of loyalty to your parents, brother, country, spouse, and family (see the first, second, third, fourth, sixth, seventh, and eighth problems), a desire to protect the innocent, to be humane, to uphold fairness, honesty, truthfulness and integrity (see the first, fifth, sixth, seventh, and eighth problems). These constitute further examples of moral considerations. When we bear in mind the many forms of suffering, courage, and truthfulness, it becomes even more striking how many moral reasons there are. Not only is the suffering of an animal that has been cruelly beaten or the discomfort it feels as a result of overcrowding and all other physical pain morally relevant, but so are the grief people feel at the loss of loved ones, the pain of a sharp insult and of rejection, which bring with them a diminished sense of their own worth. Furthermore, courage and valor can be shown not only in battle and mountain climbing, but by the citizen, artist, scientist, philosopher, and laborer tackling and braving difficulties, enduring hardship, taking risks, or making a great effort really to see, to understand, and to improve things. As Hardy observes, "To stand working slowly in a field, and feel the creep of rainwater, first on legs and shoulders, then on hips and head, then at back, front, and sides, and yet to work on till the leaden light diminishes and marks that the sun is down, demands a distinct modicum of stoicism, even of valor."[1] Truthfulness also covers a multitude of things: having integrity, being sincere, honest, loyal, faithful, and—negatively—not lying, cheating, stealing, engaging in various deceits, betraying trusts, making false pretenses, being bought by the spoils of office, and so on. You can understand why T. H. Huxley says, "Veracity is the heart of morality" (<u>Universities, Actual and Ideal</u>, 1874). Truthfulness certainly is one of the fundamental moral considerations.

Thus far we have seen that there are moral reasons, that competent and fluent speakers of the language distinguish moral reasons from those that are not, and we have looked at a few examples of each, though these are obviously not meant to be taken as exhaustive. In the next section, I want to consider whether it is possible to give a satisfactory account of moral reasons. I shall contend that it is, even though the notion is not fully definable. We shall see how Charles Stevenson's characterization makes a start in the right direction, but is unsatisfactory. R. M. Hare's analysis is better, but also needs amending. When properly simplified and supplemented, however, the latter seems to result in a quite tenable account of moral reasons.

Stevenson's Analysis of Moral Reasons

Before I give Stevenson's analysis of what can count as a moral reason, we should note that, like his fellow emotivist Ayer (see p. 25), he thinks that moral judgments cannot be logically supported by reasons, much less vindicated by appeal to facts. For example, suppose that Jeannie concludes that she ought to report her classmate for cheating. No empirical method would be capable of showing her moral judgment to be correct. Indeed, no reason could even provide evidence for or against it. According to Stevenson (1908–1980), moral judgments cannot stand in any logical relation to factual judgments. The judgments can only be supported psychologically, not logically. So in what follows I shall only be talking about moral reasons in the sense of what may count, or be adduced, as a reason for or against a moral judgment, not something that Stevenson thinks can logically support the judgment. Stevenson agrees with Ayer that there are no moral reasons of the latter kind. Finally, it will not be my aim to give a full and scholarly account of Stevenson's ethical theory. I shall only be dealing with one small part of it.

---

1. Thomas Hardy, <u>Tess of the D'Urbervilles</u> (Boston: Houghton Mifflin Co., 1960), p. 253.

Here, then, is the analysis of Stevenson that I wish to examine: "Any statement about any matter of fact which any speaker considers likely to alter attitudes may be adduced as a reason for or against an ethical judgment."[2] Notice that this contains three conditions: being a statement, being about a matter of fact, and the speaker's considering it likely to alter someone's attitudes. Simplifying, let us combine the first two conditions, giving as the new first condition that of being a factual statement; the third condition then becomes the second.

In short, I take Stevenson's statement to imply that something may count as a moral reason for or against an ethical judgment if (1) it is a factual statement that (2) the speaker believes is likely to alter the attitudes of another person. That is, (1) and (2) are together sufficient to make something a moral reason. Let us call this view the weaker thesis, to distinguish it from the stronger thesis that Stevenson suggests, but does not, I think, strictly imply—namely, that (1) and (2) are together both necessary and sufficient for a moral reason. I want to show the inadequacies of both views, beginning with the weaker one.

The weaker thesis lets any factual statement count as a moral reason providing merely that the speaker believes that it is likely to alter the attitudes of someone else. It is not necessary that it either alter, or even be likely to alter, that someone's attitudes. Suppose then that Tex learns that his wife's female lover is a registered Republican. He knows the contempt his wife, a fervent Democrat, has for Republicans. So he informs her of the fact, believing it likely that this information will make her give up her affair. We would not say that he had given her a moral reason; but, according to Stevenson's weaker thesis, we would have to say that.

Or consider the case of Leary, the high school student in the fifth disagreement, who is reluctant to give the narcotics squad the names of the local pushers of narcotics. Officer Tracy may play on Leary's vanity, fear of not being popular, his lust and greed. Suppose he tells Leary that the people in the narcotics squad all admire his graceful prose style, that they plan to give him $100, plus a lifetime subscription to Playboy, to Corset and Underwear Review, to get a doctor to cure his acne, and to make him Time's Man of the Year if he gives them the information they want. According to Stevenson's weaker thesis, we must again say that Officer Tracy's statements are moral reasons if he thinks they are likely to alter Leary's attitude. Yet this is absurd, since the statements are actually examples of nonmoral reasons.

----

2. Charles L. Stevenson, Ethics and Language (Yale University Press, 1944), p. 114.

Here are two more examples that should drive home the point that the weaker thesis has absurd consequences. Imagine that we tell Mack to kill the murderer-rapist because he will then have a chance to get the rapist's higher-paying job, which will fall vacant when he dies. Or that we urge Isabella to sleep with the deputy, remarking on his bright blue eyes, many charms, and how subtly he resembles the Fonz from the TV series "Happy Days." Suppose that in both cases we have the erroneous belief that our remarks are likely to alter the attitudes of our hearers. On Stevenson's weaker view, we must once more say that we have moral reasons. The thesis has the perverse consequence, then, that it makes many things count as moral reasons that people who are fluent in the language normally would not consider to be moral reasons. Accordingly, it fails to provide a sufficient condition for moral reasons.

Stevenson's stronger thesis, that (1) and (2) are together both necessary as well as sufficient conditions for moral reasons, even more absurdly implies that you must disregard your own moral code if you want to give moral reasons, providing you believe that appealing to your moral code is unlikely to alter the attitudes of the other person. So, on this view, you would not give the cattleman a moral reason for not cooping up and force-feeding steers if you pointed out the suffering this would cause, provided you thought your statement was unlikely to affect the other's attitudes or judgment about the matter. Therefore, I conclude that conditions (1) and (2) are neither sufficient nor necessary for moral reasons. We have already seen that they are not sufficient. They are not together necessary either, because of the second condition, which is not essential, since you need not believe that your statement will probably alter someone's attitudes in order for it to be a moral reason.

There is a final, and closely related, peculiarity of Stevenson's position worth mentioning. Because of its emphasis on trying to alter the other person's attitudes, it permits people to disregard, or even to go against, their own moralities or moral codes when they cite moral reasons in support of their moral judgments. It encourages us to play upon others with artful means and not to treat them honestly. Thus the missionary gives the Aztec cannibal a moral reason for not eating the dead warrior when he lies and says he saw the warrior run away from battle, on this view, providing he thinks that this statement is likely to dissuade the cannibal from eating the corpse.

At this point it may seem as if Stevenson is about as confused as the young rabbi who was flying from New York to Los Angeles. At 20,000 feet one of the engines fell off. The passengers were near the point of panic, whereupon the pilot asked the rabbi to do something religious; the rabbi took up a collection.[3] We smile, recognizing the rabbi's failure to understand what it is to do something religious. Stevenson also fails to understand the nature of moral reasons. Yet his characterization is not completely mistaken. I turn next to what is right with Stevenson's characterization of moral reasons.

Stevenson's analysis is right on two counts—namely, that the first condition is (1) a necessary but (2) not a sufficient condition of a moral reason. A moral reason, then, must be a factual statement or judgment, but merely being this kind of a judgment is not enough to make something a moral reason. Being factual judgments or statements, moral reasons attempt to say something true about "the world," about the way things are. They can be either true or false, but they are neither tautologies—that is, true no matter what state the world is in—nor analytic statements—statements that are true or false simply because of the meanings given the words in the statements—nor mathematical statements. Thus, "It's raining or it's not" (a tautology), "Stealing is taking what belongs to another" (an analytic statement), and "Seventy minus a score leaves fifty" (a mathematical statement), not being factual statements, cannot be moral reasons, on this account. They are not factual statements, because they do not say anything about the way things are in the world. This conclusion, that only factual judgments can be moral reasons, is sound, accords with correct usage, and also has the desirable consequence that moral reasons must make a connection with "the world." However, this is only a first step, since we still need to know how to sort out those factual judgments that are moral reasons from those that are not. R. M. Hare (b. 1919), a noted Oxford philosopher, should help us take the next step in arriving at an acceptable account of moral reasons.

Hare's Analysis of Moral Reasons

In Hare's view, there seem to be two, and only two, conditions that must be met before a factual judgment can be a moral reason or, more accurately, part of a moral reason. First, the person who makes the statement must take it to express a consideration that connects up with one of his or her ultimate values—that is, with something taken by him or her to be important as an end in itself and not merely as a means to an end. For the conclusion supported by the factual statement will be a categorical ought-statement, one of the form "We (you, I, etc.) ought (or ought not) do it." It will not be a

---

3. Harry Golden, The Golden Book of Jewish Humor (G.P. Putnam's Sons, 1972), p. 175.

hypothetical or conditional ought-statement, for example, "If it hurts him, you oughtn't do it." Secondly, Hare contends the speaker must be willing to universalize his or her judgment, both in the sense of applying it to similar cases and thus being consistent, and of backing it up with a moral principle that becomes the major premise of the resulting argument. The factual statement functions as the minor premise of this argument, which is actually a syllogism, and the categorical ought-statement, or the conclusion of the argument, follows logically from the major and the minor premises. So, if Carmen concludes that she should tell her father he is dying, because she promised she would let him know whether and when he was dying, her reason has a moral status, according to this account, providing she views promises as an ultimate consideration and she is prepared to back up her moral judgment with a major premise, such as, "You should always keep your promises." This gives us the syllogism:

P.$_1$ You should always keep your promises.
        (Major premise or principle.)

P.$_2$ If I fail to tell my father he is dying,
        I shall break the promise I made to him.
        (Minor premise or factual statement.)

_____

C.   Therefore, I should tell my father he is
     dying.
     (Moral conclusion.)

According to Hare, all moral reasoning, implicitly or explicitly, takes such a syllogistic form, and moral reasons consist of the two supporting premises. The factual statement alone is never a complete moral reason, for it is only one of those two premises and the conclusion does not follow from the factual statement by itself.[4]

Before I consider the attractive features of this analysis I want to show why it will not do. I shall discuss three main objections.

1. It is not necessary for moral reasons to take a syllogistic form. My first objection appeals to the truth (tautology?) that the real moral reasons people have for or against doing something are

_____

4. R. M. Hare, The Language of Morals (Oxford University Press, 1952). See especially pp. 48, 56, 145-46. Hare's position has undergone change in Freedom and Reason (Oxford University Press, 1963), as well as in more recent work. But I believe that most, if not all, of my criticisms also apply to his later position, at least to that part of it that I am acquainted with. However, I have not yet read his most recent book, Moral Thinking: Its Levels, Method and Point (Oxford University Press, 1981).

(normally) just the reasons that they sincerely give in seeking to justify their moral judgments. Accordingly, it is reasonable to assume that Carmen speaks her moral reason when she says: "If I don't tell my father he is dying, I'll not be keeping my promise to him; so I should tell him about the truth of his condition." To the objection that this could not be her complete moral reason, because the conclusion would not follow from it, there is the forceful, and convincing, reply that most reasons are like this—that is, they fail logically to demonstrate the conclusions they support. For instance, the weather forecaster's reasons for thinking it will rain do not logically demonstrate that it will. Nevertheless, the facts that he or she appeals to—the type of clouds seen, the speed and direction of the wind, what the barometric pressure is, its rate of change, and the like—provide evidence for the prediction made. Other facts—for example, "I promised," "It would be a lie," "It would cause great suffering," in turn have moral import; hence Carmen and others cite them in support of their moral judgments. There seems so far, then, to be no good basis for suspecting that Carmen's factual statement (premise 2 above) omits part of her moral reason(s). It is natural to assume, contrary to what Hare would say, that this is her complete moral reason, since she mentions no other in her attempted justification of her moral judgment.

If this conclusion seems precipitous, however, we can check the matter by asking our speaker, Carmen, whether she does not think that the above-mentioned syllogism more accurately represents her moral reasoning and, in particular, whether premise 1 is implicitly part of her moral reasoning. Perhaps her reason is an enthymeme—that is, a truncated syllogism in which one of the premises is understood but not stated. Suppose Carmen answers, in all sincerity, that it is not, explaining that she in fact would reject the major premise, since she can conceive of situations in which it would be right, or at least morally permissible, not to keep a promise. For example, she might say it is morally permissible to break a promise to meet a friend for coffee if you do so to help the victim of a serious car accident. Suppose, further, that Carmen says she cannot endorse any general proposition that states all the circumstances in which a person should or should not keep his or her promises. Her attitude may be that "no general proposition is worth a damn" (Oliver Wendell Holmes, Jr., a "Letter to Sir Frederick Pollock," 1920), and that "the decision [in concrete cases] will depend on a judgment or intuition more subtle than any articulate major premise" (Oliver Wendell Holmes, Jr., Lochner v. New York, 198 U.S. 78, 1905). If such is her view, it seems even more evident that this syllogism does not accurately represent her moral reasoning and we can reasonably doubt whether any other syllogism would correctly represent it either. Hare could, of course, overcome this last uncertainty by presenting some modification of the major premise that is acceptable to Carmen. Until he does this, however, or at least tells us how to do it, it would be advisable not to accept his view that factual statements have moral status only if they are backed up by general principles. It does not seem necessary that you implicitly or explicitly affirm a universal moral principle for your reasoning to be moral. (Note this is not to say that Hare is mistaken in thinking the speaker must be willing to universalize his or her judgment, in the sense of applying it to similar cases and thus being consistent. For the latter sort of willingness to universalize your judgment is not to be confused with a willingness to universalize it in the sense of affirming a universal moral principle.)

Another closely related reason to question Hare's account of moral reasons and of moral reasoning is that many of us—I do not say all of us—do not even believe that there are any true exceptionless, nonvacuous moral principles that tell us what we may, should, must, or must not do. (Nonvacuous moral principles, by definition, have content.) So, while such principles might, they need not, play a part in a person's moral reasoning. Merely consider some of the most plausible moral principles. On examination, they tend to turn out to be quite empty and unhelpful. An example is: "You may break a trivial promise to avoid great harm." The key words here are 'trivial' and 'great harm'. A trivial promise seems to be one that is not important to keep; and great harm is something you ought not to do. Thus the principle seems to be saying: "You may break a promise that it is not important to keep and if keeping it involves doing something you ought not to do." True, but hardly enlightening. Another example is: "Never cause unnecessary pain or suffering," which immediately gives rise to the question: "What is unnecessary pain and suffering?" The likely reply is, "Unnecessary pain or suffering is pain or suffering that is not required or desirable and hence pain or suffering that must never be brought into existence." Hence the principle in effect states the trivial truth: "Never cause pain or suffering that is never to be caused."

On the other hand, if we take these principles to be substantive moral principles, for example, we give a hedonist interpretation of the last one so it reads: "Never cause pain unless it brings about a decrease in the total amount of pain," all nonhedonists—people who are not concerned only with the production of pleasure and the avoidance of pain—would reject the principle as false. Indeed, moral principles that are nonvacuous, or have content, such as, "You must never lie, break promises, fail to pay back your debts, cause suffering," and so on, seem all to have exceptions and not to hold universally; that is, they are overridable, or simply not true as formulated. If you try to remedy this by building all possible exceptions into the principle, so that the principle assumes the form "You ought (or must) always do A (some action) except when_____," it seems it is impossible to fill in the blank with anticipations of all possible exceptions. Hence the temptation to revert back to the true but vacuous form of the principle: "You ought (or must) always do A except when you ought (or must) not do A."

Now I certainly do not pretend to have established that there are no exceptionless moral principles that are nontrivially true.

Perhaps there are a few. The fuller our description of the act, the greater temptation to say there are. Thus it is more plausible to say, "It is always wrong to shoot someone just for fun" than it is to say, "It is always wrong to shoot someone." But note how the more we circumscribe the act, the less guidance we can get from the principle. I wish here merely to raise the question whether—and I hope to cast some doubt on the assumption that—people generally are guided by such principles when they reason morally. Yet if we cannot be sure of this and we cannot find any principles of this kind that are acceptable to us and that guide our moral conduct, Hare's account of moral reasoning must be mistaken, since it takes for granted that we implicitly, if not explicitly, affirm such principles in our moral reasoning; at the very least they must be in the background of our thinking. Remember again, however, that all Hare needs to do to meet the challenge that there are no such principles that guide our conduct is to come up with one that we admit does guide us. The moral theories of the philosophers in Part II may be viewed as attempts to do just this. Accordingly, let us for now leave it an open question whether there are any true exceptionless, nonvacuous moral principles that guide our conduct by telling us what we may, should, must or must not do.

"But," it might be objected, "can moral principles not take a prima facie form, a 'more often than not' formulation, or be nontrivially true if properly qualified?" For example, our principles might be: "Prima facie you ought to keep your promises"; "In general, refrain from lying"; and "More often than not you should return what you have borrowed from others." Such a weakened formulation of our moral principles makes them plausible and probably both nontrivial and true. Granting the existence of such principles, however, does not help Hare answer the first criticism, since if we now use one of these moral principles in our syllogism, we can no longer derive a categorical ought-statement from it and our alleged facts. All we can infer is that prima facie, usually, or more often than not you, I, or somebody ought (or ought not) to do certain things. Yet Hare claims the conclusion of a moral argument is a categorical ought-statement, not something so weak and full of qualifications as these conclusions would be.

2. It is not sufficient for moral reasons to take a syllogistic form and to logically imply a categorical ought statement. I wish to turn now to my second main criticism of Hare's analysis of moral reasons—namely, that it is too broad. That is to say, like Stevenson's account, Hare's can be criticized for letting in too much. It allows certain things to count as moral reasons that clearly are not. Two extreme examples show how excessively tolerant it is. Suppose Tex and Emily reason in the following crazy, but logically impeccable way. First Tex, who has some rather strange ultimate values:

P.$_1$ Whenever a husband's underwear itches him,
         he should get a separation from his wife.
         (Tex's major premise.)

P.$_2$ My underwear itches me. (Factual statement.)

_____

C.   Therefore, I ought to get a separation from
         my wife. (Conclusion.)

Emily, no less absurdly, reasons:

P.$_1$ You must always accept a job offer in another state
         if it is made when the month has a 'j' in it's name.
         (Emily's principle.)

P.$_2$ This is July. (Factual statement.)

_____

C.   Therefore, I must accept the job offer in the
         other state. (Conclusion.)

Notice how the first premise applies to everyone who gets a job offer in a month with the letter 'j' in it, not just to Emily; so in reasoning this way, Emily clearly commits herself to allow others who get a job offer in a month with the letter 'j' in it to act on this principle too. Suppose she—and Tex as well—accept the implication of their words and have the requisite ultimate values. Then, accepting Hare's account, both of these syllogisms must be viewed as moral arguments, though not necessarily good ones. Yet surely the fact that a month has the letter 'j' in its name, or some other letter, or that a husband's underwear itches him are not moral reasons, or even partial moral reasons, for doing anything. They are, at best, nonmoral reasons for a husband to change his underwear and for the daughter to choose the name 'July' when doing a crossword puzzle.

Notice, further, how Hare's account not only allows such absurd arguments, but also agist, sexist, racist, and heightist arguments to all count as moral arguments, despite the fact that a person's age, sex, color, and height are not morally relevant considerations and therefore cannot be given as moral arguments. Thus if a six foot, white male, fifty years old, were to contend that no nonwhite females or persons under six foot or younger than fifty ought to be given the first amendment right of free speech, this would, according to Hare's view, be a moral principle. Consequently, it could be used to argue against Mickey Rooney's, Martin Luther King's, Jane Fonda's—and indeed most people's—being given the right of free speech. Similarly, were Leary (of the fifth moral disagreement) to have a relapse, he might argue in the following way:

$P._1$ Whatever gives a person immediate pleasure ought to be done. (Principle.)

$P._2$ It gives me immediate pleasure to get stoned. (Factual statement.)

C. Therefore, I ought to get stoned.

Not that Hare would himself, of course, ever give or accept such arguments. But his philosophy of morals, which is intended to be morally neutral, that is, to be compatible with any particular moral outlook,[5] grants them both the status and the dignity of being moral arguments.

I hope that my examples succeed in showing that logically implying a categorical ought-statement and taking a syllogistic form are not enough to make a reason a moral reason, contrary to Hare's view. My earlier criticism of him was that it is not necessary for moral reasons to take this form. Putting these two objections together I conclude that is neither necessary nor sufficient for moral reasons to take a syllogistic form and to logically imply a categorical ought statement.

3. <u>Hare's analysis of moral reasons overlooks the fact that rational people who universalize their ultimate values may be amoral.</u> This brings me to my third main criticism of Hare's account of moral reasons—namely, that it mistakenly rules out the possibility of <u>there being</u> a rational person who is prepared to universalize being amoral—that is, being outside the moral order—since all ultimate values that are consistently adhered to and universalized are held by Hare to be moral ones. I shall maintain, in contrast, that any correct account of morality must recognize that it is possible for a rational universalizer not to care about morality, not to be moral, or at least to take many moral holidays. Not that I wish to say that people can be utterly indifferent about how to live or that they can exist without any values or preferences. This is impossible, because as was mentioned in the Preface, actions and decisions themselves presuppose values, some of which are ultimate ones. Yet, it is surely theoretically possible for people to be consistent, to lack moral convictions, and to decide matters—even important ones—on the basis of values that are not themselves moral.

Here are three or four examples. Consider, first, the characters in the Weill-Brecht 1929 opera <u>The Rise and Fall of the City of Mahagonny.</u> In this mythical city there is only one sin: to be

---

5. See Hare's <u>Freedom and Reason,</u> chap. 10, "Logic and Morals," especially pp. 192-93, 195.

without money. Imagine single-minded people in Mahagonny—or in our towns for that matter--who are only concerned with making money. Their motto is: "Make money, money by fair means if you can, if not, by any means money" (Horace, Epistles, bk. I. epistle i, 1.66). Murder, rape, theft—they will not hesitate to do any of these things as long as they feel like doing them or they think it will enrich them. Being fanatics for money, they understand when others are too, and they do not morally condemn such behavior; they are ready to accept a war of all against all. Truman Capote, In Cold Blood (1966), writes about real people who are similar—"punk murderers"--who would cut someone's throat without the least compunction if they could get a few dollars for it. It seems evident that people of this sort do not think morally when they act in this way, even if they are prepared to accept a principle that permits others to do the same to them.

For a second example, consider dedicated scientists, artists, and philosophers--the "Gauguin" types--those who are ready to sacrifice everything, including themselves, for their science, art, or philosophy. Listen to Faulkner's description of the single-minded pursuit of the writer: "Everything goes by the board [for the writer]: honor, pride, decency, security, happiness, all, to get the book written. If a writer has to rob his mother, he will not hesitate; the 'Ode to a Grecian Urn' is worthy of any number of old ladies."[6] Similarly, Picasso remarks that, for him, painting "takes precedence over all other considerations" (from Francoise Gilot and Carlton Lake, Life with Picasso, 1964, pt. I). I do not wish to suggest by these quotations that Faulkner and Picasso and serious scientists, artists, and philosophers generally are completely amoral. Most of them, we know, are not that amoral. But it is reasonable to think that in the pursuit of their research or craft they are often guided exclusively, or mainly, by nonmoral values. In some cases, like the rest of us, they may also disregard relevant moral considerations.

I shall close with one brutal illustration of acting amorally; the illustration should not be taken as representative of scientific practice. In the sixties, a group of black men in Alabama were denied equal treatment for syphilis so that doctors could study the disease's progress. Had the doctors only been concerned to gain scientific knowledge, this would be a case of acting amorally.[7] Incidentally, it

----

6. William Faulkner, from an interview, New York City, 1956, by Jean Stein; from Writers at Work: the Paris interviews, 1959.

7. I say had they so acted, because the fact is these doctors did not perform their experiment merely to indulge scientific curiosity. They were not interested in scientific knowledge for it's own sake. They hoped to gain knowledge about syphilis to combat it. As James H. Jones notes in his study Bad Blood: The Tuskegee Syphilis Experiment (New York: The Free Press, 1981, pp.171, 172): "Safeguarding the

is because of a few shocking cases like this that the Federal Government ordered that institutional review boards be formed more than a decade ago as a condition of receiving Federal Biomedical research money.

We have seen that money grubbers, certain criminals, perhaps scientists, artists, and philosophers can go—and perhaps in some rare cases, for example, our imaginary Gauguin, Capote's murderers, be perpetually—on a moral holiday. We have seen how their amorality can lead to morally wrong conduct. The same is true of romantic lovers and religious worshippers. I have in mind lovers who think any means are permitted in the pursuit or retention of their loved ones. It seems love may temporarily extinguish a person's moral sense. Thus, in a recent South American film, <u>Castle of Purity,</u> the wife lets herself and her children be abused and mistreated to keep the love of a crazy husband. Many devoted wives who put up with being regularly beaten by their husbands may constitute another illustration. In <u>Fear and Trembling</u> (1843), the Danish philosopher Soren Kierkegaard (1813-1855) gives Abraham as an example of a heroic worshipper who also transcends the category of the "ethical." For in response to God's demand Abraham is prepared to go against his moral duty by sacrificing his innocent and only son Isaac as a burnt offering.

Summing up, it may be said that amoralists are people who hold that everything is lawful, morally speaking. Moral reasons neither restrain them from performing, nor motivate them to perform, actions. They are motivated solely by nonmoral considerations. Such people are, of course, also immoral, in the sense that they do immoral and morally wrong things. But not everybody who acts immorally need be amoral, since moral reasons may play a role in motivating such people's actions. I shall try to show later (in Chapter VI) that single-minded egoists are amoralists. Certainly if everyone's sole concern were "What does it matter to me?" morality would be lost. But egoism is only one of many ways of dispensing with morality. The haughty misanthrope and voluptuary who hates his neighbor but lusts for his neighbor's wife is another example. And so are conventionalists and subjectivists (who will be discussed in Chapter V), as well as those hypocrites who use morality merely to hurt others, who speak of fighting evil but feel free to employ any means in their

---

public's health was their mission." "They began the experiment because they were interested in black health." They wanted to understand the effects of syphilis on black people the better to fight it. This obviously does not excuse what they did. What they did was clearly a great moral wrong. In this sense it was not moral. But in another sense of 'moral', it was moral, that is, their conduct was motivated by moral reasons, even though they disregarded some very important moral considerations, since they acted cruelly—deceived, betrayed, and showed little respect for the poor black people they experimented on.

fight, whose talk is all of courage, candor, and justice, but who somehow never have any regard for the wishes and feelings of others. As Emerson remarks, "The louder [such a person] talked of his honor, the faster we counted our spoons" ("Worship," from the Conduct of Life, 1860). I do not want to exaggerate the point. There are extremely few, if any, pure amoralists, though many more, of course, who have their occasional moral lapses. On the other hand, there are probably equally few people who act always for moral reasons when acting on the basis of their ultimate values. Hare fails to allow for these facts because of his failure to distinguish moral from other ultimate values. He makes all ultimate considerations moral reasons if the speaker is merely prepared to universalize the claim and endorse some appropriate prescriptive principle. Although Hare is an ordinary language philosopher, and as such is presumably interested in giving a correct, discriptively neutral, nonstipulative account of our use of moral language, he, unfortunately, misdescribes the way competent and fluent speakers of the language actually use the expression 'moral reason'.

My Account of Moral Reasons

I mentioned that Stevenson's and Hare's characterization of moral reasons, despite their flaws, have several attractive features. I shall use their good points to try to arrive at a more acceptable account of moral reasons. One attractive feature of Stevenson's analysis is that it correctly recognizes that moral reasons are factual statement or judgments, that they attempt to say something about the way things are in "the world," that they are true or false, but neither analytically true nor analytically false, neither tautologies nor mathematical statements. This conclusion both accords with correct usage and has the desirable consequence that moral reasons must make a connection with "the world." Yet this is only a first step in arriving at an adequate account of moral reasons, since we still need to know how to sort out these factual statements that are moral reasons from those that are not. Stevenson deserves credit for appreciating this last point as well, since his analysis implies that being a factual statement or judgment is not a sufficient condition of a moral reason.

Hare's characterization is also correct on two counts. First, he rightly impies that the factual judgment must express some consideration the speaker takes to be of ultimate or intrinsic value. Secondly, he recognizes that satisfying this condition is not enough to make something a moral reason. Hare goes wrong in two ways as well, as we have seen. First, he thinks that his second condition is necessary—that is, that people must universalize their judgments in the sense of endorsing some prescriptive principle that, together with the

-40-

factual statement, logically implies the categorical ought-statement. Secondly, he is mistaken in implying that his two conditions are together sufficient for moral reasons. I shall therefore amend his analysis by dropping the second condition and replacing it with another one that introduces a needed restriction on ultimate values. Before I mention the restriction, however, let me explain more fully what I do and do not mean by people's taking a consideration to be of ultimate or intrinsic value.

I shall say that people take a consideration to be of ultimate or intrinsic value if they regard it as a fundamental and terminating consideration. Thus they must view it as the last member of a chain or line of reasons. They see it as something important, valuable, or desirable in itself or for its own sake, and not merely as being good as a means nor as merely having extrinsic or instrumental value. While not necessarily holding it to be the final word, they must at least take it to be a final word. Nor can they justify their claim that the consideration is important in itself. However, not being able to do this does not make them have any doubts about its importance.

An example may clarify what I have been saying. Suppose you ask me why a certain action is worthwhile. I may say that it is a means to something else. This is strictly a factual matter: either it is or it is not. For example, suppose Craig Clairborne, the gourmet cook, says he exercises daily and follows his low-salt diet—including modified use of fat and sugar in cooking—to keep healthy. Imagine that these actions are a means to this end. This still does not show they are worth performing unless the end is worth achieving. Suppose you then ask him, "And why do you want to keep your health?" He may be stumped for an answer, health perhaps being an ultimate value of his; or, alternatively, he may say, "Because sickness is unpleasant, often painful." Suppose you agree with his answer, but that it provokes you to ask still another question—namely, "What's so bad about pain?" He will now, if he did not before, no doubt shake his head and wonder about your sanity, since avoiding pain, we may presume, is an intrinsic or an ultimate value for him as well as for just about every other normal person. Avoiding pain and suffering is an end in itself for most people, and we neither feel we could nor need to justify avoiding, or give a reason for avoiding, these things. Contrast our response to the question why refrain from driving 60 miles per hour through town or why get your teeth cleaned every six months by a dental hygienist. Here reasons that justify the practices come readily to mind. Yet when we deal with considerations we take to be of ultimate value, our justifications cease and our reasons give out. As the great twentieth-century Austrian philosopher Ludwig Wittgenstein (1889-1951) says, "If I have exhausted the justifications, I have reached bedrock, and my spade is turned."[8] "The chain of reasons [and doubting as well: p. 180] has an end" (PI, § 326). Indeed, if our justifications did not come to an end, they would not be justifications. We can therefore check to find out whether a value—for example, freedom—is an ultimate or intrinsic value for somebody by finding out whether he or she cares about freedom, whether he or she cannot justify and does not feel any need to justify the importance he or she attaches to it by reference to any other consideration. Such a person takes the position that we ought to be positively concerned about freedom, period.

To prevent possible misunderstanding, however, three qualifications are needed, beginning with a negative point. When I say a consideration is taken to be of ultimate or intrinsic value, I do not mean that it in fact cannot be overridden, or that the person believes that it cannot, by other reasons. 'Ultimate' here does not mean 'conclusive' or 'decisive'; hence the consideration need not be taken, either by the individual or by others to establish acting in a certain way. That is why I said (two paragraphs ago) that even the individual who holds that ultimate value need not view it as the final word, though he or she must hold it to be a final word. That is to say, for such a person it will always be a reason for acting in a certain way. Consider the case of Gordon Liddy, in the Watergate scandal. We may assume that avoiding pain was and is an ultimate value of his; hence he always has a reason not to hurt himself. But we know that another of his deepest values is being gutsy and macho, and that the latter seems sometimes to override the former value, since he proudly tells how he burned himself with cigarettes, inflicted other pains on himself, and even forced himself to eat raw rat, which he loathed, in order to become more manly and fearless. Most of us may not be so much a macho as Liddy, but like him people generally have a plurality of ultimate values. As the English poet, Alexander Pope, puts it, human beings do not as a rule have "one master-passion in the breast [that] like Aaron's serpent, swallows up the rest" (An Essay on Man, Epistle II, 1. 131).

My second qualification is this: even though we cannot justify our claim that something is of ultimate value, we may still be able to give a certain kind of justification of such things by reference to other values of ours. We may do this by establishing that the thing is good as a means, or that it is extrinsically good—that is, that it helps us achieve something else we value. We value some things, after all, both as ends and as means to other ends. Eating, for example, is

---

8. Ludwig Wittgenstein, Philosophical Investigations, tr. G. E. M. Anscombe, 3rd ed. (The Macmillan Co., 1958), § 217. In all references to this book, section numbers generally refer to Part I, page numbers to the Preface, Part II, or unnumbered notes in Part I. 'PI' is an abbreviation of the title.

generally regarded as good in itself, but also as good as a means, since it is essential to living. Courage, honesty, and freedom, which are ultimate values for many, are also recognized to have utility, or an instrumental value, to both the community and to the people who possess them. For instance, if people were not generally honest, it would become terribly difficult, if not impossible, to conduct business, to have a stockmarket, or even to go shopping.

Thirdly and finally, we may be able to give reasons (in the sense of causes) why, or explain how, we have come to posses the ultimate values we have. Biographers and social scientists sometimes undertake to give such reasons or explanations. For example, they may speculate that Smith learned to consider others, because when he was a child he was included in conversations at home and his views were always treated with interest and respect. But such explanations, again, do not justify our having the ultimate values we have, for causes of this sort are not to be confused with justificatory reasons. In short, my three qualifications still leave us with the central conclusion that we are not capable of justifying taking certain considerations to be of ultimate or intrinsic value.

Now that I have explained what I do not mean by a person's taking a consideration to be of ultimate or intrinsic value, it is time to complete my account of moral reasons by introducing the needed restriction on ultimate values. I shall say that something is a moral reason for somebody if and only if:

> it is a factual or empirical consideration
> that person takes to be of ultimate importance
> and which expresses his or her positive concern,
> for its own sake, for either justice, gratitude,
> charity, kindness, respect of others and self,
> generosity, honesty, integrity, loyalty, fortitude
> courage, or the like.

Notice that one desirable consequence of this account of moral reasons is that what is a moral reason for me may not be a moral reason for you, since we may differ in our ultimate values. A second desirable consequence is that not every ultimate consideration will be a moral consideration. We saw the need for this when looking at Hare's view; hence the need for some restriction on ultimate values. My last requirement (what follows the 'and' in the underlined statement) provides this needed restriction on ultimate values.

We have seen that the factual or empirical condition correctly recognizes that we support moral conclusions with factual judgments. The additional requirement that the speaker, agent, or person making the judgment takes the factual consideration(s) to be of ultimate or intrinsic importance is also necessary. For suppose we allowed factual considerations that were regarded as of less than ultimate importance to be moral reasons. Moral reasons, not being fundamental

-43-

terminating considerations, would then be based on other reasons; hence they would be turned either into considerations of prudence or of expediency. We would then be dealing only with means to an end or with merely extrinsic goods, as the following illustrates. Imagine that Mack sees his wife's murderer-rapist caught in a raging fire. "It will kill him!" he yells, as he rushes to pull him out of the fire—but only to castrate and then kill him himself. In this case saving the fellow from the fire was merely a means; it was not something Mack valued in itself; hence it does not express an ultimate value of his. Knowing this, I do not think we would say his statement expressed a moral reason of his for saving the murderer. Yet we might be entitled to say this if either or both of the last two conditions (those that follow the factual requirement) were dropped.

Someone may object to the very last condition, however, claiming that it is hopelessly vague—that it is often not possible to tell when people's ultimate considerations show a positive concern on their part, for its own sake, for justice, gratitude, charity, kindness, respect for others and self, generosity, honesty, integrity, loyalty, fortitude, courage, and the like. For (the argument may continue) we have none too firm a grip on what these moral virtues consist in. What, after all, constitutes greediness as opposed to generosity, or cowardice as opposed to courage? We are incapable of giving a behavioristic analysis of these notions.

I agree that a behavioristic analysis of the moral virtues cannot be given and that it is sometimes hard to tell when people's ultimate considerations show a positive concern, for its own sake, for one of them. But that does not mean that we lack an adequate understanding of these notions or that we have no criteria to tell if a person has the right kind of positive concern for one of them. We shall see shortly that we can quite easily say in many cases that certain ultimate considerations satisfy the last condition and that others equally clearly do not. So, my account is not so obscure as it may at first seem. Indeed, I think it may sometimes help people to determine whether their actions, judgments, and conclusions are moral (as opposed to nonmoral) by helping them to find out whether they are based on moral reasons. For our actions, conclusions, and judgments can only be moral if they are grounded in moral reasons.

It must also be borne in mind that any descriptively adequate philosophical account should not make unclear cases clear. Thus borderline cases of moral reasons should remain borderline cases. So, if there is any vagueness in the notion of a moral reason—and surely there is—my account of moral reasons ought to preserve this vagueness. It will be a point in favor of my account if it does this, and the extent to which it does this. The point holds generally. Consequently, it is also desirable for analyses of democracy, of puppy dog, or of baldness, for example, to preserve whatever vagueness inheres in these notions. Hence we should reject all accounts of baldness which assert that someone is bald only if he or she has fewer that some fixed number of hairs (five hundred, one thousand?), because such accounts would make the notion of baldness more precise than it is. According to them, there would no longer be any unclear or borderline cases of being or not being bald, but we know there are such cases. The same seems to be true of moral reasons.

Before we see what sort of things will and will not be moral reasons for someone on this account, let me stress that I have not actually given a proper definition or analysis of moral reasons, since my account makes essential use of the phrase 'or the like'. This phrase, then, is not just a "lazy" 'or the like', or some abbreviated notation, for I really do not know how, or whether, the list of moral virtues could be completed. If I leave it out, I run the risk of omitting a moral virtue that ought to be on the list. That is why I have retained the phrase. Although readily within our grasp, then, the notion of a moral reason seems to elude our attempt to define it properly. At least it appears it cannot be analyzed in terms of explicitly stated necessary and sufficient conditions. Nonetheless, I think my account gives a helpful intimation of what is involved in someone having a moral reason. For, while it sometimes leaves room for doubt about what would or would not be a moral reason for somebody, in most cases it does not.

But does not retaining the phrase 'or the like' invite strange additions? Can people now not add whatever they like to the list? Suppose someone wanted to append the words 'disloyalty', 'mendacity', 'bigotry', or 'selfishness'. (Note the paradoxical and thus striking title of Ayn Rand's book, The Virtue of Selfishness: A new Concept of Egoism, 1961.) Then "It's to my exlusive advantage," "It would be a lie (a disloyal or a bigoted act)" could become moral reasons to do the act, contrary to received usage and what I imply in my account of moral reasons. My answer is that disloyalty, mendacity, bigotry, and selfishness are not sufficiently like, or not similar to in relevent respects, the items already included in my account. Disloyalty, mendacity, bigotry, and selfishness are moral vices, and the list only includes moral virtues, several of which are incompatible with these vices. Hence the phrase 'or the like' clearly rules out adding these things, or whatever someone may merely feel like adding to the list. It would, however, allow the addition of, for example, 'forbearance', and 'temperance'. We would probably get some controversy over adding 'chastity', 'modesty', 'self-discipline', 'patience', and 'purity', depending on how these traits are understood. But this uncertainty should not alarm us. It seems to reflect the previously mentioned vagueness in the notion of a moral reason.

Let us see next what sorts of things will and will not be moral reasons for someone in my view. In the end, this is the single best test of the adequacy of my account of moral reasons. I think it shows that my conditions are all necessary and in no way arbitrary. Consider, first, Carmen's statement or judgment "I promised." In my view, this is a moral reason for her to tell her father that he is dying. For (1) it is a factual judgment: either she did or did not promise to tell him this. (2) We have been supposing that she views keeping promises as an ultimate consideration. (3) This ultimate consideration shows a positive concern on her part for honesty and integrity, for their own sake.

On the other hand, suppose she concludes that she should not tell her father of his terminal illness because it would cause him great suffering. Then she would again be basing her decision on a moral reason which she has. For "It would cause him great suffering" is a factual statement; we have been supposing that avoiding suffering is an ultimate value of hers; and having such an ultimate consideration shows that she has a positive concern for charity, kindness, and possibly gratitude as well, for their own sake.

Similarly, "It would be cowardly to leave them," "It would be stealing, lying," "It's taking a human life," "It would embarrass my friend," "It would be adultery" (conceived of as the breaking of a marital vow or as an act showing lack of respect for your spouse), "I'd be betraying a trust," "I'd violate my self-respect," and so on would also be moral reasons people have, provided they have the suggested ultimate values that show they have a positive concern for either courage, honesty, justice, fortitude, respect of others and self, or the like, for it's own sake. In fact, these are ultimate values for most of us, since we think that being courageous, honest, just, and so on as good in themselves, and we neither can justify nor think we need to justify the intrinsic importance of such considerations by reference to anything external to them. I take this to be an argument in favor of my view—namely, it allows us to say that the things speakers of the language naturally would say are moral reasons for people, are indeed moral reasons for them.

Let me see next whether my account is compatible with our denial that somebody has a moral reason. If it is—and I think it is—this will provide still further evidence in its favor. Imagine, then, that Jimmy spots a classmate cheating on an important examination. Suppose he reports the cheater without the least hesitation, simply for kicks (perhaps he has a "fun morality"), to keep the lower classes in their place, or to get a reward. Jimmy may be bored and love nothing but money, power, and excitement, which we may suppose he loves for themselves alone. It is clear that we would then deny that he had a moral reason for reporting the cheater. If his reason for turning him in were that the cheater is unpopular or that the group dislikes him or simply somehow to increase the gross national product, he would again not have a moral reason, by my account. For none of these reasons satisfies the last requirement even if they all satisfy the earlier ones. The same goes for Count Dracula, one of whose ultimate values we may presume is biting people on the neck and sucking and tasting their blood. This ultimate value cannot qualify as a moral reason. (On the other hand, if he does it to stay alive, it seems this would qualify as a moral reason.) Lord Macaulay presents us with what might be another example when he observes: "The Puritan hated bear-baiting, not because it gave pain to the bear, but because it gave pleasure to the spectators (History of England, vol.I, chap.2). If true, the puritan's hatred of bear-baiting is not grounded on a moral reason, in my view, unless the puritan's attitude involved a positive regard for temperance, fortitude, or some other trait like those on my list in enough relevant respects. In contrast, if the puritan opposed bear-baiting because it gave pain to the bear, his hatred of it would be grounded on a moral reason. Once again this accords with the way we speak. Two final examples should suffice to show that things we would not take to be moral reasons won't be on my account either. For example, suppose Tex says "I drew straws and got the short one; so I'm going to stay with Felice." He would not then be basing his decision to stay on a moral reason. Similarly, should Mack decide not to kill the murderer-rapist just because it would break up a weekly poker game and inconvenience some of the guys on the block, or just because Mack heard that the President had the rapist to dinner in the White House, his decision would not be based on a moral reason, even if he foolishly thought it was. The same is true if he kills him because he thinks it will make a terrific soap opera, because he walked on a sidewalk crack, or because he finds the murderer's conversation ungrammatical. You can imagine endless examples of the same sort.

I shall close this discussion by considering another possible objection to my account—namely, that it is too static, too ahistorical, since it does not allow for moral change, especially moral progress, and because it makes no room for the moral reformer. Such an objection is incorrect on all of these counts. Jesus Christ, Mahatma Gandhi, Martin Luther King, and the German philosopher Friedrich Nietzsche (1844-1900) are all moral reformers. They brought about major moral changes, probably most of them for the better. But it was not by inventing a new kind of moral reason. In Jesus's teaching there was a changed emphasis and extension of compassion and regard for others to all people. But concern for others was a moral reason people had long before his time. The Jews and Greeks also had pity for weak and suffering human beings. Already in Leviticus 19:18 we read: "Thou shalt love thy neighbor as thyself." Jesus repeats the teaching word for word in Matthew 19:19. Nietzsche, apparently, does not hold with this emphasis on helping neighbors, including the weak, the sick, and the hungry; sometimes he even extols cruelty. He would stress the importance of strength of character and courage, which are again traditional moral virtues. We find them present in Sophocles's Antigone, in which Antigone courageously defends her brother's honor. These concepts retain their strength today, for example, in a western like High Noon. Gandhi, a twentieth-century moral reformer, also fought for justice and respect for others and self, for instance, by helping to undermine caste discrimination in India. Finally, Martin Luther King probably contributed more to the fight against racism in America than anyone else in our century. He made us more sensitive to the plight of blacks and other minorities, thereby improved our attitudes, and indirectly brought about changes in the law and many institutional practices. These changes clearly represent moral progress, and there is nothing in my treatment of moral reasons that precludes my recognizing them as such. It would probably be more plausible to say that my account actually encourages, rather than discourages, moral reformation by making us more aware of the many nonmoral ways we have of dealing with moral problems.

It is clear, then, that I allow for moral change. Indeed, I distinguish at least four kinds. First, people may either cease to have, or may aquire new, ultimate moral values. Secondly, they may change their order of priorities or preferences. For example, honesty may become the fundamental consideration when once it was not. Thirdly, certain considerations—say, avoidance of human suffering—may gain or lose in importance, but not necessarily in relation to other values. Finally, people may change their understanding of their values—for example, of what it is to have respect for a human being or of what courage consists in. When a Christian becomes a Nietzschean, or a hedonistic egoist, a Tolstoyean—or vice versa—all four of these changes may take place. Some of these changes will be for the better, some for the worse. Incidentally, for a nice example of a moral conversion from a hedonistic egoist to a Tolstoyean outlook read Tolstoy's novel Resurrection. The main character, Nekhludov, finds that the pleasure he formerly "considered good and important are actually repulsive or insignificant" (chap. 28). Such major changes in a person are of course rare.

Some of you may feel cheated at this point because I have not given any analysis of the moral virtues or of the notion of a moral virtue in general, explaining how these traits differ from those called vices. But that is a topic that deserves a book in its own right; it is too large to deal with here. I am assuming that as fluent and competent speakers of the language, we all have at least a rough, working, pre-theoretical understanding of most of the virtues mentioned in my account of moral reasons. Certainly most of us know how to correctly apply the terms 'kind', 'generous', 'honest', 'loyal', 'courageous', and the like, even if we cannot give an account, here and now, of how we use these words.

In the next chapter, I shall compare briefly moral reasoning with mathematical and scientific reasoning. Then I shall try to show why there cannot be any moral experts, though there are experts in mathematics, logic, and in the sciences generally.

CHAPTER IV

MORAL CONTRASTED WITH SCIENTIFIC REASONING AND

WHY THERE ARE NO MORAL EXPERTS

The Contrast Between Moral and Scientific Reasoning

In the formal or nonempirical sciences of mathematics and log-ic, as well as in the empirical sciences of physics, astronomy, phys-iology, biology, geology, and the like, there are experts or authorities. These are people who have a special competence in their particular fields. When we have a scientific question or disagreement, we can turn to relevant experts for an answer or enlightenment. Often they can solve the problem or settle the dispute. Even when they cannot, because they lack the data, they at least generally agree on what data or procedure would settle it. For example, a group of medical doctors may not know whether a particular patient has tuberculosis, cancer, or mononucleosis; but they do know that if they see Koch bacilli under the microscope and the patients reacts positively to the tuberculine test and his chest X-ray is positive, then the patient is almost certainly tuberculous. Were someone to reject such evidence as irrelevant or as carrying little weight, that someone would not be much of a doctor; he or she would be regarded by doctors as either irrational or else incompetent in the field. Certainly they would not pay any attention to such a person's opinions about medicine. Similarly, if someone did not know how to solve algebraic equations (say $5x + 7 = 32$) or how to answer the question, "How many Swiss francs is $850 worth, given that 1.55 is the rate of exchange?" he would obviously not be a mathematician, for he would not yet have even mastered grade school mathematics.

My point is that people who become scientists are not only trained to accept many things that are firmly founded at any given time (the theory of gravitation, the evolutionary process, quantum theory, the theory of relativity), but that they simultaneously learn procedures and methods--the various ways in which issues are settled in their science, what the relevant empirical data would be, and what would settle a scientific question. There is widespread agreement among them on these methodological matters. Thus even if nutri-tionists were to disagree about the effect on longevity of large amounts of fat in the diet of dogs, they would nevertheless agree on what sort of evidence would support or count against their different hypotheses: they share a notion of common evidence, and so are not likely to argue about basic procedures and tests for settling their dispute. This is characteristic of scientific controversies. Consequently, if students of a science rejected most of these agreed-upon procedures and methods, they would not be certified as competent in the science; for example, they would not be invited to join the fraternity of scientists by being granted degrees in science.

The same general proposition holds for simple everyday empirical, technical claims and questions, and questions about means and ends. For instance, suppose you ask whether there is a cow in the next room; whether it is snowing in Texas; how to overcome motion sickness; whether swimming and running help get rid of stretch marks; what time of day it is now in Honolulu; whether Grand River Avenue goes to Detroit; and whether an extra coating of limestone will protect the Sphinx from further air pollution. There are generally accepted criteria for deciding these matters; hence they are decidable in principle, if not in fact. If someone rejected these criteria as irrelevant, we would have reason to suspect that the person did not understand the questions asked; maybe some of the terms used were unfamiliar to him or her or were not fully understood. In the case of everyday empirical questions, familiarity with the correct use of the relevant terms often suffices to tell us how to discover the answer. In the case of the sciences, however, only those who are knowledgeable in the science know how to answer the questions that arise. Such people understand the language and the methods of the science as well as the everyday language.

So far I have been attempting to characterize the sciences in general, and I have not bothered to make anything of the distinction I alluded to earlier between the formal or nonempirical sciences of mathematics and logic, on the one hand, and the empirical sciences, on the other hand. But there is an important difference in the nature of the reasoning in each. In the empirical sciences, the best available reasons or evidence are inductive, and hence never conclusive and purely deductive in the way in which mathematical and logical arguments are. Mathematical and logical arguments consists of proofs, each step of which follows with necessity from what precedes it. As a leading nineteenth-century mathematician, Benjamin Peirce, observes, "Mathematics is the science which draws necessary conclusions";[1] the same is true of logic. And logicians and mathematicians generally agree on what is a proof. I say 'generally' since there are occasional, if rare, disagreements; for instance, intuitionists in mathematics (not to be confused with ethical intuitionists) reject traditional indirect proofs in mathematics and logic. In spite of this difference between

---

1. Benjamin Peirce, "Linear Associative Algebra," The American Journal of Mathematics, vol. IV (1881), p. 97, with notes and addenda by Charles Sanders Peirce (1839-1914), son of the author and the founder of pragmatism.

the nonempirical and empirical sciences, however, the central fact remains that there are generally recognized ways of solving problems and settling disagreements in all of the established sciences; and the same is true of everyday empirical disputes.

We can see now a major respect in which moral reasoning differs from scientific reasoning and everyday reasoning about simple, empirical, technical, and means-ends matters. In moral reasoning, there is not the same general acceptance of procedures, methods, or criteria for settling moral questions by those who are morally competent and rational. We do not share a notion of common evidence. Hence when people disagree about the way to settle a moral question, we cannot assume that at least one must lack moral competence or rationality. Take, for example, the disagreement between Isabella and her brother Claudio. The presumed fact that Isabella's sleeping with the Duke's deputy will preserve Claudio's life is taken by the brother to be sufficient moral reason for her to do it. She, on the contrary, thinks that her obligation to keep her vows and to preserve her chastity carry greater moral weight and show that she ought not do it. This difference between them gives us no ground for dismissing either as irrational or morally incompetent, even though we may personally agree with one disputant and not the other. For the relevant moral reasons each offers—or anyone else might offer—do not settle the matter for all rational and morally competent people the way comparable scientific, empirical, or mathematical reasons settle scientific, mathematical, and empirical questions. Accordingly, we do not have to agree with one side or another on pain of being found morally incompetent or irrational. Rational and morally competent people may give different solutions to moral problems, take different sides on a moral issue, and weigh considerations differently.

The contrast between moral and scientific reasoning, however, needs to be qualified in at least three ways. First, I do not want to suggest that we can settle every mathematical or scientific disagreement. For example, mathematicians have been struggling unsuccessfully for over three hundred years to prove or to disprove Fermat's Last Theorem.[2] They still do not know how to do either. Secondly, disputes in science are sometimes about the proper interpretation of the data or facts; they are not always simply about facts. Such disagreements become more common with the emergence of a new theory or a major discovery—for example, the discovery of oxygen in chemistry. These developments may so revolutionize a science that basic procedures and tools cease to be generally accepted;

---

2. Fermat's Last Theorem (ca. 1637) states that no integral values of x, y, and z can be found to satisfy the equation $x^n + y^n = z^n$ if n is an integer greater than 2. In the case of $n=2$, however, we can have $3^2 + 4^2 = 5^2$ (that is, $9 + 16 = 25$), and an infinite number of cases derived from this one, such as $6^2 + 8^2 = 10^2$.

a certain amount of methodological confusion may then ensue. In such periods, it becomes less clear what the criteria are for doing good or bad science, since the background of agreement is temporarily shaken. In time, however, a new methodological agreement emerges. Then we again have so-called "normal," as opposed to "revolutionary" science. Finally, I want to emphasize that I have been contrasting moral reasoning with reasoning within the established and "normal" sciences.

Why There Are No Moral Experts

Five bad arguments. I would like to turn now to the question whether there are any moral experts. I shall begin by examining five bad arguments for the view that there are no moral experts, since it is important, not only to come to sound conclusions in ethics—and in life generally—but also to arrive at them for good, not bad, reasons. I shall next present my argument why there are not, and cannot be, any moral experts. The discussion will conclude with replies to various objections, which should help clarify both what I am and am not saying.

The first bad argument: it is generally agreed that there are experts in the sciences. Morality is not a science; hence there are no experts in morality.

My rebuttal: even assuming that the two premises of this argument are true—and I agree with the first that morality is not a science—the argument fails. Dressmaking and marksmanship, for example, are not sciences: they are arts or skills. Nevertheless, there are experts in dressmaking and marksmanship. The French designer Christian Dior is an expert dressmaker and the pioneer Daniel Boone is an expert marksman; yet neither is a scientist. The argument makes the crucial mistake of asssuming that an expert must be an expert in a science.

Second bad argument: we have seen that when a person confronts a moral problem there is a sense in which he or she alone can decide what to do; no one can come to a conclusion for him or her. Therefore, there cannot be any moral experts.

Rebuttal: again this is a nonsequitur; that is, the conclusion of the argument does not follow fron the premises. Thus, just because there is a sense in which no one can make a decision for you in some field or area, it does not follow that there are no experts in it. There is also a sense in which no one can decide for Julia Child, or any other cook, how to make a cheese souffle; the cook alone decides how much salt to put in it, how long to beat the eggs, and so on. Nevertheless, Julia Child remains an expert in French cooking. For she knows just what ingredients to use, how to season them, how to beat the egg whites, how long to cook the dish, at what temperature, and so on, to make the ideal souffle. It is because of this recognized experise that, in another sense of 'decide', many people let her decide for them how to prepare and cook a souffle; that is, they follow her instruction on how to do it.

Third bad argument: there cannot be any moral experts since no two people have exactly the same set of values and beliefs. Hence no other person can have your moral problems and give you expert advice on how to solve them. If it were possible for two people to have exactly the same set of values and beliefs, there would be moral experts. The person who would then have your moral problem, would be a moral expert on it.

Rebuttal; this argument makes several mistakes. First, it wrongly assumes that it is necessary to have the exact same total set of values and beliefs in order to have the same moral problem. All that is required, however, is that people be torn between the same courses of action for the same moral reasons. For example, Philippe, another young Frenchman, may have the same moral problem as Francois: whether to leave for England and join the Free French or to remain with his dependent mother and help her to carry on. The same moral considerations may pull him in both directions. Yet many of his values and beliefs may differ from Francois's. Consequently, the argument is mistaken in assuming that people cannot have the same moral problem because no two people ever have exactly the same values and beliefs. Secondly, the conclusions that are thought to follow if we were to have the same total set of beliefs and values do not. To see this we need only suppose that one person perfectly replicated another and they both had the same set of values and beliefs. Admittedly, we would then have two people with exactly the same moral dilemmas. It does not follow, however, that either would be a moral expert on the moral problems of the other. They simply have the same moral problems. So the possibility of getting two people with the same set of values and beliefs is not a sufficient condition for there being moral experts. Finally, it is not apparent why this should be a necessary condition for moral experts. It certainly is not a necessary condition for expertise in other fields. Thus ballet experts from the Russian and Cecchetti schools have a different understanding of the eight body positions. Master car mechanics also differ from one another in many of their beliefs and values.

Fourth bad argument: since there are no formulae that give either necessary and/or sufficient conditions of what is morally right or wrong or what we ought and ought not to do, we cannot deduce or prove what is morally right or wrong by appeal to such formulae. That is, moral reasoning is not deductive. Consequently, there cannot be any moral experts.

Rebuttal: it still remains to be seen whether there are or are not such formulae in morality. Part II will examine various ethical theories that purport to provide us with necessary and sufficient conditions of what is right and wrong. Even if we later conclude, however, that such formulae must be rejected, this argument remains a bad one. For example, dance therapists and athletic specialists have no formulae either that enable them to prove logically what procedures will get a person to walk again or back on the field. Nevertheless, such people may be experts, and have considerable knowledge of the likely effects of motions, of what may help people move again, or improve their movements.

Fifth bad argument: it is contended that experts agree with each other and understand their fields. Yet neither this agreement nor this understanding prevails in the "field" of morality. The so-called experts—Ann, Abby, the Playboy Advisor, priests, ministers, rabbis, philosophers, and anyone else you might want to include—disagree with each other, for example, about premarital sex and other things, and they do not know how to answer all of our moral questions; therefore, there are no moral experts.

Rebuttal: the premises of this argument are false. An expert is neither defined as someone who is omniscient in a field—that is, as someone who knows everything about it and never makes any mistakes in it, nor as someone who always agrees with other experts in the same area. Two heart surgeons, for example, may disagree with each other on which technique to employ in an operation and be unable to answer many questions about surgery, and yet for all that be respected authorities in their field. Agreeing on many fundamental matters in a field and on what would settle disagreements does not imply unanimity or total agreement about everything in it.

My argument for concluding that there are no moral experts begins by considering what it means to be an expert. An expert, by definition, is someone with a special skill, technique, competence or knowledge—what can be called expertise—in a field, trade, or study. The person is an authority in it. This expertise is acquired by practice (in marksmanship, juggling, cooking) or by schooling (in mathematics, physics, architecture) or, in most cases, by both practice and schooling. But what constitutes expertise in a field at one time may not at another. For example, experts in quantum physics today know far more than they did fifty years ago. Experts are contrasted with nonexperts, people who have considerably less or hardly any knowledge or skill in the field. Necessarily, most people fall short of being experts in any given area.

Yet people can be more or less expert in something. 'Expert', like 'height', 'weight', 'temperature', is thus a degree or scalar word: it allows comparative judgments to be represented by means of a scale. The notion of an expert differs in this respect from that of pregnancy or winning, since obviously no one can be more or less pregnant or more or less win. "I won the game more than he did" and "Mary Jane is more pregnant than Mary Lu" are both absurd. Yet you can be more or less expert in something than someone else. Finally, there are tests or criteria that enable us to tell who are experts in a given field at a given time, who are not, and what a person's level of competence is. Those who do not satisfy the criteria—that is, fail the tests, or get relatively low scores—will be judged to lack competence—that is, not to be experts--or at least to be less expert than others with higher scores. For example, if about chemistry you do not know—or if _all_ you know is—that water is composed of hydrogen and oxygen, you will not be deemed an expert in chemistry.

Now my contention is that we have no comparable tests in morals, no commonly accepted criteria or tests to distinguish between experts and nonexperts, or to determine who are more or less expert, in morality. Thus, if a Buddhist monk, Dr. Joyce Brothers, Ann Landers, and Abigail van Buren all gave conflicting moral advice, there is no way to tell which of these four, if any, speaks as a moral expert and to rank the extent of that expertise. We have no such difficulty picking out experts, or judging who is more expert than who, in the different branches of mathematics or physics, in marksmanship, cooking, law, surgery, and the like. It is significant that wherever we talk of a high level of competence or of expertise, we have certifying tests, or criteria, to determine its presence or absence. We lack these in morality: so it actually makes little sense to talk of experts in morality.

Notice that my conclusion that there are no moral experts to appeal to to solve our moral problems or to settle our moral disagreements fits in nicely with a further view of mine that morality has no external object. What I mean by that is that it is not a mere means to the bringing about of some state of affairs (the external object) that is only contingently connected to it. Cooking, in contrast, may be said to have an external object or end, since it presupposes a purpose external to it: how good does the cooked food taste? Thus people can be judged to be expert cooks on the basis of how well their cooking contributes to producing tasty dishes. If morality, like cooking, presupposed an end external to it, we could similarly judge people to be moral experts on the basis of how well their advice contributed to attaining that end. (I return to this topic of morality being an end in itself and not merely serving some external purpose in my concluding chapter.)

That we have no tests or criteria to pick out experts in morality, in contrast to the sciences, is directly related to the point made in the previous section that in scientific, but not in moral, reasoning there is a general acceptance among those who are competent in the field of procedures or methods for settling questions that arise and arriving at knowledge in the field. Earlier I claimed that students who reject these agreed-upon procedures and methods are not admitted into the fraternity of scientists. Morally competent people, on the other hand, realize that they cannot presume a notion of common evidence. Thus something may be enough evidence or reason for one person (Claudio was one example I gave), but not for another (Isabella). Most of us recognize that people can weigh moral considerations quite differently without either being morally incompetent or irrational.

Suppose, however, that a charismatic reformer arose who converted everyone to a morality that emphasized strict rules of honesty, the sanctity of promises, and the like—and that thereafter all moral judgments were made in terms of that morality. Would we not then have a situation comparable to what we now have in the sciences? I think not, as a second thought experiment shows. Imagine that another moral reformer arose—say, one who preached in addition the need to love your neighbor. Even if the people never accepted this new morality, with its emphasis on loving your neighbor, they could not properly regard its proponent as morally irrational or incompetent. (They might, of course, throw him into jail or even crucify him for being a rabble-rouser, but that is another matter.) I think this shows that moral, unlike scientific, deviants cannot just be dismissed as incompetent or irrational because of their marked disagreement from what is considered acceptable in the group. I therefore draw the strong conclusion that not only are there at present no moral experts, but there never could (logically) be any, regardless of how much moral agreement were achieved at any given time. My argument in a nutshell:

1. If there were an expert in morals at any given time, then there would be a commonly accepted set of criteria for applying the expression 'moral expert' at that time that everyone would have to agree with on pain of being found either irrational or morally incompetent.

2. There cannot be such a commonly accepted set of criteria.

3. Therefore, there are no experts in morals, never were any, and never will be any.

Objections and replies. First objection to the view that there are no moral experts: it might be thought that my view cannot be correct, since some people's moral judgment is expert in the same way that Daniel Boone's aim is: their individual decisions are always "on target." Most of us believe there are people now and in the past who make better moral judgments than others. Such people are said to possess practical wisdom. This quality of judgment reveals itself over time in the individual decisions they make. Consequently, there is indeed such a thing as moral expertise. The moral experts are simply those people who display this quality of judgment to the greatest extent.[3]

Rebuttal: this objection fails to respond to the main difficulty: it provides us with no test or criteria to tell who has this quality of judgment and to measure the extent to which someone has it. Talk of being "on target" and having a "track record" of making the right moral decisions is metaphorical and unhelpful. In markmanship, there are literally targets that do or do not get hit; thus we can show that Daniel Boone hits the target more than most people. Similarly, in running for speed, we can show that some athletes have better track records than others: we have records showing how they cover a certain distance in less time than the other people. We can clock this. But how are we to establish superior "track records" and who always "hits the target" in moral decision making? It seems we have no criteria for answering these questions that morally competent and rational people must agree upon.

Second objection: if my view is correct, the advice of others should be worthless to people with moral problems or to those who are involved in moral disagreements. But clearly it often is not. Consequently, there must be moral experts.

Rebuttal: this is a nonsequitur. I am not denying, either explicitly or implicitly, that it is possible to give others useful advice on moral matters. Moral leaders like Gandhi and Martin Luther King sometimes propose creative ways of dissolving moral problems and moral disagreements. Moreover, it is often possible to help people troubled by moral questions by pointing out to them the nature of their conduct, the consequences of their acts, alternative actions available to them that they may have overlooked, and so on. Thus it is advisable to listen, for example, to individuals possessing that special and important literary, philosophical, and political talent for tracing "the implications of things" (Henry James's phrase, from his essay "The Art of Fiction"), or who have a knack for describing what people are doing, for uncovering their motives and intentions. Such individuals may open our eyes to some relevant factors we have missed. To admit this is quite compatible with denying that there are any moral experts. For I am not conceding that such people's answer on what we ought morally do are authoritative and generally ought to be followed.

Third objection: there actually are tests to find out whether someone understands various notions—tests that not everyone will pass or pass equally well, that is, receive the same score. Why not call those who pass these tests moral experts? Or equate moral experts

---

3. Thomas Nagel suggests such an objection in "The Fragmentation of Value," Mortal Questions (Cambridge University Press, 1979), pp.128-141. See especially pp.135, 136, 139-41.

with people who understand moral language?

Reply: the first point about tests is certainly correct. Thus we can check to see whether someone knows how to use moral words, whether a person grasps the implications of moral judgments, and the like. For instance, we can find out whether someone is aware that morally right acts are those that we ought morally to do; that the concept of guilt is logically connected with the moral notion of wrong action; that if an act is said to be morally permissible, it is implied that is is not morally wrong; that one of the main functions of the word 'good' is to commend things; and that saying that the Roman emperor Nero was a vicious man implies that you should not (morally) imitate him. But almost everybody—all normal people anyway, idiots and imbeciles excepted—will pass these tests, even though they may not receive exactly the same score. It would thus be inadvisable to call these people, that is, people who have a reasonable and normal command of the moral language, moral experts, for doing so will tend to undermine the contrast between experts and nonexperts mentioned earlier. In short, if we adopt this linguistic recommendation and call everyone who demonstrates a satisfactory grasp of moral notions a moral expert, we shall most likely misuse the notion of an expert, which presupposes that there can only be a few experts in a given area or field. Even were this not so, however, there remains a second and more important objection to the proposal, namely, that there is no reason to believe that people who have such linguistic competence will also have a good understanding of what is morally right and wrong. Some will and some will not. Certainly it would be absurd to defer to the opinions of a Stalin, Hitler, or some other villain about how we should conduct ourselves just because they do well on such tests.

Fourth objection: it might be thought that my view implies—falsely—that there are no people with special knowledge of moral concepts, of ethical theories, and of moralities. But there are such people. Philosophers, for example, have knowledge of ethical theories and special metaethical understanding of moral concepts—that is, knowledge of the meaning of ethical terms, the nature of moral language, discourse, reasoning, and the like, along with the usual understanding of moral notions mentioned in the previous objection. Sociologists and anthropologists in turn often have considerable knowledge of different moralities; so do priests, ministers, rabbis, and theologians. For example, the Ayatollah Khomeini probably knows in greater detail how his sect of Moslems feels about moral questions than do the rest of us. And a Catholic priest or theologian may be an expert in Catholic moral law and doctrine, and thus give instruction on these matters.

Reply: all of this is true, and not denied by me when I say there are no moral experts. Notice I distinguish between being an expert in any particular morality, for example, Lutheran morality, and being a moral expert. If we did not make such a distinction, we would have to say that people lacking knowledge of a particular

-58-

morality are morally incompetent, which would be absurd. Even the Catholic, the Protestant, the Jew, Buddhist, Moslem, and the like recognize the absurdity of such a claim. In short, the special knowledge of the philosopher, anthropologist, sociologist, and religious leader may give them expertise in certain areas, but it does not make them moral experts; hence it is not the case that we must defer to their opinion about what is the morally right or wrong thing to do.

Fifth and final objection: it may seem that I am denying that anyone has any kind of moral authority. But what about papal authority, parental authority, and the like? For example, Roman Catholics believe that they should always abide by what the Pope says excathedra, that is, in the exercise of his office, when it comes to matters of faith and morals.

My reply: here we are dealing with a different kind of authority. Parents, the Pope, Khomeini, and others lay down the moral law on certain matters to others. They have moral authority over these people, which is not to be equated with having moral authority that rests on moral expertise. To see this compare the M.D. who is director of a hospital. Such a person clearly has authority over the hospital staff. But this is different from the authority medical doctors have in virtue of their knowledge of medicine. Hence this doctor has two distinct kinds of authority. Similarly, the authority of the state is obviously different from "the authority of experts in scientific and other fields."[4] So just because there are people who have moral (or legal or political) authority over others, in the sense that people defer to them, obey them, follow their moral (or legal) directives and the like, it does not follow that they have any authority based on moral expertise. (Of course, it does not follow that they do not either.) For the reasons already given, I do not think that they in fact have any authority based on moral expertise, which is not to deny that they may have some kind of authority over others in regard to certain matters. To put the point as Robert Louis Stevenson might have: every man is his own doctor of morality, in the last resort.[5]

This brings to a close Part I. In Part II we shall examine some important ethical theories, beginning with approbative ones: ethical subjectivism, conventionalism, divine-command theory, and the golden

---

4. Rush Rhees's examples, from his book Without Answers (Schocken Books, 1969), p.69.

5. Robert Louis Stevenson's actual remark probably also expresses an important and related truth: "Every man [I presume he means adult human being] is his own doctor of divinity, in the last resort." From his chapter "Noyon Cathedral," An Inland Voyage (Charles Scribner's Sons, 1905).

rule, and ending with objectivist theories: ethical egoism, utilitarianism in several different forms, the appeal to nature for moral guidance, two versions of Kant's ethics, and agapism or the ethics of love. We shall examine each of these to see how helpful it is in dealing with moral problems and disagreements.

PART TWO

SOME MAJOR ETHICAL THEORIES

CHAPTER V

APPROBATIVE THEORIES

I shall call a theory approbative (approval, attitudinal) if it determines what is morally right (wrong), good (bad), solely on the basis of someone's, or a group's, approving (or disapproving) or having a pro (or con) attitude towards it. Interest theories in ethics, for example, those of Thomas Hobbes (1588-1679), William James (1842-1909), and Ralph Barton Perry (1876-1957), are approbative theories, since they hold interest in, or concern about, things to be the source of their positive and negative value. Hobbes takes the words 'good' and 'evil' to name objects of our desires and aversions; and Perry says that value is that which attaches to any object of any interest. For William James, "the essence of good is simply to satisfy demand."[1] The popular dictum "Do your own thing" often expresses an approbative viewpoint as well. Likewise for the view that says that whatever is popular, is right. I shall call the conviction that "there is nothing either good or bad, but thinking makes it so" (Hamlet, II, ii, 259) ethical subjectivism or conventionalism. It will be classified as subjectivism if the thinking that is held to make something morally right or wrong, good or bad, is that of an individual; as conventionalism, if the thinking that is held to make something right or wrong is that of some group. Both of these last two kinds of theories are approbative theories, because they make what is morally right or wrong rest on its being approved or disapproved of by someone or by a group of people. Protagoras (ca. 490-420 B.C.), the most famous of the Sophists, or itinerant educators who toured the cities of Greece in the fifth century B.C., thus can be interpreted as either a subjectivist or a conventionalist when he contends that "man is the measure of all [including moral] things," or that things are the way they seem to us. If it is individual people that Protagoras has in mind, he is a subjectivist; if it is groups of people, he is a conventionalist.

Ethical Subjectivism and Conventionalism

---

1. William James, The Will to Believe and Other Essays in Popular Philosophy (New York: Longmans, Green & Co., 1897), p. 201.

Subjectivism takes the form:

Action A (any particular action) is morally right
(wrong) if and only if some individual thinks
or believes that A is morally right (wrong).

Conventionalism says something of the form:

A is morally right (wrong) if and only if the group
thinks or believes that A is morally right (wrong).

These theories have an appealing simplicity: they seem to provide us with a neat decision procedure to deal with our moral problems and moral disagreements. The idea that everyone must decide for himself or herself easily gives rise to one form of subjectivism; the desire to be able to justify almost anything, to another. Some forms of subjectivism, and all forms of conventionalism, appear to take the burden of making moral decisions off our shoulders. Conventionalism thus appeals especially to teenagers and to people who tend to be peer-oriented--to those who, in David Riesman's words, are "other-directed" rather than "inner-directed." (The sociologist Riesman develops these concepts in his book The Lonely Crowd (1950).) The other-directed person looks to what other people think is right or what is wrong; the inner-directed does not: his or her concern is simply to do what is right, even if others disagree. But this, of course, does not mean that inner-directed people must be subjectivists. They may or may not be.

A criticism that seems to apply to all forms of ethical subjectivism and conventionalism: the circularity and infinite-regress objection. Before I consider how these formulations are to be interpreted, we should note that they contain an apparent circularity. Specifically, they appear to explain the notion of moral rightness (wrongness) in terms of itself, since the phrase 'A is morally right (wrong)' appears on both sides of the connective 'if and only if'. This is why the statements seem to lead to an infinite regress—that is, to a never-ending act of reasoning backward. For, if to avoid the circularity, I replace the phrase 'A is morally right (wrong)' wherever it occurs on the righthand side of the 'if and only if' with the whole clause that explains it, I shall have to go on doing this without end, since the phrase will keep on reappearing with each substitution. To illustrate, suppose you give the definition, "Tom's lie is morally right (wrong) = Df James (or the local bowling club) believes that Tom's lie is morally right (wrong)." We see immediately that the phrase 'Tom's lie is morally right (wrong)' appears on both sides of the special sign of equality that indicates that the expression on the left is always replaceable by the expression on the right. (I have underlined the phrase in the above definition to emphasize this fact.) So that phrase is both what is being defined and also an essential part of what is doing the defining, making the definition appear circular. But (the objection continues) if I did not initially understand the phrase, I won't understand it after hearing the circular definition.

Suppose now that to get more enlightenment, I ask you what you mean by the phrase 'Tom's lie is morally right (wrong)' when it occurs on the righthand side of the equal's sign. You will repeat your definition, what you said originally. If I now substitute the phrase that is doing the defining for the phrase that has been troubling me in that original definition, I shall get the following stutter: "Tom's lie is morally right (wrong)=Df James (or the local bowling club) believes that James (or the local bowling club) believes that Tom's lie is morally right (wrong)." Once more we see the troublesome phrase (underlined). No matter how many substitutions I make, it will keep on reappearing there, each time with an increased stuttering effect. Thus the next substitution will give me: "Tom's lie is morally right (wrong)=Df James (or the local bowling club) believes that James (or the local bowling club) believes that James (or the local bowling club) believes that Tom's lie is morally right (wrong)." The regress that I am embarked on appears to have no end.

There is a possible counter, however, to this criticism. Someone may reply that we understand the longer expression in the original statement, namely, 'some individual (or the group) believes that A is morally right (wrong)', independently of, and maybe even better than we understand the phrase 'A is morally right (wrong)'. Indeed, we have seen (p.25) that emotivists like A. J. Ayer deny that sentences of the form 'A is morally right (wrong)' have any cognitive significance or that any thoughts can be expressed with them; hence, in his view, strictly speaking, they lack truth-value and they cannot be understood. But Ayer is confident that we can understand what it is for someone, or a group, to believe that something is morally right or wrong. Pollsters and sociologists, after all, compile data on public opinion on moral issues. In short, someone might claim that the question whether something is morally right or wrong either lacks cognitive significance or, more moderately, that it is at least less well understood than the question whether some individual or group believes that that actions is morally right or wrong.

Leaving this criticism up in the air, let us return to the question how we are to interpret 'some individual' and 'the group' in our two formulations. There seem to be at least two ways to take them. 'Some individual' might be taken to mean some specific individual, for example, the Reverend Jim Jones, or the man who first married Marilyn Monroe. Similarly, 'the group' may be interpreted as some definite group, such as Michigan State University students in 1984. Let us call these two theories specific or individual ethical subjectivism or individual ethical conventionalism, respectively. Alternatively, we may take 'some individual' or 'the group' to mean any individual, or any group. I shall now examine and rebut both of these subjectivist and conventional theories.

-65-

1. Individual or specific variants of ethical subjectivism and conventionalism. We are supposing here that 'some individual' or 'the group' can be replaced by a proper name or definite description (something of the form 'the such and such') that picks out one unique individual or group. Then by finding out what this individual or this group believes to be morally right (wrong), supposing the theory to be correct, we shall find out what is morally right (wrong). So it appears that this kind of theory might be quite helpful to a person facing a moral problem. Suppose, for example, that the special individual is Billy Graham. Then all Gauguin (see the second moral problem) needs to do, if he is this sort of subjectivist, is to find out which of the alternative courses of action Billy Graham believes to be right, which not. This will tell him which action he ought to perform, which not. Alternatively, if Gauguin is a specific or individual ethical conventionalist and if the Moral Majority is the group, all he needs to do is to find out what the Moral Majority believes he ought to do. This, again, will be what he ought to do.

Objection about the criteria of moral rightness and wrongness. The theory implies that the only reason for saying something is morally right (wrong) is that some specified individual or group believes that it is. Accordingly, the claim that something is morally right can only be false if we misreport or misinterpret the individual's or that group's beliefs about what is morally right (wrong). Such a theory thus runs counter to our ordinary views about how the assertion that something is morally right (wrong) is to be justified or shown to be unjustified. The whole emphasis has been shifted from the question whether this or that is right to the question whether a particular person or a particular group believes this or that is right. If we are not the key individuals, our own opinions about the matter are irrelevant, along with the characteristics and consequences of the action. We are to disregard such things and simply get on the bandwagon—that is, conform to the views of the specified individual or group.

A moral criticism. Suppose the key individual is a deranged or vicious person, someone like the Rev. Jim Jones, who believed that it is morally right for his followers to be beaten, tortured, humiliated, sexually assaulted, and finally, that it is right for them to take a fatal dose of cyanide. We must then say that all of these things are morally right, which most of us would say is absurd as well as immoral. We know that there were many people—apparently a majority of his followers—who obeyed the Rev. Jim Jones willingly. They did not doubt their leader. He had immense power over them. The attitude of such People's Temple Cult members was "to go with Dad," even when "Dad" urged them to commit suicide and to kill their children. (About 900 died in Guyana in November 1978.) These people seem to have been individual or specific ethical subjectivists, whether or not they realized it, and we see the horrors that such a theory can lead to. However, if you find the example of the Rev. Jim Jones objectionable in one way or another and hence unpersuasive, substitute your own favorite villain—the Roman Emperors Caligula or Nero, Attila, King of the Huns, Stalin, or Hitler. The point can be made using any one of these, as well as with other people. Essentially the same moral criticism can be made of individual or specific conventionalism. To see this we need merely suppose that the relevant group consists of Nazi SS troopers who believe that it is morally right to exterminate all non-Aryans. If we accepted this ethical theory, we would have to conclude that such an act is morally right, which is again absurd.

A possible reply. It might be urged that we choose our individual and group with greater care; that we could then avoid these criticisms. Suppose instead we take as our group the majority and that we choose Mother Theresa of Calcutta, Joan Baez, or Abraham Lincoln as our individual. Henry David Thoreau would object to the first suggestion, asking, "When were the good and the brave ever in a majority?" ("A Plea for Captain John Brown"). The evidence indicates that majorities are sometimes wrong, even though they are not usually entirely wrong. Henry Sidgwick (1838-1900), the important English moral philosopher, say that "all or most men in whom moral consciousness is strongly developed find themselves from time to time in conflict with the commonly received morality of the society to which they belong." He thinks that we can even imagine that some of our moral beliefs might collide with those of the "whole human race" (The Methods of Ethics, bk. I, chap. III). So it seems that the opinions of the majority cannot be taken to be definitive of what is morally right or wrong. Mother Theresa, Joan Baez, or Abraham Lincoln may be better moral guides, yet why should we favor a specific variant of subjectivism that makes them the key individuals instead of Xaviera Hollander (the author of The Happy Hooker), the Rev. Jerry Falwell, or Hugh Hefner? The same problem occurs with competing groups. If our appeal is to a particular variant of individual or specific subjectivism or conventionalism, our reasoning is circular and we beg the question by assuming the point at issue. If our basis of choice rests on another theory of what is morally right or wrong, we abandon individual or specific subjectivism or conventionalism. Consequently, we can offer no moral reason for choosing one person or group over another without either abandoning our theory or begging the question.

2. General or universal variants of ethical subjectivism and conventionalism. Let us turn now to the second variants of these theories, which say that 'some individual' equals any individual and 'the group' means any group. According to these theories, if any individual, or any group, believes that an action is morally right (wrong), it is. Pure subjectivists or conventionalists of this kind must be very rare, though it often seems as if many people act to some degree as if they were such subjectivists or conventionalists.

Besides the moral objection that such theories lead to the slimy conclusion that anything goes, morally speaking, we have the further fatal criticism that the theories lead to a contradiction, assuming merely that one person or group—for example, Simone de Beauvoir or the American Civil Liberties Union—believes that a certain act is morally right or permissible and another person, or group—for example, the Rev. Jerry Falwell or the Moral Majority—believes that such an act is morally wrong. We know that the two organizations mentioned disagree on the morality of abortion; Simone de Beauvoir (the author of The Second Sex) and Jerry Falwell presumably do so as well. We must then conclude that it both is and is not morally right to have an abortion. Hence this second version of the two theories must also be rejected, along with the first one. It settles nothing.

3. <u>Relativistic variants of ethical subjectivism and conventionalism.</u> There is a way we can get around the last objection to general or universal variants of subjectivism and conventionalism. All we need to do is modify the theories slightly, as follows:

> A is morally right (wrong) <u>for a certain individual</u> if and only if that individual believes that A is morally right (wrong).

> A is morally right (wrong) <u>for a certain group</u> if and only if that group believes that A is morally right (wrong).

Note the expression 'right (wrong) for . . .' here. Adding it makes the new theories thoroughly relativistic. Accordingly, given the same facts, we no longer get a contradiction. Instead, we arrive at the conclusions that having an abortion is morally right for Simone de Beauvoir and for the ACLU, but that having an abortion is not morally right for Jerry Falwell and the Moral Majority. These conclusions do not contradict each other.

<u>A reductio ad absurdum of the third variants of subjectivism and conventionalism based on the intensionality of belief.</u> That is, supposing such theories to be true, I shall demonstrate (indirectly) that they could not be true, since they can lead to a contradictory conclusion given human fallibility and the intensionality of belief. The intensionality of belief is a characteristic of belief that distinguishes it from certain other notions and relations, such as shooting, wounding, hitting, touching, and so on. Let me explain by comparing believing with shooting. Both may be conceived of as two-place relations between people and objects that are either believed or shot. That is, we distinguish those who shoot from what they shoot and distinguish believers from what they believe. Thus a potential assassin (the shooter) shot and wounded Mr. Reagan (the object shot), on March 30, 1981. Similarly, there are people (call them believers) who believe that Ronald Reagan is the 40th President of the United States (what follows the 'that' expresses the object of their belief). So far the relations seem to be similar, but now notice two differences between the cases. First, belief and shooting take different kinds of objects:

-68-

the objects of belief are propositions or sentences, whereas objects of shooting are nonpropositional, nonsentential, physical, and (too often) flesh-and-blood entities. Secondly and more importantly for our purposes, when the potential assassin shot and wounded Mr. Reagan in March, 1981, he shot and wounded the 40th President of the United States, whether or not he knew or believed that Reagan is the 40th President of the United States. Contrast believing (along with hunting, looking for, and the like). Someone may believe in March, 1981, that Reagan is the President of the United States without believing that Reagan is the 40th President of the United States, even though he is. In a word, something believed under one description (something of the form 'the such and such') may not be believed under another description of one and the same thing. But something shot under one description must be shot under another description of one and the same thing. We mark this difference between believing and shooting by calling the first an intensional and the second a nonintensional (or extensional) relation.

We are ready now to make use of this characteristic of belief in developing the promised reductio ad absurdum of the two relativistic theories. I shall show how someone can believe that a certain act, A, is morally right and at the same time that act B is not morally right, even though A=B. The play, King Oedipus, provides a famous literary illustration of the point. Presumably Oedipus believes that it would be morally wrong to sleep with his mother, yet that it is not morally wrong to sleep with Jocasta (his wife). But Jocasta, unbeknownst to him (at least until the end of Sophocles' play), is his mother. So, given these facts about Oedipus's ignorance, the present relativistic subjectivist theory leads to the conclusion that it is both morally right and not morally right for Oedipus to sleep with Jocasta. The theory must therefore be rejected.

Next, let us apply the reductio ad absurdum to the relativistic conventionalist theory—namely, to the theory that holds:

> an action A is morally right (wrong) for a
> group of people if and only if that group
> of people believes that A is morally right
> (wrong).

Again we make use of the intensionality of belief. Suppose we have a group consisting of Michiganders, or as they are coming to be called these days, Michiganians. Suppose Michiganians overwhelmingly believe that it is morally all right, or permissible, to sell the Pigeon River Country State Forest for $100 million to some rich Arabs or Swiss in order to assist the state treasury. Suppose that 100 million barrels of oil and 100 cubic feet of natural gas lie beneath the forest, and that taxes on the oil and gas would pump at least one billion dollars into the state treasury, but the Michiganians do not know this. Polls show that they agree that it would be morally wrong to sell any Michigan state forest with that much oil and gas to anyone for a mere $100 million, since they think that would rob the state of money it needs to relieve the suffering of the poor and the unemployed. Our hypothesis and theory, then, entitle us to infer that it is morally right for Michiganians to sell the Pigeon River Country State Forest for $100 million and also that it is not morally right for them to sell this state for a mere $100 million. We must, therefore, reject this form of ethical conventionalism, along with the corresponding form of subjectivism.

There are two possible misunderstandings of what I have just said that I would like to guard against. First, it may be thought that the intensionality of belief somehow relies, or depends, on ignorance. It does not, even though my reductio depends on it. As explained, intensionality is simply a characteristic of belief that distinguishes it from certain other relations (hitting, shooting, touching, and the like). Thus, if I touch (or hit) the Sears Tower in Chicago in 1982, I touch (or hit) the tallest building in the United States, if the Sears Tower is the tallest building in the United States in 1982, for touching is not an intensional relation. Yet if I believe in 1982 that some building is the Sears Tower, we cannot infer that I believe that it is the tallest building in the United States in 1982, even though it is. This, in a nutshell, is the intensionality of belief: that something believed under one description might not be believed under another description of one and the same thing. It is this possibility, coupled with the right kind of ignorance of an identity, that gives rise to the aforegoing reductio of these theories.

A second possible mistake is to think that this reductio implies that it is a contradiction to say either that Oedipus believes his sleeping with Jocasta, his wife, is all right, but that his sleeping with his mother is not all right, if Jocasta is his mother, or that it implies that the two theories are both self-contradictory. It does not inply these things. The contradiction the argument derives from the theory and the supposed ignorance of an individual (Oedipus) and of a group (Michiganians) about some identity is that an action is both morally right and not morally right for that person or group. I am of course assuming that any adequate ethical theory will not lead to a contradiction, given the facts of life, which includes the fact that human beings are fallible and, in particular, are often ignorant of various identities. Finally, it is no part of my intention to criticize either Oedipus or Michiganians (they both have enough problems as it is). Oedipus's ignorance is certainly highly unusual, but he cannot fairly be blamed for it, given the circumstances of his life. Michiganians could hardly be blamed, either, for the possible ignorance ascribed to them in my second example.

A problem about agreements and disagreements. Before I close this discussion of relativistic subjectivism and conventionalism, I want to mention one more difficulty these theories run into. They have a problem accounting for moral agreement and moral disagreement. As we have seen, it is quite compatible to say "A is morally right for NM

-70-

(one person or group)" and "A is not morally right for NN (another person or group)." How, then, can individuals or groups either agree or disagree with each other? Suppose Ms. White says that shoplifting is morally right for her. Ms. Black can only agree with her by saying, in effect, "Yes, you do believe it is morally right to shoplift," and only disagree with her by saying something like, "No, you do not believe that it is morally right to shoplift." For if she said instead, "Yes, I agree. I believe shoplifting is morally right too," she would merely be establishing that shoplifting is morally right for her (Ms. Black), which is not to assert what Ms. White asserted. The same point holds for groups.

These theories, then, leave no room for any nonrelative sense of 'right' and 'wrong'. Yet people often discuss—sometimes agreeing, sometimes disagreeing—what is morally right or wrong. They do not only, or always, talk about what is morally right for somebody or for some group. This again shows the inadequacy of these relativistic theories: they ignore, or dismiss as irrelevant, a major portion of our discourse and deliberations. The nonrelativistic versions of subjectivism and conventionalism do not make this mistake; however, we have seen that they are untenable for other reasons. Consequently, we should reject, along with ethical subjectivism, all versions of groupism or the Gospel of Getting on the Bandwagon. Neither our own nor our neighbor's opinion settles what is morally right; it does not even constitute a moral reason in support of such judgments. Yet many people seem to be guided mainly by the views of others. They ask fearfully, "What will the Joneses say? What will the Joneses think?" John Masefield says that custom is "a God worshipped by the herd" ("Lines on the Tercentenary of Harvard College," 1936). Operating solely at such a conventional or subjectivist level—accepting only the ready-made opinions of others about what is good and right—means you have not yet learned how to think morally or how to make moral judgments. For moral reasons do not guide your judgments and conduct. The same is true if you are a subjectivist who thinks the only "justification" you can offer for thinking something is morally right is that you think it is. You are then like the child who when asked why he makes a certain claim can only answer, "Because," which is not to give a reason, much less a moral reason. Subjectivism and conventionalism in the end reveal themselves to be only pseudo-ethical views.

The Golden Rule

I would like to turn now to an ancient principle that continues today to be widely accepted in both East and West, the golden rule. In the Bible it is given a positive formulation: "All things whatsoever ye would that men should do to you, do ye even so to them: for this

-71-

is the law and the prophets" (Matthew 7:12). Confucius's statement of the principle is negative: "What you do not want done to yourself, do not do to others" (The Confucian Analects, bk.15, chap.23). Then there are the jocular formulations: "Do unto the other feller the way he'd like to do unto you an' do it fust" (Edward Noyes Westcott, David Harum, chap.20). "'Do other men for they would do you.' That's the true business precept" (Charles Dickens, Martin Chuzzlewit, chap.11). Or: the one who has the gold rules. Finally, there is the claim that "The golden rule is that there is no golden rule,"[2] which is my personal favorite, since I do not think there are any true exceptionless, nonvacuous moral principles that tell us what things we should and should not do (see pp.34-35 as well as Chapter VII). The whole of Part II will establish just how appropriate Shaw's formulation is. However, I shall only discuss the first two versions of the golden rule, from Matthew and the Analects. These can be interpreted literally and nonliterally. In this chapter, I shall only examine the literal interpretation of the golden rule. I shall try to show that, so interpreted, both the positive and the negative formulations of the golden rule could easily lead—though obviously they won't always--to the justification of immoral acts; hence the golden rule, taken literally, is immoral. Finally, I shall propose a reductio ad absurdum of the literal version of the golden rule based on the intensionality of desire.

Why the golden rule, taken literally, is an immoral doctrine. Suppose I am a sadomasochist and I enjoy and want twisted things done to me. Then I can justify doing such things to others, according to the positive formulation of the golden rule, for it says whatever I want people to do to me, I may and should do to them. Time magazine gives the following decadent example. A Viennese artist, Rudolf Schwarzkogler, recently "decided to make a modernist artistic statement by amputating, inch by inch, his own penis, while a photographer recorded the process as a work of art" (10 September 1979). Suppose Schwarzkogler really would have preferred to have someone else amputate his (Schwarzkogler's) penis—he was just too embarrassed to ask. Then he could use the positive formulation of the golden rule to justify cutting off another man's penis to produce still another work of art. Or consider the following less gruesome example. Suppose you have a fetish for other people's toenail clippings. You make presents of your toenail clippings to your friends, thinking, as a good golden ruler, how delighted you would be to get their toenail clippings. Those who receive your parcels are, no doubt, disappointed: it was not what they really had been hoping for. Some of them are even likely to be disgusted. (Could they think that it is the thought that counts?) It is probably too strong to say that what you did was immoral, but it was certainly tasteless. Yet your moral

---

2. George Bernard Shaw, Man and Superman, Act III, "Maxims for Revolutionists: the Golden Rule."

theory and desires led quite directly to the erroneous conclusion that this was what you ought morally to do, which is absurd. Finally, the negative formulation of the golden rule, no less than the positive, can also justify immoral and other unacceptable behavior. For example, if I do not like courtesies to be shown to me or to be treated with respect, the principle, interpreted literally, entitles me to treat others without respect or courtesy.

Why can following the golden rule have such disastrous and bizarre consequence? Because the principle determines the moral rightness of the action on the basis of a person's wants or desires, or rather, on the wants or deires they would have in different circumstances. And as people's positive and negative desires can be nonmoral or immoral, so can the desires and attitudes and inclinations they would have in other circumstances. So merely affirming—no matter how sincerely—that you want to do something or that you would like to have something done to you, is not yet to give a moral reason for doing it. But if your act is not motivated by moral considerations, it cannot be a moral action. The golden rule, then, when taken literally, no more rules out immoral behavior than does the dictum that we should do our own thing or whatever we feel like doing. For that principle, too, will only result in moral behavior if "our own thing" or what we feel like doing happens to be moral.

A reductio ad absurdum of the literal version of the golden rule based on the intensionality of desire. This argument takes essentially the same form as the previous reductio directed at the third variants of subjectivism and conventionalism. Desire, like belief, is an intensional relation because you can desire something under one description (something of the form 'the such and such') and yet not under another, even though both descriptions are of one and the same thing. For example, if I were a young child and it was Halloween, I would probably like very much to be given some candy. Suppose Joe is a young child and it is Halloween. It follows from the golden rule and our suppositions that I ought to give Joe some candy. Suppose further that if I were deathly allergic to candy and worried about it, I would not want to be given any candy, and that Joe is deathly allergic to candy and worried about it. It follows from the golden rule and our suppositions that I ought not to give Joe some candy. Thus, given certain plausible factual assumptions, the golden rule easily leads to a self-contradictory conclusion, namely, that a certain act ought to be done, or is morally right, and also that it ought not to be done, or is morally wrong. Interpreted literally, then, the theory must be rejected.

Two nonliteral interpretations of the golden rule. I mentioned above (p.72) that the golden rule could be interpreted literally or nonliterally. So far only the literal interpretation has been considered. A defender of the golden rule is likely to object that my literal interpretation misrepresents its substance. What the golden rule is, in effect, telling us (the objector may continue), is that we should always consider the wishes, desires, and feelings of others; we should always try to put ourselves into other people's shoes, try to see things through their eyes and, above all, have regard, a certain kind of love, or respect for them. If this is correct, the golden rule seems to be one version of Kant's ethics (the second) or to be a form of agapism, that is, an ethics of love. This theory (or theories) is (or are) examined at the end of the next chapter (see pp.114-125). According to a second possible nonliteral interpretation of the golden rule, it urges us to test our moral norms or principles of action by some sort of universalizability test; that is, we are to ask ourselves whether we can consistently will that everyone act on the principle in question. Certainly the golden ruler's question: how would you like that done to you—for example, have slavery tried out on you—leads easily and naturally into the Kantian question: can you universalize that principle, say, of slavery? If we can universalize the principle, it is okay; if not, it is not. This interpretation of the golden rule seems to make it still another version of Kant's ethics (the first) which is also discussed in the next chapter (see pp.108-114). Since both forms of Kant's ethics and agapism are only examined later, along with other objectivist theories, we must defer for now a final evaluation of the golden rule. I believe it is these nonliteral versions of the golden rule that account for its enormous and perennial appeal in so many different cultures and religions. Interpreting the doctrine literally, however, as I have here, it surely must be rejected, along with the other approbative theories discussed—subjectivism and conventionalism—which try to determine what is morally right, or morally right for somebody or for a group of people, on the basis of an individual's or a group's beliefs about what is morally right. I shall examine next one final approbative theory, divine-command theory. Then we shall turn to objectivist ethical theories.

Divine-Command Theory

The divine-command theorist says that those, and only those, actions God commands (orders, wills, love, or wants us to do) are morally right and those he forbids are wrong. Thus it is the voice of God, His commands, that settles all moral questions. This is an approbative theory, since it makes moral rightness and wrongness depend on someone's approval or disapproval—God's. Atheists and polytheists will of course reject the theory. Certainly if there is no God, or there are many Gods, it must be mistaken. If you are an agnostic, you will also have doubts about the theory.

The Euthyphro objection. This criticism of the divine-command theory comes from Plato's dialogue the Euthyphro (9b-11b). The objection neither presupposes the existence nor the nonexistence of God; it simply bypasses that question. So it should not get up the hackles of either theists or atheists.

There are two superficial features of Plato's discussion in the Euthyphro that may make us overlook its relevance. First, the topic of the Euthyphro is the nature of piety, not of right. But piety, or holiness, Plato regards as part of justice, or of what is morally right, since it is concerned with right-dealing towards the Gods. In other words, what is pious must be right, though not everything that is right need be pious. Plato's notion of right or just is broader than the notion of piety: he conceives of piety merely as a species of rightness. Secondly, Plato talks here always about gods, not about God. To bring out the relevance of the argumentation of the Euthyphro I shall therefore substitute 'right' for 'pious' and 'God' for 'gods' wherever they occur in the text. This will also avoid uninteresting complications and make the discussion more suitable to our monotheistic culture.

Socrates and Euthyphro are the two characters discussing the nature of piety in this dialogue. (The historical Socrates (ca.469-399 B.C.) is also the famous teacher of Plato (ca.427-347 B.C.).) Let us begin at the point at which Socrates has just amended the definition of 'piety'--or of 'right'--offered by Euthyphro, to read as follows: what is right is what God loves. In short, the claim is:

A is morally right=Df A is loved by God.

Euthyphro and Socrates agree to inquire into the truth of this proposed definition. Euthyphro is confident that the statement will stand the test of inquiry. Socrates now fires his loaded and famous question: "Is what is right loved by God because it is right or is it right because it is loved by God?" Euthyphro does not understand the question; Socrates gives various analogies which we shall skip since they are not very helpful. Let us instead re-ask the question: "Is what is right loved by God because it is right, or is it right for some other reason?" In the end, Euthyphro inconsistently replies: "No, that is the reason; that is, God loves what is morally right because it is morally right." This implies that it is not morally right because God loves it. Rather, it is loved for the reason that it is morally right. In brief, God's loving it does not constitute its being morally right. Euthyphro has therefore abandoned the definition he originally proposed. To be consistent he should say instead: "No, God doesn't love what is right because it is right: His loving it constitutes its being morally right, is its very essence." Then he would not be guilty of the inconsistency of implicitly rejecting his own proposed definition of moral rightness.

Socrates concludes from Euthyphro's response: "But then that which is loved by God is not right, nor is that which is right loved by God: they are two different things." What he means is that being loved by God and being morally right must then not have the same essence, since what is morally right is not morally right in virtue of being loved by God, but rather it is loved by God because it is morally right. Therefore, these cannot be one and the same notion. Or to put it another way, the terms 'morally right' and 'loved by God' may have the same extension (apply truly to the same things), but they cannot have the same intension (meaning or sense). As Socrates says, Euthyphro has only given us an attribute or inessential characteristic of what is morally right (it is loved by God), whereas what we wanted to know was its essential nature.

Consequently, when the divine-command theorist states that what is morally right is what God commands, and nothing else is right, we should follow Socrates' lead and find out which of two distinguishable assertions the theorist is making. The claim might be that what is right is right simply in virtue of God's commanding it; this and nothing else is what makes it right, for this is what being morally right consists in. According to this version of the divine-command theory, God's will or command defines morality; so without God there could be no morality. William of Ockham, the important fourteenth-century English philosopher, is one of a small number of thinkers who apparently accepts this view. The Protestant reformer and theologian, John Calvin (1509-1564), may well be another proponent of this view. For he declares: "God's will is so much the highest rule of righteousness that whatever He wills, by the very fact that He wills it, must be considered righteous" (the Institutes of the Christian Religion 3.23.2).

The second claim the divine-command theorists might be making is that what is right is right, not because God commands it (this would be the first view), but for some other reason, and God commands such morally right actions because they are morally right. According to this version, there is only an extensional equivalence between God's commands and what is right; that is, there is no direct and necessary connection between God's commanding something and its being morally right, but both expressions, 'God commands it' and 'it is morally right', nevertheless apply truly to the same things. St. Thomas Aquinas, the great thirteenth-century theologian and philosopher, seems to make this second claim when he says "God cannot will evil."[3] He commands what is morally right, and nothing else, because He "grasps the good [and what is morally right] by His intellect,"[4] which is perfect. He makes no mistakes about such matters. Knowing every moral truth, God, in this view, might be called the supreme moral expert, contrary to the view I defend at the end of Part I that there cannot be any moral experts. But Aquinas adds that God is endowed with will as well as intellect, and it is with His will

---

3. St. Thomas Aquinas, Summa contra Gentiles, tr. Anton Pegis (Notre Dame: University of Notre Dame Press, 1975), bk.I, chap.95, sec.1.

4. Ibid., chap.72, sec.2.

that He commands us to do what He knows to be good and morally right.

I shall now attempt to evaluate these two positions. The first gives rise to the following absurdity. If God had willed the elimination of all black people, the extermination of the Jews, the institution of child-battering, or any other act we clearly regard as immoral, for example, rape, or even acts we think of as silly, such as running around naked and covered with mustard, the theory implies that we would have a moral duty to do these things. But such things few would ever think could be our moral duty. It might be thought that this criticism can be rebutted if we grant either that God's will is eternal—that is, that He wills whatever He wills eternally, or that He would never actually command that we perform such acts, since "He is the Giver of Life and perfect in every way." Yet neither of these replies has any force, because both of them are quite compatible with the criticism. Thus even if we agree with them, the criticism still seems sound.

However, there is a further and independent reason to doubt that God's will defines morality. Suppose that Scriptures give us the word of God. According to the Bible, God commanded Abraham to kill his innocent son Isaac and to offer him up as a burnt offering in the land of Moriah, three days away (Genesis 22:2). Admittedly, when Abraham was about to carry out this cruel deed—"Abraham stretched forth his hand, and took the knife to slay his son"—an angel of the Lord held him back from it (Genesis 22:10-12). Yet think of the anguish father and son must have gone through during those three long days! We also learn from the Bible that God allowed one of His most faithful worshippers, Job, to be tormented to make a point to the devil (Job 2:7); and God told Joshua, the commander of the Israelites, to wipe out all of Jericho. Except for Rahab and her kindred (she turned traitor to her people and collaborated with the Israelites), every "man and woman, young and old, and ox and sheep, and ass [were utterly destroyed], with the edge of the sword" (Joshua 6:21). Moreover, we read in the Koran that "the recompense of those who fight against God and His Messenger" is that they will "be slaughtered, or crucified, or their hands and feet shall alternately be struck off, or they shall be banished from the land." It appears from the text that it was God's will, at least at that time, that these people suffer such "a degradation . . . in this world." God added: "in the world to come [there] awaits them [an additional] mighty chastisement, except for such as repent, before you [presumably Muhammad and his followers] have power over them" (Koran 5:37-38). In short, it seems we need not attack the divine-command theory solely by appeal to contrary-to-fact suppositions of the sort mentioned in the last paragraph. The Bible and Koran themselves give us reason to doubt whether God's commands are always morally sound. But if they are not, we do not have an extensional equivalence between God's commands and what is morally right; hence the second version of the divine-command theory is false. However, if it is, the first version must also be false, since if they are not extensionally equivalent, they cannot be intensionally equivalent.

Some believers may object here at this presumption to measure God by human standards of justice and morality, saying that He transcends them. Indeed, He is the standard of right and wrong. So the designation 'unfair', 'immoral', and 'morally wrong' cannot be applied to God's commands and actions. Paraphrasing the Voice out of the Whirlwind that spoke to Job (see Job 38:1-42:6), it may be asked how we—who are mere ignoramuses and pip-squeaks in comparison to God—dare to question and to challenge Him. I answer that this sort of argument from God's superior credentials is really irrelevant. The basic fact is that it is impossible for us to refrain from judging in terms of the moral values we actually have. And given those values, most of us judge it to be morally wrong to make a burnt offering or sacrifice of our children, to torment a good man simply to illustrate a point to someone, or to commit genocide. If we refuse to acknowledge these moral convictions, we only deceive ourselves and perhaps others.

This second claim (God commands what is morally right because it is right and He recognizes that it is morally right), unlike the first, does not purport to tell us what the nature of moral rightness is. As we have seen, it merely contends that there is an extensional equivalence between God's commands and what is morally right. We determine that there is or is not such an extensional equivalence by finding out what acts are morally right, what acts God commands, and then seeing whether these acts are one and the same. If they are, we have the alleged equivalence; if not, we do not. One of my contentions has been that there is some reason to doubt whether we have such an extensional equivalence if we go by the Bible or the Koran, since there seems to be Scriptural evidence that God sometimes commands immoral acts. However, it may be that we are actually pretty much in the dark how to settle the question what God wills. Certainly if we take any controversial question—for example, our Salvadoran policy, racial desegregation, homosexuality—we shall find that those who accept the Bible as the word of God are likely to disagree whether God favors, permits, or condemns it. Thus some declare that homosexuality is clearly prohibited by both the Old and the New Testaments. They quote Leviticus 18:22 and Leviticus 20:13 which say it is "an abomination" for a man to lie with a man as he would with a woman, and Romans 1:18-32, which condemns both lesbianism and male homosexuality. In the recent book, The Church and the Homosexual (1976), Father John McNeill, a Jesuit priest, replies that the Law of Moses is actually a protest against the use of homosexuality in pagan rites, and that when St. Paul censures men for burning "in their lust one toward another; men with men working that which is unseemly" (Romans 1:27), this is to be read as opposition only to homosexual activity by people who are naturally heterosexual. But (comes the counter) then why did God create Eve—and not Steve—as "a suitable partner" for Adam (Genesis 2:18-25)? And why did He

-78-

destroy Sodom (Genesis 19:1-29), and say that sex is for heterosexual marriage only (I Corinthians 7:1-9 and Matthew 19:1-12)? McNeill answers that Sodom was destroyed, not for practicing sodomy, but for its "inhospitality" to strangers (see Ezekiel 16:49-50), and that men, no less than women, can fulfill God's purpose by providing "companionship and a cure for loneliness" for men; hence these passages do not provide a clear-cut condemnation of homosexuality by God. It depends on how they are interpreted. Father McNeill and others conclude that the homosexual condition, like the heterosexual, is according to the will of God. Others are equally certain that homosexuality opposes God's biblically-revealed wish for humanity.

This example shows how elusive the Almighty's cogitations can be. Curiously, the Bible itself gives us reason to question whether we can ever know God's will when it asks the rhetorical question, "For who hath known the mind of the Lord?" (Romans 11:34). Russell Baker puts the skeptical position nicely when he says:

> A proper respect for God might start with the
> assumption that He is a power surpassing all
> understanding and that to profess to grasp
> any message emanating from such a source is,
> at best, to give yourself airs about your own
> superiority and, at worst, an act of arrogance
> which calls for the corrective medicine of
> humility. I hesitate to commit such foolishness
> by stating flatly that God sends mortals so
> many contradictory messages to teach them how
> inadequate their auditory equipment is. In
> view of the low quality of our mortal talent
> for humility, such a lesson would probably be
> wasted on us anyhow.
> [The New York Times Magazine, 19 October 1980]

Of course, if we can never know God's commands, we shall never be able to know whether they are extensionally equivalent to what is morally right. We shall then have to withhold judgment about the second version of the divine-command theory, and consequently also about the first.

Finally, remember my earlier charge that God seems sometimes to command immoral acts. One reply to this is that He could not because He is both morally perfect and omniscient, and that hence we must reinterpret those Scriptural passages on which this claim rests. But this reply seems to me to be saying only that we are adopting the view that whatever we know to be morally right, God commands, and whatever we know to morally wrong, God forbids. Thus people say God commands us to be kind, honest, loving, and the like. And when the "Yorkshire Ripper" says he bludgeoned, stabbed, strangled, and mutilated thirteen women during a five-year reign of terror because God ordered him to, the usual response will be that God would never have ordered such a thing since it is obviously wrong. The theory, then, does not seem to be used to help us discover what is morally right or wrong. Rather, we simply use our independent and antecedent convictions about what is morally right and wrong to say what it is that He commands and forbids. We are like the politician who not only always has the ace of spades up his sleeve, but who has the gall to say that God put it there.

I conclude that the divine-command theory is either absurd (the first interpretation) or else unhelpful (the second). It should therefore be rejected along with the other approbative theories discussed—subjectivism, conventionalism, and the golden rule, interpreted literally. In the next chapter, we shall begin the examination of objectivist ethical theories to see if they give us any better answers to the questions, "How ought we, or what is the morally right way, to live and to behave?"

CHAPTER VI

OBJECTIVIST THEORIES

I shall call a theory an objectivist theory if it satisfies the following two conditions. First, it refuses to equate either an act's seeming to be morally right (wrong), or someone (or a group's) thinking that it is right (wrong), with its actually being so. If it is morally right (wrong), it is so whether or not it either seems to be, or whether someone or some group believes that it is. This is therefore a nonapprobative viewpoint. Hence none of the four normative theories discussed in the last chapter is an objectivist theory. Secondly, objectivist theories hold that moral judgments are true or false—that is, that they have a truth-value. But the truth (or falsity) of such judgments does not depend on whether anyone, or any group, thinks that those judgments are true (or false). It follows that flatly contradictory and contrary moral judgments cannot both be true; at least one must be mistaken. And a person can have a true (or false)—that is, a correct (or mistaken)—belief about what is morally right or wrong, good or bad. We have seen in Chapter III that emotivists, for example, Ayer and Stevenson, deny that value judgments are true or false; hence emotivists are not objectivists.

We must not assume, however, that just because objectivists say that there is truth in ethics, they are committed to a particular view of truth (correspondence, coherence, pragmatic, or the like). They may quite consistently deny that there is any acceptable theory of truth. Nor are they committed to the view that moral truth is either easy to attain or that there is a decision prodecure—or that there are even criteria—to determine whether, much less to demonstrate that, someone has got it. Finally, objectivists can recognize—though not all do—that there are important differences between disputes about moral issues, and disputes about either mathematical, scientific, causal, or straightforward everyday empirical matters. G. E. Moore (1873-1958) and David Ross (1877-1940), for example, are two British intuitionists as well as objectivists, in the above sense. Yet they both stress how difficult it is to know our actual duties, how it differs from knowing scientific or purely empirical truths, and they both insist that it is impossible to prove what is morally right or wrong. In Chapter III, we saw that the intuitionist and objectivist H. A. Prichard takes a more extreme view, contending that there are not even any moral reasons, or criteria, to appeal to in defense of the moral judgment that an action is obligatory or morally right (wrong). It is simply a question of "seeing" that it is or is not. So some ethical intuitionists have criteria for what is right or wrong and some do not. Almost all intuitionists, however, are objectivists, though not conversely. We shall begin the inquiry into objectivist theories by examining a form of objectivism that is generally not intuitionist: ethical egoism.

"Ethical" Egoism

Ethical egoism could be called "me-ism," the I-me-mine approach, looking out for number one, the cult of the self, or narcissism. The Narcissus of mythology loved only himself. He pined away gazing at his own reflection in a pool of water because he could not consumate his self-love. Walt Whitman, though apparently not himself an ethical egoist, beautifully captures the spirit of the doctrine when he says, "I celebrate myself and I sing myself. . . . I dote on myself, there is that lot of me and all so luscious. . . . nothing. . . is greater to one than one's self is" (Leaves of Grass, "Song of Myself," 1, 24, 48). Egoists may value other individuals--they may even think some are of tremendous value—but only if, and the extent to which, they view them as a means to furthering their own self-interest. If they are consistent egoists, they won't value them in and for themselves. The works of the ethical egoists Ayn Rand (1905-1982) and Jesse G. Kalin (b. 1940) are among the most influential in America today. But there are many others who advocate the position, for example, Nathaniel Branden, J. A. Brunton, John Hospers, Tibor R. Machan, Eric Mack, S. M. Sanders, and S. A. Smith. Two variants of ethical egoism will be considered here, each a conceptually coherent and rational position. They are rational in at least the minimal sense that they are neither logically self-contradictory nor preclude the egoist from taking the most effective means to given ends. What both of these variants of egoism have in common is that they are consequentialist positions--that is, they try to determine the moral rightness or wrongness of an action solely on the basis of the goodness or badness of its actual or probable long-range consequences. But the only consequences that count in the end, according to egoists, are consequences for the self.

1. Personal (individual or specific) ethical egoism takes the form:

> A (a particular action) is morally right if and
> only if A is actually or probably in my overall
> self-interest—that is, it actually or probably
> benefits me in the long run. A is morally wrong
> if and only if it actually or probably damages
> my overall self-interest or harms me in the
> long.

The word 'me' here is to be replaced in all of its occurrences with a proper name or a definite description. It always refers to some specific or definite individual, functioning thus as a constant rather than as a variable. The special individual might be the first Egyptian pharaoh or somebody like J.R Ewing. Suppose it was the latter. Then we would find out whether an action is morally right by finding out whether it is actually or probably in J. R. Ewing's overall self-interest or whether it actually or probably benefits him in the long run. If it does, it is morally right; if it harms him, it is morally wrong and therefore not right. The doctrine has an appealing simplicity. It offers a code of values that is applicable to everyone and which people could, at least theoretically, live by, providing the key individual exists and can be harmed or benefited. One of the peculiarities of the theory, however, is that it allows only one person to be an egoist—the special individual referred to. Everyone who wants to do what is morally right must serve that person's well-being. Not surprisingly, most egoists prefer the impersonal version of the theory.

2. Impersonal (universal or general) ethical egoism takes the form:

A is morally right if and only if A is actually
or probably in the overall self-interest of the
agent performing it—that is, it actually or
probably benefits him or her in the long run.
A is morally wrong if and only if it actually
or probably damages the overall self-interest
of the agent performing it or harms that person
in the long run.

This theory, unlike the previous one, contains no implicit proper names or definite descriptions. It gives no one any special normative role. Instead, it allows—and indeed encourages—everyone to be an egoist. For it implies that any and all of us do right if and only if we further our own self-interest and disregard those of others unless their interest contribute to our own.

Notice that the word 'probably' appears in both the personal and impersonal variants of ethical egoism. This is because of the difficulty of knowing the actual long-range consequences of our acts. Accordingly, the doctrines do not require that we know the actual consequences: it is enough if it is reasonable to expect, or we have good reason to believe, that the act we perform either will serve our over-all self-interest (the second theory) or the self-interest of the key individual (the first theory). In other words, if suffices if such over-all beneficial outcomes are probable.

I turn next to the evaluation of these normative doctrines.

The problem about benefit and self-interest. Since both of these versions of ethical egoism involve the notions of what is to a person's self-interest or benefit (good, well-being, welfare), as well as what harms someone, each raises the questions what is in someone's self-interest, what is beneficial, and how benefit and self-interest (as well as harm) are to be measured. Until we get satisfactory answers to these fundamental questions of value, each theory of what is morally right or wrong remains incomplete and therefore lacks a certain clarity. Many ethical egoists agree with this point, and some try to answer these questions. For example, hedonistic ethical egoists reply that pleasure and the avoidance of pain are, ultimately, the only two things in our self-interest. Ayn Rand thinks it is that that contributes to the survival of man qua man, that is, as a human being—what is pro man. Eudaemonistic egoists give the perhaps more promising answer that happiness and the avoidance of unhappiness are the only things that are truly in our overall self-interest and benefit. Other egoists says it is personal self-realization. These views give rise to many difficult questions: "How do we determine what contributes to the survival of man qua man or what is pro man? How do we establish that something is or is not? What constitutes happiness, unhappiness, and self-realization? And how are we to achieve these things?" It seems to be an open question whether the ethical egoist can give a satisfactory answer to the basic problem about benefit and self-interest. An adequate response must give both a correct and illuminating account of benefit, harm, and self-interest, and without having the effect of transforming ethical egoism into a nonegoistic theory. I shall attempt to show next why we should reject both variants of ethical egoism, beginning with the first one.

Personal ethical egoism's insurmountable problem of who is to be the special individual. We see that there are at least as many versions of this doctrine as there are people. It all depends on who is chosen to be the key individual, whom I shall call "NN." Why should one person and not another be given such an important position? The theory provides no guidelines or criteria for deciding this question. So either we make the choice arbitrarily or we have to appeal to something outside the theory. If the latter, we see still another way in which this theory fails to be a complete ethical doctrine.

Personal ethical egoism is both morally and psychologically unacceptable to the vast majority of us. Most of us would reject the doctrine regardless of who NN is. Proof: there are only two possibilities: either we are NN or we are not. Suppose we are not NN. Then we shall be morally obligated to disregard our own well-being and that of others, our friends, loved ones, our children—we all count for nothing—except in so far as we are a means to serving NN's overall self-interest or well-being. Now since most people have at least some regard for themselves as well as for others, they would reject the theory given our present supposition that they are not NN. Only someone drunk with NN's glory and goodness, who loves NN adoringly or idolatrously (the way perhaps Romeo and Juliet loved each other or the way some people love God) could accept such a doctrine. Certainly most of us would reject the deification of Joe Schmoe. We would hate to be his slave and to live by his interests alone.

Suppose next that you were the key individual, NN—that it was your own overall interest alone that counted. This second possibility would also be unacceptable to normal people, for, as has been implied, such people care about more than one person and are not concerned only about themselves. I am assuming here the falsity of psychological egoism—namely, the doctrine that every voluntary act is determined solely by a desire of the agent to maximize his or her own welfare.[1] NN would have to have a massive, and not what most psychologists would consider to be a healthy, ego—in fact, be an egomaniac—to accept this form of ethical egoism. Like certain potentates, such a person would regard everything as created for himself or herself, have no care at all about others for their own sake, no respect for their work or labors, no concern whether something caused them suffering, unless that suffering adversely affected him or her. A person like this would be incapable of friendship, of forming attachments to others, of love, or of having respect for others. We would despise the selfish wretch, as we do those who think only of themselves, and care about other people's well-being only if, and in so far as, it contributes to their own. As Joaquin Miller says, "That man who lives for self alone, lives for the meanest mortal known" (Walker in Nicaragua, Chat I, st.I).

We also have moral and psychological reasons for not consenting to impersonal ethical egoism, since we recognize that we are not only agents, but also the objects of the actions of others. According to the second doctrine of ethical egoism, the only morally relevant consideration is what in the long run actually or probably benefits the agent performing the act. Thus if your doing A—setting my house on fire to roast some eggs (Francis Bacon's example)--benefits you in the long run, we must judge it to be morally right, on this theory, which is absurd. At a mimimum, then, neither personal nor impersonal ethical egoism is true by definition.

----

1. Joseph Butler (1692-1752) and David Hume (1711-1776) offer excellent refutations of psychological egoism (not to be confused with ethical egoism). See Butler's Preface to his Fifteen Sermons, Sermons 1 and 11, "A Dissertation upon the Nature of Virtue," from The Analogy of Religion, and Appendix II of Hume's Enquiry Concerning the Principles of Morals. In The Transcendence of the Ego (chap.1, sec.c), Sartre presents some strikingly similar objections against what he calls "the theory of the 'self-love' moralists." Joel Feinberg sums up the case against psychological egoism in his collection of readings, Reason and Responsibility (Dickenson Publishing Co., 3rd ed., 1975), pp.501-512.

Ethical egoists may grant that this shows that it is impossible to define what is morally right in terms of a person's actual or probable long-range self-interest or benefit. They may still object, however, that, though logically possible, the supposition offered is farfetched. That is, it is unrealistic to suppose that it would ever be to anyone's overall self-interest to set someone else's house on fire to cook some eggs. In a normal situation, it certainly would not be. It would be better if you inquired whether you might use the stove. For if you burned down the house, you might get caught and punished. And even if you did not, it could result in your getting a bad reputation or reprisals if you were later suspected of the act.

Suppose, however, that none of these external considerations apply. Nobody is around and people think you are in another part of the world. Moreover, it is the house of your enemy who is trying to drive your highly profitable sex shops out of Times Square and replace them with ethnic restaurants and specialty food shops. Could not cool self-love now advise you that it is probably in your overall self-interest to set the house on fire and afterwards to roast your eggs on the hot ashes?

The ethical egoist may counter that it still would not be in your overall self-interest to do this, for you would feel guilt and a diminished sense of self-worth even if you did get away with the act. Hence you would have compelling internal or psychological reasons not to do it. My answer is that you can only feel guilt if you do what you believe is morally wrong. But if you think the act is actually or probably in your overall self-interest and you are an impersonal ethical egoist, by hypothesis, you think it is morally right. Consequently, you cannot feel guilty about doing it; at most you may feel towards it "some quasi-moral likings and aversions." (Sidgwick uses this phrase in The Methods of Ethics, bk.II, chap.V.) Notice that these quasi-moral feelings may be positive as well as negative: they may be either likings or aversions. Finally, as for feeling a diminished sense of self-worth, again you may or may not feel this. For some this sense might be enhanced when burning down an enemy's house. Even supposing, though, that you would feel a diminished sense of self-worth, along with a quasi-moral aversion, if you set the house on fire, we are not forced to conclude that it would not be in your overall self-interest to do it. As Sidgwick observes, "I see no empirical grounds for believing that such [negative] feelings are always sufficiently intense [and lasting, he might add] to turn the balance of prospective happiness [or for that matter self-interest] in favor of morality. This will hardly be denied if the question is raised in respect of isolated acts of duty" (ibid.). Putting it another way, if we focus on particular acts that actually or probably further our overall self-interest, we shall find that there is ample evidence that some of them involve doing things we regard as unfair or immoral. For example, in the absence of controls it is often in the interest of factory owners to damage the health of the rest of us by polluting the air and water. There are many examples like this in which the overall good of one can best be achieved by not respecting others. This is especially true if the individual is strong and powerful and the other people negatively affected are relatively weak and powerless. In such circumstances, there are no good reasons for a egoist to accept the restraints of equity and justice.

We have seen now that both variants of ethical egoism are immoral doctrines, since they could be used to justify performing acts that are morally wrong. This is because they have excessively modest moral-right-making conditions. If I actually or probably benefit NN in the long run, I do right, according to the first theory. On the second, all that is required is that agents actually or probably benefit themselves in the long run. It does not matter whether they harm someone else.

An impersonal ethical egoist might try to meet this criticism by modifying the doctrine, saying an act is morally right if and only if it is actually or probably in the overall self-interest of the agent performing it _and_ (what follows is the new part) it either does not harm someone else and/or it violates no one else's rights. This harm or rights proviso may get around the criticism, but only at the cost of making the theory non-egoistic. For now the theory requires that we consider the rights and/or well-being of others and not just of ourselves.

Notice that this problem would not arise for the egoist if the world were different--in particular, if there were always a perfect harmony of interest among people. Then the conflicts of interest I am imagining--in which what is to one person's benefit may be to another's detriment--would never occur. But experience tells us that this is not the nature of the world we live in. It is true that one person's interests are often compatible with another's and that many relationships in life are mutually advantageous. Think, for example, of the mother and the baby breastfeeding. Yet we know that sometimes conflicts of interest between people are real, deep, and irreconcilable. In some situations, for example, when food becomes scarce, one person may only be able to save his life if another loses his or hers. Consequently, the egoist cannot just assume as a dogma that what is to one person's long-range benefit or overall self-interest never will have a damaging or even disastrous effect on the well-being of someone else.

Why it is a misnomer to even call ethical egoism an ethical doctrine. We have seen that by either variant of egoism discussed, an ethical egoist recognizes only one kind of morally relevant consideration: Is the action actually or probably in my overall self-interest—that is, will it actually or probably benefit (or harm) me in the long run? I contend, first, that such considerations are never moral reasons (my stronger thesis) and, secondly, that they are not the only morally relevant considerations (my weaker thesis). If either of the theses is correct, ethical egoism should be rejected, since it

-87-

implies the negation of both. I shall give two arguments in support of these claims.

My first argument is based on the way we speak. Fluent and competent speakers of the language (at least those who are not in the grip of some philosophical or normative theory) would deny that someone who acts solely out of self-interest acts morally (as opposed to nonmorally) or for a moral reason. For example, should they learn that Carmen decided to lie to her father solely on the basis that it was likely to contribute to her overall self-interest, they would naturally—and quite correctly—say that her decision was not based on a moral reason and therefore it was not a moral one. This linguistic fact supports both my stronger and my weaker theses.

My second argument has to do with linguistic instruction. If speakers of the language were asked to give a child who does not quite understand the notion of a moral reason examples of one, they would not cite as their illustrations: "It's to my interest," "I'll probably benefit (profit) from it," or "It's to my advantage," for they recognize that these are never moral considerations. Instead, they would give nonegoistic reasons of the kind mentioned in Chapter III, for example: "I promised," "It would prevent human death, injury, suffering," "It would be cowardly, a lie, cheating, stealing," or "I wouldn't be respecting him—or myself—as a person if I did that." So again we get the conclusion that egoistic concerns neither exhaust nor are included in the class of moral reasons. What may obscure this fact is that we cannot be indifferent to the question of benefits, or to our interests and the interests of others, if we are to respect ourselves and others. This discussion should also remind us of the more general point (made in Chapter III) that not anything supports a moral judgment: only ethical considerations can. Moral decisions have to be made on the basis of moral reasons. Considerations that are not moral ones are therefore irrelevant to moral questions, problems, and disagreements. Hence a moral approach to a problem can never an I-me-mine approach.

I conclude that ethical egoism, not being an ethical doctrine, is misnamed. It is actually a nonmoral normative theory, that is a theory that may offer guidance and tell us how we should act, but one that will always fail to tell us how we should act morally; hence it is not an alternative ethical view. Even if I were mistaken on this last point, however, we have seen that there is ample and independent reason for rejecting both forms of so-called "ethical egoism" that have been considered: they are psychologically unacceptable doctrines that lead to the legitimation of immoral behavior.

Utilitarianism

Utilitarianism is the view which states that the moral rightness or wrongness of particular actions or sorts of actions is determined by the amount of goodness of badness they bring about. It is common to distinguish between "act" (or extreme) and "rule" (or restricted) versions of the doctrine. I shall examine both forms, beginning with the first.

Act (or Extreme) Utilitarianism

In its "ideal" (nonhedonistic and noneudaemonistic) form, the normative theory of act utilitarianism says that a particular act

A is morally right if and only if A actually or probably produces at least as much intrinsic good (value, utility) as any other action open to the agent.

G. E. Moore, probably the most influential ideal utilitarian, judges an act to be morally right provided it "will not cause less good than any possible alternative" (Principia Ethica, sec.89). That is, it is the actual production of good that counts. In a 1910 essay, Bertrand Russell (1872-1970), one of the best known philosophers of the twentieth century, defends a slightly altered version of the doctrine: "the objectively right act is that one which, of all that are possible, will probably have the best consequences."[2] As with ethical egoism, then, the basic aim of ideal utilitarianism is to promote the good, but not just for yourself; hence this is not an egoistic doctrine. Another leading ideal utilitarian and ethical intuitionist at the turn of the century is Hastings Rashdall (1858-1924). Like Moore, he believes that intuitions can tell us what ends are intrinsically good and the relative degree of their goodness. In denying that the good is confined to either happiness or pleasure, ideal utilitarians imply that their view is neither eudaemonistic nor hedonistic—that is, they neither define or explain moral obligation by reference to happiness nor by reference to pleasure.

Hedonistic utilitarians, starting from a different conception of value, quite naturally arrive at a different theory of obligation and right:

An action A is morally right if and only if A actually or probably produces at least as great a total balance of pleasure over pain

---

2. Bertrand Russell, "The Elements of Ethics," reprinted in Readings in Ethical Theory, ed. W. Sellars, and J. Hospers (New York: Appleton-Century-Crofts, 1952), p.14. Russell remarks that not long after publishing this essay, he came to depart from ideal utilitarianism.

as any alternative action open to the agent.

Thus the aim is to maximize pleasure, but not necessarily the pleasure of the agent. Jeremy Bentham (1748-1832), his friend and disciple, James Mill (1773-1836), his son, John Stuart Mill (1806-1873), and Henry Sidgwick are generally grouped among the most celebrated of the classical hedonistic utilitarians. (Sidgwick, however, is difficult to classify, since he seemed to be equally drawn to egoistic hedonism.) In his Works (vol.X, p.142), Bentham claims that "Priestley was the first (unless it was Beccaria) who taught my lips to pronounce this sacred truth—that the greatest happiness of the greatest number is the foundation of morals and legislation."[3] Like the Mills, Bentham thinks of happiness as nothing but pleasure and the avoidance of pain. In fact, it seems that this "sacred truth" has its orgin in Francis Hutcheson (1694-1746), who says: "That action is best which procures the greatest happiness for the greatest numbers" (Inquiry Concerning Moral Good and Evil, 1720, sec.3). Hutcheson also develops a fairly complex calculus prior to Bentham's.

In more recent times, John J. C. Smart (b. 1920), a prominent Australian philosopher, gives a spirited defense of what may be called eudaemonistic act utilitarianism. According to this view, we may say, roughly:

> An action A is morally right if and only if of all
> the actions open to us (including the null-action
> of doing nothing) A is likely to maximize—or
> better, it in fact does maximize—the total
> balance of happiness over unhappiness.

Note that this theory, like hedonistic utilitarinism, does not exclude animals. Both have the virtue of making morality apply to animals as well as to us. Smart, however, opposes the hedonist view that pleasure alone is good or the only thing that makes life worth living, preferring instead happiness as the sole intrinsic good.[4] He also recognizes that happiness is something different from mere pleasure

---

3. Robert Shackelton, "The Greatest Happiness of the Greatest Number: the History of Bentham's Phrase, "Studies on Voltaire and the Eighteenth Century 90 (1972): 1461-82, argues that Bentham actually got the "greatest happiness" formula, as well as the first four dimensions of his calculus (intensity, duration, certainty, and promptness) from Beccaria's little book, On Crimes and Punishment 1764 and not from Priestly.

4. John J.C. Smart and Bernard Williams, Utilitarianism: For and Against (Cambridge: Cambridge University Press, 1973). See pp.12-47. Bernard Williams offers a powerful critique of utilitarianism in the second half of the book.

and the avoidance of pain.

These three forms of act utilitarianism—the "ideal," the hedonistic, and the eudaemonistic—remain today among the dominant and most popular ethical theories. It is therefore especially important to examine each with care.

Objections to act utilitarianism. I shall look at four objections to these versions of act utilitarianism, and consider how successful are the ideal, the eudaemonistic, and the hedonistic utilitarian's responses to them. I shall then briefly discuss another kind of utilitarianism called "rule (or restricted) utilitarianism," showing that in so far as it is a genuinely utilitarian view, it is not a logically distinct theory. Thus rule utilitarianism collapses into, or is reducible to, act utilitarianism. If this is correct, they must both give the same answers to questions about what is morally right and wrong. Accordingly, criticisms made of one also apply to the other.

1. The problem about what is good. Since all the versions of utilitarianism we are considering involve maximizing what is intrinsically good, to understand the theories we have to know what is intrinsically good. It may be objected that the ideal utilitarian fails to answer, and that the hedonist and the eudaemonist give incorrect answers to this question; hence ideal utilitarianism is incomplete and unclear, and hedonistic and eudaemonistic forms of utilitarianism are both false doctrines.

I agree with this criticism of hedonistic and of eudaemonistic utilitarianism. Producing pleasure or happiness and avoiding pain or unhappiness are not the only morally relevant considerations. Indeed, producing pleasure is not even a moral reason for doing something; the same seems to be true of making someone happy. Thus if a psychotic or misogynist got exquisite pleasure and a great deal of happiness from strangling women, it is unlikely that we would count this as his having a moral reason to strangle them. Moreover, such an action would not be wrong only because it would cause the women pain, bring misery or unhappiness to their relatives and friends, and produce apprehension in the community. It would also be wrong because it would be the intentional taking of human life—that is, murder--which is bad in itself. Hedonistic and eudaemonistic utilitarians, however, cannot say that murder is bad in itself, since they hold that only pain, unhappiness, or the absence of pleasure or happiness, is bad in itself. Murder may, of course, be bad as a means, be morally wrong, on their view, but only because, and insofar as, it produces a lower surplus of pleasure or happiness over pain or unhappiness than some alternative action open to the agent. According to hedonistic and eudaemonistic utilitarianiams, any action is morally okay so long as it actually or probably produces the most pleasure or happiness.

Another way of stating this criticism of hedonistic and eudaemonistic utilitarianism is to say that their views are too simple-minded: they oversimplify and misrepresent moral reasoning. They just consider the consequences to the pleasures or happiness and pains of all affected by the action. Special ties, relations, and loyalties are viewed as irrelevant. For example, that it is your son, daughter, colleague, friend, spouse that you are considering turning over to the police, or that the children you are about to feed are your own, these are irrelevant facts, unless they affect the total amount of pleasure, happiness, or pain produced. Hedonistic and eudaemonistic utilitarians can give no preference to one human being over another simply because that being is their father, wife, daughter, or the like; they have a fine or a callous--a fine and callous--impartiality. I cannot help feeling that the world of the hedonistic utilitarian, to quote John Donne:

> 'Tis all in pieces, all coherence gone;
> All just supply, and all relation:
> Prince, subject, Father, Son, are things
>   forgot.[5]

This is because most of the relevant considerations will simply be dismissed as irrelevant on this doctrine. Hence it does not represent a view most people could accept. Most of us would quite rightly contend that these things have value independent of their utility.

Let us see next whether ideal utilitarianism has more success than the hedonistic and the eudaemonistic varieties in rebutting the first criticism concerning what is good in itself.

Moore must, and certainly would, acknowledge that he does not give any definition of intrinsic goodness. It would be inconsistent for him to do so, since he argues that good is indefinable. He tries to prove the indefinability of good in the first chapter of Principia Ethica, beginning with an argument from simplicity. This argument claims that good is too simple to be defined; only complex concepts can be defined, for definitions divide things into their parts (sec.7). Moore also gives a second argument for the indefinability of good that has come to known as the "open question" argument. This argument asserts that good cannot be defined because you can always intelligibly ask of something that satisfies any proposed definition of good, "But is it--such a thing--really good?" (sec.13). Using this question we can show that the concepts of goodness and, say, giving pleasure must be two distinct concepts. Moore says those who fails to recognize the indefinability of intrinsic goodness commit the "naturalistic fallacy," since they confuse one thing with something else and nothing can be

---

5. John Donne, An Anatomy of the World, the First Anniversary of the Death of Mistress Elizabeth Drury (1611), 1.205

anything other than itself.[6]

But even if intrinsic goodness is indefinable, this does not mean that we cannot be aware of what is intrinsically good. In the last chapter of Principia, Moore mentions several things that he thinks belong among the best things imaginable: aesthetic enjoyment, knowledge, courage, compassion, and so on. We simply "see" that these things are good in themselves, when we consider them, even though it is impossible to give any reasons or evidence for saying that they are. Judgments of intrinsic value are like that, according to Moore. They are neither provable nor disprovable. "Intuition alone" (sec.104) settles the question whether they are or not. But that does not mean we cannot know what is good in itself and what is not. Moore would say we have no more reason to be skeptical about our judgments of intrinsic value than we have about or perceptual judgment that something is yellow. In the color case it is just a matter of seeing as well, although here the seeing is literal seeing.

I have sympathy for this answer, in spite of its difficulties. The fact is that we are confident about our judgements of ultimate or intrinsic value, and we should not pretend we are not. Yet there is an obvious problem here that Moore cannot handle: what are we to do when two ideal utilitarians disagree--and they often do--about what is intrinsically valuable? They are then likely to come to different conclusions about what is morally right. So it seems that the first criticism still stands: Moore's version of utilitarianism is unclear because it is incomplete; that is why it can be completed in different ways, depending on the ideal utilitarian's intuitions about what is good in itself. Finally, accepting Moore's way of completing the doctrine seems to lead to another serious criticism--that he makes certain things moral reasons that in fact are not. For example, that an action gives aesthetic enjoyment or results in knowledge would be one of the more powerful moral reasons to do it, on his view, since these are alleged to be two of the most intrinsically valuable things. Yet both are actually illustrations of nonmoral reasons. Thus dropping an H bomb on a million people may teach someone the concept of a megacorpse and the colorful explosion this produces may give some spectators immense aesthetic enjoyment, yet these facts would not constitute two moral reasons in support of doing such a thing. What Moore seems to overlook is that not every ultimate or intrinsic value is necessarily a moral value. Hence the need, which I emphasized in my account of moral reasons in Chapter III (see p.43), to put a restriction on ultimate values when explaining what moral reasons

----

6. It would be less misleading if Moore called this view he opposes the "definist mistake." For an excellent discussion of the so-called naturalistic fallacy see W. K. Frankena's "The Naturalistic Fallacy" (Mind, 1939), reprinted in Readings in Ethical Theory, ed. W. Sellars and J. Hospers (New York: Appleton-Century-Crofts, 1952), pp.103-14.

are.

   2. We can never know what is morally right if we accept either
ideal, hedonistic, or eudaemonistic utilitarianism. Moore pretty much
admits that this is true. For to know what is right we have to know
all the relevant long-range consequences of our acts and of all
alternative acts open to us, and what human being can know this? We
would have to be omniscient, and no human being is. Thus Moore
asserts, "we cannot hope to discover which is the best possible
alternative in any given circumstances, but only which, among a few,
is better than the others." And it is at most only probable "that what
is better in regard to its immediate effects will also be better on the
whole" (sec. 94). This is tantamount to confessing that we can never
know what is our duty or what is morally right. On Moore's view, it
is strictly speaking impossible to establish the moral rightness of any
particular action, because we cannot have certainty about all of the
consequences of our actions. Other versions of ideal utilitarianism,
such as Russell's, which are couched in terms of the probable rather
than the actual consequences of acts, do not have to admit that we
can never know what is morally right just because they say we can
never know all of the consequences that in fact would occur.

   Hedonistic and eudaemonistic utilitarians tend to be less
skeptical than Moore about the possibility of our knowing what is
morally right or wrong. Bentham even entertains the possibility that
we can use a hedonistic calculus to determine our duty. (See Chapter
IV, The Principles of Morals and Legislation [1789].) There are seven
things about an action, according to him, we have to consider. First,
if the action involves immediate pleasure or pain, how intense is it?
The more intense the pleasure and the less intense the pain, the
better, all other things being equal. Thus sexual pleasures are likely
to rate higher for most, if not all, people than those they derive from
attending committee meetings. Hobbes (1588-1679) asserts that the
gratification of curiosity—which he calls "a lust of the mind"--in turn
far exceeds in intensity "the short vehemence of any carnal pleasure"
(Leviathan VI). And a blow to almost anyone's mid-section will produce
a more intense pain than a gentle slap on the back. After getting
clear on the intensity of people's pleasures and pains, the next thing
to consider is the duration of both, that is, how long the pleasures and
pains last. We know, for example, that the joys of the glutton tend
to be more fleeting than the more refined pleasures of the artistic
connoisseur, critic, and historian. Similarly, the pain of squeezing a
ripe pimple is likely not to last as long as a bad hangover headache.
We then multiply the duration of the pleasure and of the pain by the
intensity of each. Thirdly, the certainty or uncertainty of the
pleasure and pain has to be considered, by which Bentham means the
probability that it will occur. Fourthly, we must take into account
the fecundity of the action—that is, the chance the act has of being
followed by sensations of the same kind. For example, if Pushkin's
poetry got to Bentham, he would believe that reading Pushkin's poetry
is more fecund than playing pushpin (tiddlywinks), since the original

pleasure of reading this Russian poet tends to be followed by other pleasures, unlike pushpin. Similarly, getting a cavity filled by a dentist is less fecund than being tortured, since it will tend to be followed by less rather than more pain, unlike being tortured. Fifthly, we should examine the purity of the action's pleasure or pain. All other things being equal, better a painless pleasure than one that contains a mixture of pain or discomfort, and better a pain mixed with some pleasure than one that is a pure pain. These five considerations show that in some ways Bentham is a rather complex hedonist. But he adds as a sixth point that we should consider the pleasure's or pain's propinquity or remoteness--that is, whether the pleasure or pain is to come sooner or later. He sees these as relevant considerations because they are mixed up with certainty or uncertainty: the more remote the pleasurable act, the more uncertain or improbable that it will occur, in his view. But since this dimension has already been taken care of by that of certainty and uncertainty, Bentham's sixth circumstance is really unnecessary. Finally, he mentions extent, that is, the number of people who are affected by the act. Knowing these six dimensions of an action (I say six rather than Bentham's seven, because of the previously mentioned redundancy of propinquity or remoteness) we are ready to calculate the value of the act. We do this by adding the positive values of the pleasures and subtracting the negative values of the pains, which gives us the value of the act. We then compare the value of this act with that of others open to us, choosing whatever gets the highest hedonic score. According to Bentham, that will be the act that is right or that we ought morally to do.

But is this decision procedure really as clear and useful as it sounds? I think not. Consider the question of the probability that a pain or pleasure will arise. The chances of getting the flu or of having certain other kinds of pains are often incalculable. Pleasures may be even harder to predict than most pains. And can we actually measure the intensity of pleasures or pains? Duration surely can be measured, but it seems to be nonsense to say that one pain is twice as bad or intense as another, or that you enjoyed Gone With the Wind, say, three times as much as your last hot fudge sundae or calculus lecture. Moreover, it is questionable whether it is possible to multiply the duration of pain or pleasure by its intensity. To do that we would have to express its intensity in numbers, and we do not know how to do that. For example, how do you put a numerical figure on the intensity of the pleasure derived from swimming in an unpolluted versus a mildly polluted Mississippi River? Or suppose you are not admitted to graduate school. You feel hurt and your mental distress lasts for a period of time. But how in the world can you multiply the duration of that pain by its intensity and then subtract that from the value of various attendant pleasures? All of this is unclear. I conclude that Bentham is deluded if he thinks he has given us anything like a workable hedonistic or felicific calculus. It does not seem that there can be such a thing.

Later hedonistic utilitarians have given up this calculus, and no longer try to draw up the neat balance sheet Bentham wanted. They reject the notion of a moral arithmetic and acknowledge that it is often difficult to determine which action is best, because of our meager and only rough knowledge of what causes pleasure and pain. For example, who could have known, according to a hedonistic utilitarian point of view, that Hitler probably should have been admitted to art school in Vienna when he applied, since then he would most likely never have gone into politics, in which case he would never have come to power, and that would (plausibly) have spared the world a great deal of misery and unhappiness? There are surprising cases like this. Yet hedonistic utilitarians still maintain that their theory offers guidelines possible, even if not easy, to follow. The formal calculus may fail, but it does not follow that hedonistic or eudaemonistic utilitarianism must be abandoned. Writes Sidgwick, " I think it must be admitted that the Hedonistic method cannot be freed from inexactness and uncertainty . . . ." Yet it is "not useless for practical guidance," since we can make rough calculations of the required sort, especially when this method is supplemented by appeals "to the judgements of common sense respecting the sources of happiness" or pleasure (The Methods of Ethics, bk.II, chap.IV, p.158). Finally, it might be argued that the fact that it is often hard to tell what we ought to do, going by these theories, is actually a point in favor of them, for that is the way it is in life too. The utilitarian, like other moralists, may offer us an unattainable ideal, but nevertheless an ideal to strive after.

3. Ideal, hedonistic, and eudaemonistic utilitarianism justify unjust or inhuman behavior and other immoral acts, for whatever act produces the most good, or the greatest balance of pleasure or happiness over pain and misery, or which is likely to do this, is judged to be morally right, according to these theories. Yet such an act may in fact be unjust. Suppose, for example, that we present an innocent man on TV, but the public does not know he is innocent. Instead, we portray him as a rapist and castrate him on TV. Suppose, further, that this event dissuades 90 to 95 percent of rapists (I am assuming that not all rapists watch TV). Suppose in time the crime becomes practically nonexistent. From a utilitarian point of view, we may then have done the morally right thing; yet we would still think the act of castrating such a man on TV was unjust. Or take a second example. A healthy solitary, with no relatives or friends, goes to a hospital for a checkup. He is found to be in excellent condition. However, five other patients in the hospital will die unless each gets an urgently needed transplant. The utilitarian doctors decide quietly to cut up the healthy man, and to give his organs to the other five people, who are all highly productive scientists needed for the national defense and who would be sorely missed by the community if they died. Let us suppose the doctors are convinced that they have thereby performed a public service, that they have furthered the general good. We would still think, even granting that their act maximized the good, that they would be guilty of a terrible thing. To quote William Blake:

> He who would do good to another must
>   do it in minute particulars:
> General good is the plea of the scoundrel,
>   hypocrite and flatterer. . . .
>
> [Jerusalem, chap.3, sec.55.]

A third example is provided by Crime and Punishment. Raskolnikov overhears a student, whom he does not know, giving the following utilitarian argument to a young officer in support of the morality of killing Alyona Ivanovna, the old pawnbroker:

> . . . look here; on one side we have a stupid,
> senseless, worthless, spiteful, ailing, horrid
> old woman, not simply useless but doing actual
> mischief, who has not an idea what she is living
> for herself, and who will die in a day or two
> in any case. . . On the other side, fresh young
> lives thrown away for want of help and by
> thousands, on every side! A hundred thousand
> good deeds could be done and helped, on that
> old woman's money which will be buried in a
> monastery! [The old woman has already made
> her will leaving all her money to a monastery
> that prayers might be said for her in perpetuity.]
> Hundreds, thousands perhaps, might be set on
> the right path; dozens of families saved from
> destitution, from ruin, from vice, from the lock
> hospitals [hospitals which treat venereal
> diseases]—and all with her money. Kill her,
> take her money and with the help of it devote
> oneself to the service of humanity and the
> good of all. What do you think, would not
> one tiny crime be wiped out by thousands
> of good deeds? For one life thousands
> would be saved from corruption and decay. One
> death, and a hundred lives in exchange—it's
> simple arithmetic!

Can the utilitarian answer this criticism that utilitarianism legitimates immoral acts? Let us begin by considering a possible response of the ideal utilitarian. Moore could point out, first, that it is a mistake to think his is a consequentialist view, in the sense of being one that find the necessary and sufficient conditions of a right act in its consequences. Granted, ideal utilitarianism is an axiological

---

7. Fyodor Dostoyevsky, Crime and Punishment, tr. Constance Garnett (Random House, 1950), pp.66-67.

-97-

theory, and in the strong sense (at least in Principia), in that it defines the rightness of an action by the goodness of something. The theory of right (duty and obligation) is therefore entirely dependent on the theory of value. But that does not entail that the rightness of an action is dependent on, much less only on, the value of its consequences. "With regard to [actions]," Moore says, "we may ask both how far they are good in themselves and how far they have a general tendency to produce good results" (sec.17). Moreover, he makes it very clear that you must consider both the action's value as well as its consequences in determining whether the action is morally right or a duty. Thus the choice for the Moorian ideal utilitarian (the same may not be true of all other ideal utilitarians) is not to consider actions or their consequences, in the exclusive sense of 'or': both are viewed as relevant and indispensable considerations; hence my classification of Moore as a moderate deontologist, for he does not determine the rightness or wrongness of an action solely on the basis of the goodness or badness of its consequences, yet he obviously takes consequences into account. According to him, by definition our duty is to do the best thing. In the first chapter of Principia, he explains: "In asserting that the action is the thing to do, we assert that it together with its consequences [my emphasis] presents a greater sum of intrinsic value than any possible alternative" (sec.17).[8]

Secondly, were Moore to consider these examples--namely, castrating an innocent person as a rapist to discourage rape, and killing an innocent or spiteful and mischievous person simply to distribute his vital organs or her money to others--there is no reason why he should not say that these are examples of injustice and murder, and that he intuits such unjust or murderous acts to be intrinsically bad. The injustice (or justice) or murderous nature of an act is then always a relevant consideration, one never to be

----

8. Unfortunately, some of Moore's other remarks about duty and right make him sound like a consequentialist. A nice illustration of this can be found in his fifth chapter. There he writes that he has already shown in section 17 of chapter 1, that "the assertion 'I am morally bound to perform this action' is identical with the assertion that 'this action will produce the greatest possible amount of good in the Universe'" (sec.89). The irony is that such an apparently consequentialist formulation, strictly speaking, is incompatible with the position he develops in section 17. The fact that Moore could overlook this may help explain why so many of his readers have also failed to realize that he is actually a moderate deontologist and thus not a consequentialist. Even Moore seems sometimes not to grasp his own normative position. How else can you explain his bizarre and purely consequentialist defense of the rule "do no murder" when a much more plausible deontological defense comes readily to mind? See my paper, "Moore's Defense of the Rule 'Do No Murder'," The Personalist 54 (1973), pp.361-75.

disregarded. Accordingly, it must not be permissible to decide to perform such bad acts solely on the ground that their consequences are on the whole good. This sort of reply should dispose of the objection that Moore's ideal utiliitarianism cannot deal with justice, in the sense of giving weight to considerations of justice and fairness. He could certainly admit the relevance of such considerations as do other moderate deontologists.

The hedonistic and eudaemonistic utilitarian can also take a moderate deontological stance. That an act is immediately pleasurable or painful, for example, is a morally relevant consideration for a hedonistic utilitarian quite apart from what the consequences of the act are. This shows again that you can be a utilitarian and not be a consequentialist. Moreover, the hedonistic and eudaemonistic utilitarian have this further answer to the scapegoat objection and to the charge that the doctrine encourages unjust acts. As Hare says, we should just imagine what the consequences would be in the actual world "if hospitals shanghaied casual visitors and pinched their organs for transplants. . . would not all the hospitals have to close their doors? . . . It is not the technology that is fantastic [in these examples], but the assumptions about keeping the thing dark; and, as I said, moral principles are for the actual world" (The Listener, 6 April 1978). So it is implausible to think that a utilitarian would think that either of these outrageous acts would be for the best. The hedonistic and eudaemonistic utilitarian could object to them just as much as the rest of us.

This answer has considerable force. I just have the following reservation: is it not a huge—an perhaps even a dubious assumption—to in effect answer the third criticism by saying, as Hare and other utilitarians do, that fairer and juster things are better, because their long-run consequences are always better in the actual world? Can this assumption be established? How? Finally, the objection does seem to show at least one thing—that you cannot define 'what is morally right' as 'that which produces the highest surplus of pleasure or happiness over pain', since it is not logically self-contradictory to conceive of an act that does this but is not morally right. But, of course, just because you cannot define moral rightness in these terms does not mean that these two expressions are not extensionally equivalent. Consequently, this third criticism does not clearly refute either ideal, eudaemonistic, or hedonistic utilitarianism.

4. Utilitarians have a double standard. This charge is leveled against all three versions of utilitarianism, on the grounds that, according to these doctrines, an action may be morally right (or wrong), yet it may not be morally right to say such an act is morally right (or wrong)—that is, to praise (or to condemn) it. For example, given what we know now, a utilitarian today might believe that Hitler's baby sitter did wrong in not smothering, drowning, or in some other way doing away with him when she had the chance. However, since omissions of this sort are generally thought to be more

beneficial than infanticide, the utilitarian might also say of the baby sitter that she did right in taking good care of baby Hitler. In short, utilitarians may praise all "scrupulously conscientious acts," even though in particular cases some of these acts give rise to infelicific conduct. Similarly, as Sidgwick points out, "although, in the view of a Utilitarian, only the useful is praiseworthy, he [the utilitarian] is not bound to maintain that it is necessarily worthy of praise in proportion as it is useful" (Methods of Ethics, bk.IV, chap.III). Hence utilitarians could consistently condemn the murder of baby Hitler, even though they considered the act to be morally right, provided that they believed it was more useful or expedient to condemn than to praise it. For utilitarians do not assume that the utility of an act and the utility of praising (or condemning) it are necessarily one and the same.

All of this is correct: act utilitarianism is committed to distinguishing between these acts and to recognizing that just because one is right (or wrong), it does not follow that the other is too. But I do not see this as a flaw in utilitarianism. On the contrary, it would be unfortunate if the theory failed to appreciate these very real distinctions. Strangling baby Hitler is one act; saying it would have been morally right to have strangled him is an altogether different act. Nor does the utilitarian reveal a double standard by sometimes treating such different acts differently: he or she judges both acts—indeed all acts—by one and the same standard. It is true that the children of utilitarians may be momentarily perplexed to hear their parents praise (or condemn) acts that they (the children) know their parents believe are morally wrong (or right). Yet in time the children will come to understand that their parents' lack of openness is itself based on utilitarian considerations and that they are acting in a perfectly intelligible and consistent way.

In summary, the act utilitarians have powerful answers to most of these criticisms. Nevertheless, hedonistic and eudaemonistic utilitarianism both flounder because of their overly simple and restricted conception of what morally relevant considerations are, as was brought out in the first objection that deals with the problem of what is good. This criticism relates to what was said in Chapter III (see especially pp.26-28, 40-48) about what are and are not moral reasons. Ideal utilitarianism comes to grief for essentially the same reason. We saw that this form of utilitarianism is an incomplete and unclear theory; thus it turns out to be a different doctrine with each change in an ideal utilitarian's intuitions about what is intrinsically good. When the doctrine is completed with particular intuitions about what is intrinsically good—for example, Moore's—certain things become moral reasons that are not. What ideal utilitarians overlook is that not every ultimate or intrinsic value is a moral reason, a view which I took issue with in the third chapter.

Rule (or Restricted) Utilitarianism

I claimed earlier that rule (or restricted) utilitarianism, in so far as it is a genuine utilitarian view, is not a logically distinct theory from act (or extreme) utilitarianism; that is, rule utilitarianism collapses into, or is reducible to, act utilitarianism. Hence criticisms made of the one also apply to the other. I shall now try briefly to establish this claim.

Recall that act utilitarianism says that an act A is morally right if and only if it produces, or is likely to produce, at least as much good as some alternative act. Rule utilitarianism, in contrast, asserts that an act A is morally right if and only if A is required by a rule that, if adopted, would produce, or probably would, at least as much good as the adoption of some alternative rule. The rule need not be hedonistic or eudaemonistic, though it may be either; so the present distinction between act and rule utilitarianism cuts across the trichotomy of the previous section: ideal, hedonistic, and eudaemonistic utilitarianism.

Let us address ourselves now to a particular problem, say, Mack's in the eighth moral problem, or Raskolnikov's in Crime and Punishment, to see whether a rule and an act utilitarian, possessed of the same information, would come to different conclusions about what these people ought to do. Mack, remember, is considering whether he should take the law into his own hands and kill a certain rapist-murderer. Raskolnikov is considering killing an old and ailing woman pawnbroker. A rule utilitarian might plausibly point out that since A here in both instances is the deliberate taking of a human life, there is a consideration against the act, for it is generally beneficial to follow the rule "Don't murder!" In contrast, if A were keeping a promise, this would be a reason for doing it—the rule being "Keep your promises!" which it is also generally useful to follow. Suppose that it is known that in this case, however, the most expedient act would be quietly and secretly to kill the rapist-murderer or pawnbroker, since this would produce more good than any other act available to the agents by saving lives, preventing several rapes or much destitution. We are supposing that the acts would have no appreciable effect on people's respect for law and order, because it would not even be known that any murder had been committed. An act utilitarian would then hold that the acts ought to be performed. Could rule utilitarians legitimately come to the conclusion that the acts would be morally wrong simply on the ground that it is usually useful not to murder? No, they must show more than that. In particular, they need to show that it is more expedient to follow the rule "Do no murder!" rather than any other. Even if this rule is preferred as a general rule to "Always murder!" yet it is surely possible to formulate other rules that are more justifiable on utilitarian grounds. Moreover, if the facts are as we have supposed, a more useful rule should include certain exceptions, for example, "Never murder unless you can do it secretly and in doing so save lives, prevent several rapes, and/or much destitution."

In short, rule utilitarians, if they are not to cease being utilitarians and if they are to avoid blind obedience to rules, must justify their rules on a utilitarian basis. But if they do that, the rules must include all the relevant exceptions. So whatever act passes the act utilitarian test—that is, is most expedient, or is likely to produce more good than any alternative action—will also pass the rule utilitarian test: that is, it will fall under a rule that if adopted would be more likely to produce more good than any alternative rule. Conversely, any act that falls under a rule that passes the rule-utilitarian test—that is, that falls under a rule that if adopted would be more likely to produce more good than any alternative rule—will be an act that also passes the act utilitarian test—that is, it will be most expedient or be likely to produce more good than any alternative action. Accordingly, given the same information, consistent act and rule utilitarians will agree perfectly on what acts are morally right and morally wrong. Fundamentally, they are judging them on the same basis. I therefore conclude that the distinction between act and rule-utilitarianism is a distinction without a difference, and the two positions are susceptible to the same criticisms. So, rule utilitarianism cannot meet the objections considered in the last section (see pp.91-100) any better than act utilitarianism does.

The Appeal to Nature for Moral Guidance

This may be called the view that the morally right thing to do is what is natural or in harmony with nature. If we just keep with the ways of nature, we shall be on a morally correct course. To sin is to go again nature. Many very different thinkers make an appeal to nature of this sort. Lao Tzu (sixth century B.C.?), the founder of Taoism, one of the great Asian religions, for example, holds that we should follow Tao, the Natural Way. He writes that "[the sane man's] one care is . . . to let nature renew the sense of direction men undo" (The Way of Life, tr. Witter Bynner, 64). Henry David Thoreau (1817-1862), a New England transcendentalist and naturalist, and Walt Whitman, the poet, have been mentioned as two of Lao Tzu's more eminent American disciples. The ancient Roman stoics, Seneca (ca. 5 B.C. - 65 A.D.), Epictetus (ca. 55-ca. 135 A.D.), and Marcus Aurelius (121-180 A.D.) also celebrate nature. Epictetus says we must live "in harmony with nature".[9] Marcus Aurelius urges that we follow both our "own nature and the common nature."[10] Aristotle (384-322 B.C.) and the natural-law theorists, for instance, Thomas Aquinas (ca. 1224-1274) and John Locke (1632-1704), think that there are implicit standards of right and wrong in nature, which our reason can grasp and which we can use to guide us in life. Finally, philosophers of evolution, Herbert Spencer (1820-1902) and Thomas H. Huxley (1825-1895), and in a different way, Lecomte du Nouy (1883-1947), try to derive guidance from the processes of evolution. Spencer's view is "that the conduct to which we apply the name good is the relatively more evolved conduct; and that bad is the name we apply to conduct which is relatively less evolved."[11] Lecomte du Nouy concludes that whatever supports or is in harmony with our moral and spiritual evolution is good. By the same token, he says "anything which opposes this evolution in the moral and spiritual realm, anything which tends to bring about a regression toward the animal, to replace man under the dictature of body is contrary to the directing Will [which manifest itself through evolution] and represents absolute Evil."[12] Because some of these theories--for example, Lecomte du Nouy's, Lao Tzu's, the ancient Roman stoics--can be interpreted as either approbative or objectivists, and hence nonapprobative, doctrines, I shall consider both kinds of interpretation. However, since the appeal to nature is usually interpreted in the second way, it is discussed here, in the chapter on objectivist theories. We shall see in the next few pages why neither the approbative nor the nonapprobative variety of this theory will do.

1. Interpreted as an approbative theory, it gives rise to the objection, first, that the appeal-to-nature doctrine is either nonsensical or at least guilty of outrageous anthropomorphizing. In this interpretation, the theory says that whatever nature intends, wants, is interested in, approves of, aims at, wills, and the like is morally right; whatever it opposes is morally wrong. Yet it seems nonsensical to say that nature wills, intends, wants, or approves of anything. Nature is not the sort of entity, if it is an entity at all, to take such psychological predicates, since it is not a person. The metaphor of Mother Nature may be responsible for such crude anthropomorphizing.

---

9. The Works of Epictetus, tr. E. Carter (Boston: Little Brown, 1865), chap.1, p.6.

10. The Meditations of the Emperor Marcus Aurelius Antoninus, tr. George Long (New York: A.L. Burt, 1864), chap.5, p.2.

11. Herbert Spencer, The Principles of Ethics (New York: D. Appleton, 1895), vol.1, p.15.

12. Pierre Lecomte du Nouy, Human Destiny (New York: Longman, Green, 1947), pp.225.

Incidentally, Russell Baker questions the aptness of the metaphor. He finds, "There is nothing motherly about nature. Nature is more like one of those ugly drunks you are always in danger of encountering in a strange bar—short-tempered, quixotic, dangerous."[13] He notes that she gives us tornadoes, northeast gales, leaf mold, and poison ivy, as well as stampedes of tomato worms. In his brilliant essay "Nature," John Stuart Mill agrees that the ways of nature frequently oppose us: "her [nature's] powers are often toward man in the position of enemies, from whom he must wrest, by force and ingenuity, what little he can for his use, and deserves to be applauded when that little is rather more than might be expected from his physical weakness in comparison to those gigantic powers."[14]

The Euthyphro criticism. Waiving the first objection, let us suppose we succeed in making sense of nature's having wishes, a purpose, intentions, interests, and the like. Suppose that nature really is a peculiar kind of mother. We now run into the Euthyphro objection, discussed in the section on divine-command theory: is what Mother Nature wants or approves of morally right simply in virtue of Mother Nature's wanting or approving of it, or is it rather that Mother Nature simply wants or approves of those things, and only those things, that are morally right? If we opt for the first alternative, we get the absurdity that morally wrong things would be morally right if Mother Nature approved of them. If we opt for the second alternative, we still do not know what makes things morally right or wrong.

The theory gives no guidance. We can see this if we ask the epistemological question, how are we to determine what nature wants? For example, does she prefer us to eat the "natural" foods advertised on television, or to forage for our dinner in wilderness areas? to visit glaciers or the library? Are we to go to bed when the sun goes down and rise whenever, and only when, it gives us light again? Or may we divide our time between sleeping and waking the same in winter and in summer with the help of electricity? Should we act like other animals? Which ones? Like scavengers, predators, parasites? Would it be hostile to nature to wear panty hose, use mouthwash, and a shampoo to free yourself from dandruff? Is it unnatural to be vaccinated against polio, to phone a daughter in Europe? And have you somehow lost touch with nature (a question Russell Baker asks) when you become an airline stewardess, a system analyst, a cop, a fashion model, or a surgeon, and you no longer say "By golly!" and "There's a heap of goodness in this old world of

----

13. Russell Baker, So This is Depravity (New York: Congdon and Lates, 1980), p.73.

14. John Stuart Mill, Nature and Utility of Religion, ed. George Nakhnikian (New York: The Liberal Arts Press, 1958), pp.14-15.

ours"? Nature gives either no replies to these questions or at best ambiguous ones. Thus you could, I suppose, find in nature the following queer argument against bathing in the nude: if nature had wanted others to see your genitals, she would have put them on your neck. But she did not put them there; so she must be against bathing in the nude. Of course, to this there is the equally persuasive counterargument that if nature had wanted others not to see your genitals, she would have brought you into the world fully dressed instead of in your birthday suit. A better example may be the second moral disagreement over birth control. We noted that Patricia, the Roman Catholic housewife, contends that birth control is unnatural, because it is designed to prevent conception, which is the natural consequence of sexual intercourse. Jan does not agree. She thinks that the "pill" and the "IUD" are actually more natural than the "rhythm" method Catholics recommend, since these devices in no way restrict our behavior, unlike the rhythm method, which requires abstention from sex, which we would naturally engage in if it were not for the fear of pregnancy. It seems impossible to settle these disagreements by inquiring into what nature wants or what her purpose or will is. If we try to evade this attack by retreating to a theist-nature view that says it is not a question of what nature wants or does not want, but of what God does or does not want to happen in nature, the theory is still vulnerable to the objections leveled earlier against divine-command theory (see pp.74-80). There is the Euthyphro argument, and as we have seen, even if we grant that God exists, there are lots of problems about whether, and how, we can know what God wants.

2. Let us, then, interpret the appeal-to-nature doctrine as a nonapprobative and objectivist theory: an act is morally right if and only if it conforms to the laws of nature; it is wrong if and only if it is a violation of the laws of nature. Now the question is: what do we mean here by 'a law of nature'? There are two possible interpretations of the phrase. First, we may mean by it simply a scientific law, like the law of gravity. Then, by definition, nobody can go against it. All acts physically or psychologically possible--including spouse-abuse, rape, and murder--must consequently be judged to be morally right. Which would be absurd. So we must search for another and a better interpretation of 'law of nature'. Certainly when Tolstoy says that sexual relations between a husband and wife during pregnancy are a violation of the law of nature or a Roman Catholic that contraception and homosexuality go against natural law, they are both aware that neither contraception, homosexuality, nor having sexual relations during pregnancy violates any laws of science. We are therefore only to be guided by certain aspects of actual behavior.

This, of course, raises the question: which ones? Richard Wollheim points out: "For [the] natural-law doctrine to be viable, we need a criterion for distinguishing within nature (where this is equated with the whole range of natural phenomena) those aspects to which we can, and those aspects to which we cannot, attach normative significance" ("Natural Law," The Encyclopedia of Philosophy, vol.5, ed. Paul Edwards). We must keep distinct, then, two senses of 'nature': (1) the sum total of natural phenomena and (2) a thing's nature or essence, that is, the quality or qualities that make something the kind of thing it is. It is the second sense of 'nature' that natural-law theorists see as being especially relevant to ethics. Thus Aristotle attempts to provide a criterion for distinguishing within nature, in the first sense, those aspects that have normative significance, by saying what human nature is in the second sense. His answer is that we are rational animals. Accordingly, those natural phenomena that further the end of being a rational animal are to be approved of and those that do not are not. I shall now mention three criticisms of this nonapprobative appeal-to-nature theory; the second and third, if not the first, I believe are decisive objections to it.

We may question the natural-law theorist's account, for example Aristotle's, of human nature. Why accept, say, that being a rational animal is our essence? We could equally well say that our nature or essence is to be versatile and highly adaptable, or that it is to make things, to use language and tools, or to be featherless bipeds that play, love, make war, tell jokes, do philosophy, write poetry and music, and create art. Perhaps the key thing about human beings is that they are self-conscious and are aware, unlike other animals, that one day they will die. The French philosopher Blaise Pascal (1623-1662) says our nature is to be "but a reed, the weakest in nature, but [man] is a thinking reed" (Pensees, no.347). The fictional character, Lancelot, thinks this is only half the story. "What man is," he claims, "is a thinking reed and a walking genital." Lancelot is struck by what he calls the elementary facts that "of the three million species on earth the human female is the only one capable of living in a state of constant estrus; of having an orgasm; of making love face to face with her mate. . .[15] . [Woman] is the only creature on earth in perpetual heat." Should we cite these characteristices as distinctively human and as essential attributes of human beings? The discussion shows how hard—perhaps impossible—it is to give a satisfactory account of human nature. As Wittgenstein says, "there is not always a sharp distinction between essential and inessential" (PI, § 62).

Why should not we try to transcend our human nature or essence? Even accepting that Aristotle, or some other theorist, has put his or her finger on our essence, a second objection arises: why should not we try to deviate from, or go beyond, it? For example, suppose it is found that our nature is to have little regard for anyone outside the family circle and that we have a strong propensity to

---

15. From Walker Percy's novel Lancelot (New York: Farrar, Straus and Giroux, 1977), p.223.

engage in violent sex and to be pornographic. Should not we try to overcome these tendencies and to cultivate whatever small capacity we have to care for other people? Alternatively, if we cannot do this, because there is no way we can transcend or deviate from our essence, then is it not pointless to say that we have a moral obligation to live in accord with it? For we shall do so in any event.

The doctrine, as at present interpreted, provides no substantive moral guidance. Even supposing that we can, to a greater or lesser extent, live in accordance with our human nature, that it is as Aristotle or some other natural-law theorist describes it, and that it has been established that it is desirable to conform to it as much as possible, there is a third objection: it seems unlikely that we can derive any substantive moral guidance from the doctrine. For example, does it mean that we should be sociable? So much so that wives may engage in the custom of polyandry and husbands in polygamy? We could probably have a spirited debate whether the doctrine permits people to struggle to gain power over others, whether it allows us to let crippled and palsied children die or whether we should try to help them survive. Is lying a sin against nature, according to this doctrine? Is homosexuality unnatural? Is it wrong, permissible, or morally obligatory to have abortions sometimes? Should we strive to live like Henry David Thoreau, Billy Graham, Gloria Steinem, Ayn Rand—or like none of these? Ought we to try to make the deserts bloom, and fence off our fields with hedges? Is it morally correct to charge interest on loans? The theory does not seem to give any definite answers to these questions, although Aristotle and medieval thinkers, including Thomas Aquinas, seem to think it does, at least to the last one: they contend that charging interest on loans is usurious and immoral. Aristotle gives the implausible argument that "of all modes of getting wealth this is the most unnatural" and hateful, since "money was intended to be used in exchange, but not to increase at interest" (Politics 1258b 2-8).

I believe that the appeal to nature fails to provide definite and convincing answers to these, as well as to the most basic questions concerning matters of life and death, because there are countless ways of living that are in accord with our human nature; hence appealing to our nature gives us precious little, if any, moral guidance in determining how we ought to live or what a morally good life is. After all, the key questions are not so much what human nature is and whether we are living in accord with it, but what kind of life we want to live and what kind of human being we want to become. We are not like can openers that are made to serve one definite purpose (opening cans and bottles). Beside, even in the case of the can opener, it seems reasonable sometimes to use it in ways that are not its purpose. For example, you may use it as a paper weight when grading papers on the porch and a slight breeze is coming through the open door. It does not seem, then, that appeal to any distinctive human function or end can provide us with criteria to determine whether a person is or is not living in a morally correct way. Indeed, conformity to nature generally appears to afford no criterion at all of what we should do.

In conclusion, however, I would like to concede one important point to the natural-law theorists. While it is true that we cannot read off our moral duties from any discoveries of nature, including human nature, these discoveries are nevertheless relevant to ethics in the following way. Because 'ought' implies 'can' (but not conversely)—that is to say, it must be possible to do what we ought to do (though we ought not to do whatever we can do)—knowledge of what we can and cannot do may rightly affect the legitimacy of our ought judgments. Hence the study of human nature can—quite properly—change our view of our duties and obligations. For example, if we conclude that it is humanly impossible to love all of our fellow human beings, we shall think it inappropriate to say that we ought to love all of them. Similarly, when we discover that industrial pollution, smoking cigarettes, putting nitrite into our food, and cooking food in aluminum pots undermine our health, most of us will conclude that we should, if we can, stop doing these things. It is thus morally important to understand nature, including human nature. That is why anthropology, ecology, and many other sciences are morally relevant. As Mill wisely observes: although the precept to follow nature is useless, the "precept to study nature—to know and take heed of the properties of the things we have to deal with, so far as these properties are capable of forwarding or obstructing any given purpose . . . [is] the first principle of all intelligent action" (ibid., p.12). The study of nature gives us knowledge that helps provide needed constraints on our moral judgments as well as other information that is morally relevant. This is the truth in the appeal-to-nature doctrine.

Kant's Ethics

I shall consider two versions of Kant's ethics: one based on the first and the other on the second basic formulation of what Kant calls the Categorical Imperative in his work the Groundwork of the Metaphysic of Morals. I shall not deal with his third main formulation of the Categorical Imperative requiring us to treat human beings as members of the kingdom of ends, since it is in a way a synthesis of the other two. That is, it combines both the form of the first formulation (universal law) and the matter (ends in themselves) of the second. It is the view of Immanuel Kant (1724-1804), probably the greatest German philosopher, that these are merely different formulations of one and the same principle. The first two main formulations seem to me to represent two distinct ethical theories. Thus, despite Kant's beliefs and intentions, certain actions are likely to be endorsed by the one imperative that are not endorsed by the other. A particular lie, for example, may be justified by appeal to the first formulation but not be justified by appeal to the second, or vice versa.

Before delving into these two theories, however, some clarification of Kant's terminology is called for, beginning with his distinction between categorical and hypothetical imperatives. Categorical, unlike hypothetical, imperatives are unconditional commands for Kant. There are no "ifs" and "buts" about them. For example, "Never lie!" "Shut the door!" Contrast: "If you want to collect honey, don't kick over the beehive" (one of Dale Carnegie's prudential imperatives). This would be classified as a hypothetical imperative by Kant, because it is conditional; that is to say, it only applies if you happen to want to collect honey. Kant's Categorical Imperative, in its capitalized formulation, not only gives an unconditional command, but also provides a general rule to judge the maxims of your actions, where "'maxim' stands for a particular principle of action adopted by an individual, such as 'Always tell the truth' or 'Always tell lies'."[16]

1. The formula of universal law: "Act only on that maxim through which you can at the same time will that it should become a universal law."[17] Kant believes that when you consider performing any particular act, A, you must always ask yourself what maxim or principle you would be acting on if you did A. As an extreme deontologist, or someone who holds that the goodness or badness of an act's consequences never has anything to do with its moral rightness (wrongness)—according to Kant all that counts is the motivation—he denies that the value of the consequences of A is relevant in determining A's moral rightness (wrongness). The sole moral question is whether you can will the maxim of your action to be a universal law or one valid for everyone (ibid., p. 71). William Frankena (b. 1908) sums up the position nicely as follows: "An action is morally right and/or obligatory if and only if one can consistently will that the maxim or rule involved be acted on by everyone in similar circumstances, and an action is morally wrong if and only if one cannot consistently will this."[18] In brief, self-contradiction is the basis of wrongdoing; consistency, the basis of right-doing, according to

---

16. Sir David Ross, Kant's Ethical Theory: A Commentary on the Grundlegung zur Metaphysik der Sitten (Oxford: Clarendon Press, 1954), p.44.

17. Immanuel Kant, The Moral Law: or, Kant's Groundwork of the Metaphysic of Morals, tr. H. J. Paton (London: Hutchinson, 1964), p.88.

18. William K. Frankena, Ethics (Englewood Cliffs: Prentice-Hall, 1963), p.25.

Kant's first formulation of the Categorical Imperative, which is held by him to be the supreme principle of morality. We shall explore three different things the formula of universal law might mean, and then turn to the second main formulation of the Categorical Imperative.

Before we examine the three interpretations, however, let us see how Kant himself applies the first formulation to one of his favorite examples: lying. Imagine that you are considering telling a lie by making a false promise. You are in need of money, and believe you cannot get it unless you promise to pay it back by a certain date. Suppose you also know you cannot repay it by that date. Kant formulates the maxim of this contemplated action as follows: "Whenever I believe myself short of money, I will borrow money and promise to pay it back, though I know that I will not pay it back." He then denies that this maxim can ever "rank as a universal law of nature and be self-consistent," that is, satisfy the first formulation of the Categorical Imperative. According to Kant,

> [it] must necessarily contradict itself. For the
> universality of a law that every one believing
> himself to be in need can make any promise he
> pleases with the intention not to keep it would
> make promising, and the very purpose of promising,
> itself impossible, since no one would believe he was
> being promised anything, but would laugh at
> utterances of this kind as empty shams.
>
> [The Moral Law, p.90]

First interpretation of the first formulation of the Categorical Imperative. Kant's argument may appear to be the following: you cannot consistently will that everyone always act on the above lying maxim, because if everyone did act on it, no one would believe promises any more; thus the practice of promising would be destroyed, which is undesirable. A similar argument could be developed against telling lies that assert what you believe to be false. If people did that whenever they thought it was to their advantage (so goes the parallel argument), no one would believe assertions any more; hence assertions would lose their function. Thus Carmen (of the sixth moral problem) should not lie to her father about his terminal illness, or for that matter, to anyone else about anything. The same goes for the rest of us.

I shall consider two objections to this apparent Kantian position that you should not act on certain maxims—for example, the lying maxim—because to do so would have bad consequences. First, it may be questioned whether the results would actually be as he imagines. Certainly, the consequences he mentions need not follow. For assertions and promises might be believed as much as they are now. Indeed, if some cynics are right, assertions and promises might be believed more than they are now. It has been said that "If you want

-110-

to be thought a liar, always tell the truth" (Logan Pearsall Smith). We know that liars are in fact often believed, and that even they are occasionally taken in by other liars. Suppose, then, we were all to act on the maxim Kant disapproves of and uses as an example—what he calls "this principle of self-love or personal advantage" (ibid., p.90)—making promises with no intention of keeping them unless we think it is to our advantage to do so. We might find that it is usually to our advantage to keep most of them, or at least as many of them as we now keep not acting on this maxim. Similarly, if we were to act on the closely related egoistic principle of asserting what we believe to be false with the intention thereby of deceiving someone, but only when we think that we have something to gain from the deception, we might still rarely tell such a lie, because we might believe that only rarely will we have something to gain from doing so. Thus everyone acting on this maxim would not necessarily give rise to the consequences Kant suggests it would of increasing the number of lies told.

A second objection may be even more important. Does not Kant's argument against lying run counter to his own theory? Kant says the moral worth of an action lies "not in the purpose to be attained by it, but in the maxim in accordance with which it is decided upon" (The Moral Law, pp.67-68). Here again we see Kant's concern with the motives of actions rather than their consequences. Nothing is good without qualification, he says in the first sentence of his Groundwork, but a good will. And you show your will is good when your conduct is guided by maxims that you recognize conform to the Categorical Imperative. Then you do what is morally right, regardless of the consequences of your conduct, according to Kant's theory. Kant's argument, however, clearly asks us to consider the consequences of actions, which are contingent matters of fact. But how then can the rightness of an action be independent of the value of its actual or intended consequences, as he claims? Wrongdoing seems, after all, not to be simply a matter of not contradicting yourself. Kant might reply that he is asking us to consider the consequences of everyone's acting on such a principle, not the consequences of this particular act. So it could remain the case that the morality of the particular act does not depend on the value of its consequencs. Thus Kant could still be a consistent deontologist at the level of acts. Even if we grant this, he would now be open to the charge that he has ceased to be a rule-deonlogist—that is, one who holds that the validity of a moral rule or maxim is not determined solely by whether it promotes the good. Kant's doctrine begins to sound suspiciously like rule utilitarianism, a doctrine we have already found reason to reject (see pp.89-102).

Second interpretation of the first formulation of the Categorical Imperative. Some readers of Kant think that the interpretation just given misinterprets him. They deny that he is arguing that you should not, for example, give lying promises because the consequences of everyone doing so would be bad. That is how a rule utilitarian would argue, and Kant is not any kind of utilitarian. Frankena writes in support of a second and different interpretation in the following passage:

> Kant, however, is contending that one cannot even will such a maxim to be universally acted on, because in so doing, one would be involved in a contradiction of will; one would be willing both that it be possible to make promises and have them credited (else why make them?) and that everyone be free to break promises to suit his own purposes. In other words, he is arguing, not that the results of everyone's always acting on the deceitful promise maxim are bad [as the first interpretation of Kant maintains], but that the results are self-defeating [call this the second interpretation], since if that maxim were universally acted on, we could not even have the institution of promise making which that maxim presupposes.
>
> [Ethics, p.90]

Even supposing that this is a correct interpretation of Kant's argument—and it seems as plausible as any—we see that the argument still fails for the reason given earlier: namely, it does not follow that if such a maxim were universally acted on there could be no more false or lying promises; hence the results need not be self-defeating. This is even more evident with the qualified maxims: "Lie whenever you can save a man from a murderer," or "Lie when a thief has you by the throat." These can be universalized without the results being in any way self-defeating. So Kant's conclusion that lying is always wrong does not seem to follow from his ethical theory even when we go by the second interpretation of his theory. The same is true of the three other examples he considers in his Groundwork: that it is immoral to commit suicide to end a miserable life, to neglect your natural gifts and talents if developing them interferes with your having a pleasant and enjoyable life, and that it is immoral not to help others in distress if you do not feel like doing so (The Moral Law, pp.89-91). The results of everyone's always acting on these three disapproved maxims need not be—and indeed are not even likely to be—self-defeating. Hence Kant is mistaken in supposing that his theory, at least as here interpreted, rules out acting on such maxims. It seems that the only way he can show what he wants to show to be immoral is to rest his case on several dubious empirical assumptions, thus inconsistently grounding his morality on variable factors—what people would will, want, do, be content with, and the like.

Third interpretation of the first formulation of the Categorical Imperative. There is a last possibility that remains to be considered. Kant might argue that there is a kind of inconsistency in the cases we have been considering that has nothing to do with the consequences at all or with the claim that the results would be self-defeating if everyone acted on the maxim. He might simply argue, for example,

-112-

that promising necessarily incurs an obligation, that it is a necessary part of making a promise that you are obligated to keep it. As Carritt observes, "It is hard to see what a promise is if it is not, as Hume said, 'binding oneself to the performance of an action'. A man could not without self-contradiction make a promise while explaining that he was under no obligation to keep it. Possibly this is what Kant really meant. . . ."[19] In short, if it is an analytic statement that promises entail the obligation to keep the promise, we cannot (logically) generalize the principle of promising without incurring any obligation of keeping our promises. Accordingly, it would be logically self-contradictory to will that no one should be obligated who makes a promise. But if this is Kant's point, there is the objection, first, that his theory still does not rule out lying, or anything else for that matter. The third interpretation merely shows that what purports to be an action—promising without incurring an obligation to keep your promise—is not an action; it is no more an action than marrying once and divorcing twice, or meeting your husband six months after living with him, or in a week's time getting a month behind in your work. Because these things are logically impossible, we know they could not be actions, since actions must (logically) be performable, whether or not they actually can be performed. Secondly, and as a corollary, it neither establishes that you cannot consistently universalize the principle of promising without intending to keep your promises nor that it is impossible to universalize the principle of lying in some other way.

Therefore, if Kant's first formulation of the Categorical Imperative is interpreted in the third way, it is vulnerable to the fatal criticism that it provides no moral guidance whatsoever, in the sense that it fails to rule out any action or practice of any kind: all it rules out are nonactions. Moreover, we have already seen that the first interpretaion makes him inconsistently appeal to the badness of the consequences of following certain maxims as a ground for rejecting those maxims, and that that interpretation seems to turn his position into rule utilitarianism, which was rebutted earlier along with act utilitarianism (see pp.89-102). Finally, if Kant is interpreted in the second way, he again rests his case on various empirical and hence contingent claims—and dubious ones at that—contradicting his position that his moral law is necessary and universal, and therefore one that cannot be based on anything empirical. For example, Kant argues that if you were to allow yourself lying even to a thief who has you by the throat, you would set yourself "in opposition to the condition and

----

19. E. F. Carritt, "Moral Positivism and Moral Aestheticism," an excerpt from which is reprinted in Readings in Ethical Theory, eds. W. Sellars and J. Hospers (New York: Appleton-Century-Crofts, 1952), p.410.

means through which a human society is possible."[20] So even on this, the second and most plausible of the three interpretations, Kant still cannot seem to make out his case against acting on certain maxims. Once more he appears inconsistently to ground his morality on a shaky, empirical, and contingent base.

In conclusion, I shall present a brief reductio ad absurdum of Kant's first formulation of the Categorical Imperative. This criticism is independent of the problem of applying his theory which we have been considering. Interpreting it in any of the three ways mentioned, the theory will have the consequence of making some acts morally right that are not even moral acts. To see this, let us suppose that I like to do easy exercises and that I am fond of meaningless rituals. Suppose that the maxim of my actions is to stand erect every couple of hours when I feel like it. I then touch my chin to my chest, slowly, and try to chirp like an alligator. Let us suppose that that if everyone acted on this maxim it would have little or no consequence. I could now will that everyone act on the maxim of my action without doing anything either logically self-contradictory or self-defeating. It seems, then, that Kant must say that whenever I perform this exercise, what I do is morally right. Yet this is absurd, since the action is not even a moral action. It is nonmoral, because it is based on a nonmoral reason. As we saw in Chapter III, "the principle or maxim of the action is coherent and can be universalized without contradiction" is neither a moral reason why someone should or should not cannibalize a human corpse. Worse yet for Kant, it is not a moral reason for doing anything. Therefore, actions based on this consideration are not moral actions, much less morally obligatory actions.[21]

2. The formula of the end in itself: "Act in such a way that you always treat humanity, whether in your own person or in the person of any other, never simply as a means, but always at the same time as an end" (The Moral Law, p.96). This formulation of the Categorical Imperative gives us moral guidance that does not depend on our making dubious empirical assumptions, unlike the ought-statements derived from the first formulation. It tells us both to do and to avoid doing certain things, whether or not we have the desire to do so. These positive and negative obligations hold for every

----

20. Immanuel Kant, Lectures on Ethics, tr. Louis Infield (New York: Harper and Row, 1963), p.227.

21. It might be thought that Kant can answer this last criticism. Perhaps he would reply that an action is not moral, in the sense of being morally right, simply by being in accord with the Categorical Imperative. All we can infer from such a fact is that the action is not immoral. I doubt, however, if such a rejoinder would be consistent with his theory.

rational being. The basic idea is that all human beings or other rational creatures are intrinsically good or ends in themselves, because of their capacity to act morally. Therefore, they count, and not just as a means to something we may want to achieve. We may treat them as means, but never simply as means. Kant wisely recognizes that the qualifiers 'simply' or 'merely' are essential here, since otherwise you would not be able to go into a shoe repair shop and treat the shoemaker as a means for getting your shoes fixed, anthropologists could not use people to study, and you could not take a class and treat the teacher as somebody who can help you learn the subject. Unfortunately, Kant himself apparently overlooks the need for the limiting 'merely' when he contends that prostitution is immoral because both the prostitute and the customer treat themselves and each other as a means. (See his Lectures on Ethics, pp.164-66.) What he should say is that it is immoral for either the prostitute or the customer to treat either himself or herself or the other as a mere means (to attain pleasure, relief from sexual frustration, money, or the like). For everyone must (morally) be treated as a person--that is, with respect. It does not matter whether that person is a prostitute or a prostitute's customer.

Some acts this doctrine rules out. You should not put a human being into a fire to warm a chilly room. Nor put yourself up to be raffled into slavery, no matter how worthwhile the cause. People are not to be used merely as a medium for social protest, like the guy who painted "Oink," "Right on," "Legalize pot" all over a girl's body. Nor are you to sell someone into the military, or in any way deprive people of their freedom (Lectures, p.165). Or take advantage of another's vulnerability. Former President Ford would have done wrong if he had Ronald Reagan crated and shipped to Senator Goldwater as a birthday present (Russell Baker's example). It is also wrong to knock somebody off to pass the time of day or because he or she is a utilitarian philosopher from whom you hope to get oil.[22] Or for doctors to impose treatments on their patients without letting those who can, choose from among the several available alternative treatments. Doctors should neither experiment on human beings without their consent nor give kidney machines only to the rich. Nor

---

22. When Bentham's body was dissected in accordance with his will, James Mill reported one day to Peacock, a friend of Bentham, "that there had exuded from Mr. Bentham's head a kind of oil, which was almost unfreezable, and which he conceived might be used for the oiling of chronometers which were going into high latitudes. 'The less you say about that, Mill,' said Peacock, 'the better it will be for you; because if the fact once becomes known, just as we see now in the newpaper that a fine bear is to be killed for his grease, we shall be having advertisements to the effect that a fine philosopher is to be killed for his oil'" (The Oxford Book of Literary Anecdotes, ed. James Sutherland [Pocket Books, 1976], p.235).

are students to treat their instructors as TV sets who exist merely to entertain them. Although the doctrine allows you to treat other people as sex objects—and even to be a sex object or sex symbol yourself—contrary to the view of some feminists, it insists that you must never treat either them or yourself merely as sex objects. It is morally all right, then, to appreciate people for their beauty and sexual attractiveness, among other things. But do not just order, "Hey, get in the car!" and not talk to the man or woman you are sexually interested in. For the same reason, it is morally wrong, according to this doctrine, to whisper and twitter behind the back of someone who is a Playgirl or a Playboy centerfold. Nor should radical Lesbians say to heterosexual women, "You have pig in the head!" as a way of sneering at them for being sexually attracted to men. (Such extremists argue that a feminist can only have "true" relationships with other women.) Again, although "we are entitled to form opinions about our fellows, we have no right to spy upon them," Kant says (Lectures, p.231), or, for example, to read their diaries without their permission. Privacy must be respected. Respect of others and for yourself also entails that we should not overeat and overdrink or encourage others to do so and that we should take care of our health. Given what we know today, that seems to rule out smoking. Moreover, we should avoid the "satanic vices" of envy, ingratitude, and malice (ibid., p.159). As Kant rightly observes, "an habitual scoffer betrays his lack of respect for others" (ibid., p.239); so do not scoff.

Speaking more positively, we should always recognize the dignity of people and treat them, and ourselves, as their moral status and ours requires—that is, respecting their freedom and feelings. This means we must act with integrity—with honesty—as well as kindness towards people. It is not, however, because integrity, honesty, and kindness are independently valuable, according to this view. The second main formulation of the Categorical Imperative implies that the one and only thing of independent moral value is respect of persons. While this consideration gives moral guidance, you should not expect that it will always tell you clearly and unambiguously what you should do in any given situation. It won't. Nevertheless, the second version of the Categorical Imperative seems to me to be an improvement over the first. Since Kant himself maintains that his moral doctrine "agrees very well with [the command to love thy neighbor as thyself],"[23] I shall save my final evaluation of it for the discussion of agapism.

---

23. Immanuel Kant, bk.1 ("Analytic of Pure Practical Reason"), the Critique of Practical Reason and Other Writings in Moral Philosophy, tr. Lewis W. Beck (Chicago: University of Chicago Press, 1949), pp.189-90.

Agapism

Agapism, or the ethics of love, says that what is morally right is to love your neighbor—that is, everyone—equally and as much as yourself. We find this doctrine in both the Old and the New Testaments. The words of Leviticus 19:18, "Thou shalt love thy neighbor as thyself" are repeated in Matthew 19:19 and 22:39, in Mark 12:31, and Romans 13:9, and James 2:8. In Galatians 5:14, we even read: "For all the law is fulfilled in one word, even in this; Thou shalt love thy neighbor as thyself." The Good Samaritan story (Luke 10:25-37) defines your neighbor as anyone and everyone. It would be a mistake, however, to suppose that agapism is an exclusive Judeo-Christian teaching. We find essentially the same doctrine of universal love in the Chinese tradition. Thus I Chih, the Mohist, speaking to Mencius (371-289 B.C.?), the Confucian, says:

> Even according to the Confucians, among the ancients
> the right way to treat others was "as if caring for
> an infant" [here I Chih quotes one of the Confucian
> Classics, in which this is recommended as an attitude
> for a king to have toward his people]. To me this
> means that we are to love all without difference of
> degree.[24]

In other words, I Chih argues that "even Confucian authorities sanction our doctrine of universal love" (ibid., p.741). Agapism, then, though connected in our tradition with a belief in God, does not presuppose the existence of such a being.

If we are supposed to love everyone equally, including ourselves, a natural question arises: in what sense of 'love'? The relevant love here is human agape—a "brotherly" and "sisterly" love—love in the Judeo-Christian sense of charity, care, regard, or respect. Such love is compassionate and forgiving, as the Parable of the Prodigal Son shows (Luke 15:11-32). It involves a commitment to each person's well-being. When we love people in this way, we value them as ends in themselves, fulfilling Kant's second formulation of the Categorical

---

24. Quotation from David S. Nivison's 1980 Presidential Address to the Pacific Division of the American Philosophical Association, "Two Roots or One?" reprinted in the Proceedings and Addresses of the American Philosophical Association, vol.53 (1980), p.740.

Imperative. So this love is neither to be confused with erotic love, which may or may not contain agape, nor with romantic love, which is never pure agape. Agapism is not to be confused with the bumper sticker philosophy: "Make Love Not War." It may be compatible with our making love, but it does not prescribe it.

Agapism and utilitarianism are also fundamentally different, in spite of perhaps sounding similar. Agapism's focus is on the motive of the act rather than on the actual or probable good it produces; hence it is a deontological theory. Some, if not all, utilitarians, on the other hand, are consequentialists. Moreover, while utilitarians are maximizers of the good, or at least of the probable good, agapists are not. Hence someone may always act in the most loving way possible—and thus do what is morally right, according to agapism—and yet fail to maximize the good, or even fail to do more good than harm. As Walter Bagehot observes, it is a melancholy reflection whether benevolence does more of one than of the other (Physics and Politics, 1869, chap.5). In other words, it is not clear whether a loving or kindly disposition to promote the well-being of others actually does more harm than good. Anatole France expresses an even more pessimistic view, remarking that "thoses who have given themselves the most concern about the happiness of people have made their neighbors very miserable" (The Crime of Sylvestre Bonnard, pt.II, Chap.4).

Another difference between these two doctrines is that utilitarianism does not require that you love everyone, in the aforementioned sense. Thus utilitarianism sometimes gets criticized (see above, pp.96–99) for condoning cruel and unjust acts. There is no temptation to make such a criticism of agapism, since a consistent agapist could never accept a nonloving act as morally right because it maximized the good. Genuine agapists have an active concern for everyone; so they would of course never sacrifice one person for another or for several others.

A second criticism that cannot plausibly be made of agapism is to say that it provides no moral guidance. Frankena makes this objection to agapism, writing: "It is not clear how the injunction to love provides us with any directive, any way of telling which act to perform or which rule to follow. . ."[Ethics, p.44]. Besides the illustrations already mentioned when discussing Kant's second formulation of the Categorical Imperative, I shall add here a few more. It rules out working on a firing squad, tossing cinder blocks off tall buildings onto pedestrians, genocide, or even putting a doormat outside that says "Scram!" Doctors should not perform a caesarean section on a patient just to speed up delivery or tie up a woman's fallopian tubes (a form of sterilization) without her permission while she is half-paralyzed by anesthesia. The doctrine rules out your buttonholing passersby and babbling out another person's most cherished anatomical secrets (Perelman's example). Nor should you expunge another from the human race because you no longer find fulfillment with him or her. Agapism implies further that you are not to gloat over the defects of others or to trifle with them. You must never act arrogantly, rudely, boastfully. Or act selfishly and bear grudges. Or be nice to your parents, say, only when you want money or the car. Or, on the other hand, think of your children just as tax deductions. A child should mean more than that. You are not to show false humility or live in filth if you can help it, for these things would be an affront to your self-respect and violate the command to love all people equally, including yourself. Positively, agapism implies that you should always show as much regard for the life and wishes of a humble file clerk or road sweeper as for a famous entertainer or president. Agapists will do what they can to fill empty stomachs, to prevent disease, poverty, and suffering, to help others in distress, and to oppose economic and political oppression. So it is clear: if your aim is to live in accordance with this doctrine, you must refrain from certain acts and be concerned to do others. Indeed, it seems it is likely to have quite radical effects on your conduct, confirming William James's thought that "All the higher, more penetrating ideals are revolutionary."[25]

Another dubious criticism of agapism and Kant's second basic formulation of the Categorical Imperative is to contend that all people do not really deserve to be loved or respected. We should only love and respect people who are lovable and deserving of love or respect, not those who are not. In his book, Civilization and Its Discontents, Sigmund Freud (1856-1939), the founder of psychoanalysis, writes: "My love is something valuable to me which I ought not to throw away without reflection. . . If I love someone, he must deserve it in some way."[26] Earlier he remarks that "not all men are worthy of love" (ibid., p.49). Along much the same lines, Nietzsche says, "There is not enough of love and goodness in the world to throw any of it away on conceited people" (Human, All Too Human, tr. Alexander Harvey, 129). If we suppose that the people in question are not only conceited, but also intolerant, cruel, and even criminal, would it not be absurd to love or respect them? Surely Charles Manson deserves our contempt (the objection continues), not our love and respect, and maybe he should even be commended "to cold oblivion" (Shelley's phrase, from Epipsychidion, 1821, 1. 149). An agapist will reply that there is an ambiguity here in the word 'respect'. People like Manson admittedly do not deserve our respect, in the sense that they are entitled to a high or special regard, esteem, or honor; quite the contrary. Yet in another sense of 'respect', even they deserve it; that

---

25. William James, "The Moral Philosopher and the Moral Life," Essays in Pragamatism, ed. Alburey Castell (New York: Hafner Publishing Co, 1957) p.68.

26. Sigmund Freud, Civilization and Its Discontents, tr. James Strachey (New York: W. W. Norton and Co, 1961), p.56.

is, we should have regard for their well-being, concern for their feelings, and the like. We should never assign them "to cold oblivion." In other words, an agapist may reply to this first criticism that people's rightly not being loved or respected in one sense does not mean they are not to be loved or respected in the special agapist and Kantian senses of these words. According to agapism and the second formulation of the Categorical Imperative, all human beings deserve the latter respect and love, no matter how vicious or bad they may be; hence it is not irrational to love or to respect them in this way. The Kantian and the agapist would agree with George Bernard Shaw's remark, "The worst sin towards our fellow creatures is. . . to be indifferent to them: that's the essense of inhumanity" (The Devil's Disciple, 1901).

I shall now discuss four more serious criticisms of agapism and the second version of Kant's ethics.

First, there is the objection that neither agapism nor Kant's second formulation of the Categorical Imperative includes animals; they both make morality apply only to persons, but it applies to animals as well. Most of us believe that we ought to be kind towards animals, and that it would be morally wrong to shoot our dog or to turn out our horse because age has made them incapable of serving us.

The agapist and Kant will answer that their moral theories do include animals, if only indirectly. Kant admits that on his view "we have no direct duties" to animals: "Our duties towards animals are merely indirect duties towards humanity" (Lectures, p.239). We should not cause them needless suffering or do away with them when they cease to be useful to us, he argues, because were we to do such things, we would damage in ourselves "that humanity which it is [our] duty to show towards mankind." The psychological fact is, "he who is cruel to animals becomes hard also in his dealings with men" (ibid., p.240); that is why we should not be cruel to animals. Aquinas reasons in much the same way: we should not mistreat animals, not because they are themselves direct objects of moral concern, but because treating them this way will tend to make us mistreat other people. Agapists can give exactly the same argument.

This answer, however, still fails to make agapism and Kant's second main formulation of the Categorical Imperative square with our moral judgments. It is a mistaken moral outlook to think we should avoid being cruel to animals only because—and in so far as—acting this way is likely to make us cruel to human beings. It would be wrong independently of its having this consequence. For suppose that we could mistreat animals without developing any tendency to mistreat people. Acting this way would still be morally wrong. Finally, we may question Kant's and Aquinas's psychological assumption that there is a causal connection between behaving cruelly towards animals and behaving cruelly towards other people. Certainly there seem to be many people who are extremely kind and generous to other human beings, but who are nevertheless very callous and harsh in their treatment of animals, and vice versa. Just what the connection, if any, between these two things is is a question that remains to be answered.

It is interesting to note that this first criticism of agapism and the second version of Kant's ethics cannot be made of utilitarianism, at least not in its hedonistic and eudaemonistic forms. For the latter theories require that we take account of the suffering of all creatures. Jeremy Bentham, the eighteenth and nineteenth century hedonistic utilitarian, stresses the moral relevance of all pleasures and pains, regardless of who has them (see pp.89-96). Australian philosopher Peter Singer (b. 1946), applying this theory in his book Animal Liberation, argues for radical changes in the way we treat animals.

Kant and the traditional agapist could sidestep the first criticism if they simply extended the notion of neighbor and person, or rational being, to include animals. But it is unlikely they would, or even consistantly could, accept such an extension of these terms. However, there are philosophers—for example, Robert S. Downie and Elizabeth Telfer (see their book, Respect for Person (1974))—who maintain that all animals as sentient beings, as well as people, should be treated with respect or agape love. Such a view—whether it is called "agapism," "neoagapism," or "quasiagapism"—clearly escapes the first criticism, but not necessarily the second, to which I now turn.

Agapism and Kant's second formulation of the Categorical Imperative disregard the moral relevance of our standing in certain relationships to one another—that of parent to child, husband to wife, that we are friends or lovers. According to these views, all people are owed precisely the same thing and nothing more: respect and an equal regard for their well-being. No place is accorded to loyalty or personal attachment. Maybe this is why Jesus says, "Whoever does the will of God, that one is My brother and sister and mother" (Mark 3:35), in effect, repudiating the significance of the filial and parental relations. Yet surely we have special obligations to our children, spouses, and friends, and these obligations do not apply to other people. For example, we have a duty to feed, nurture, and educate our children, and we do not take ourselves as having the same obligation towards other people's children. It seems, then, that to love all equally, the stranger as much as my family, would be wrong. "For," as Freud notes in Civilization and Its Discontents, "my love is valued by all my own people as a sign of my preferring them, and it is an injustice to them if I put a stranger on a par with them" (pp.56-57). This second criticism should not be confused with favoring nepotism. Nepotism is of course to be rejected, since it is favoritism shown to nephews and to others relatives, especially by giving them positions because of their relationship rather than on their merits. Consequently, it is a form of corruption and an abuse of power. It is not equivalent to the fulfillment of a moral obligation to one of our relatives.

The third formidable objection is that we have other moral values besides the agapist and Kantian one of showing respect to, caring for, and loving people. For example, we also value integrity, courage, honesty, and sincerity. These other values have been with human beings since the earliest times. Thus we read in the Iliad (bk.IX, 1. 312), "Hateful to me as the gates of Hades is that man who hides one thing in his heart and speaks another." Sophocles agrees: "To tell lies is not honorable" (Creusa, frag.323). It is because we have these other moral values, and value them in and for themselves, that we can admire the integrity and courage of a Jake La Motta, the former middleweight boxing champion (put on the screen in Raging Bull), even though we recognize how brutal, uncaring, and repulsive the screen character is. We morally value his integrity and courage, despite the fact that neither furthers his love of others. Again, as N. J. Dent points out (Mind, 1980, p.153): "if someone honors the truth, despises any cheap and easy way with intellectual problems, does this not display a moral attitude on his part? But," Dent continues, "this has nothing particularly to do with caring about others," or with agape love. Further, compassion and respecting others do not seem to be involved in all of our moral duties. For example, the duty to keep a particular promise may have nothing to do with agape love. Nor can the agapist or Kant plausibly make out a case for saying that integrity, honesty, and sincerity are important and valued by us simply because they further our love and respect for others, for we see that often they do not do this but even come into conflict with our showing compassion towards others.

Agapists and Kantians might of course try to rebut the third criticism by demonstrating that all of the aforementioned moral values are merely dependent or derivative values—that is, that they have value only because, and in as much as, they are means of showing respect for people or expressing brotherly or sisterly love. In Agape: An Ethical Analysis (1972), Gene Outka (b. 1937) suggests that this is possible. Rodger Beehler (b. 1938) tries, unsuccessfully, to establish the point in his book Moral Life (1978). To my knowledge, no one has yet made out the claim. I doubt that anyone ever will.

These three criticisms are probably the most damning of the four major ones I shall consider. What they show, mainly, is that agapism and Kant's second formulation of the Categorical Imperative (like hedonistic and eudaemonistic utilitarianism) oversimplify our moral reasoning. These views, like the others, disregard many morally relevant considerations: in particular, that the suffering of an animal, as well as of a human being, counts morally; that we take into account the personal relations people stand in to each other (mother to child, wife to husband, and the like); and, finally, that we have many other moral values besides respect and concern for people, such as integrity, courage, honesty, and sincerity. For these reasons alone agapism and the second version of Kant's ethics cannot constitute an adequate theory, though an additional reason to reject them may well be that they ask more of us than most of us are capable of, thereby violating the requirement that whatever we ought to do we must be able to do. I turn next to this fourth and last criticism of agapism and of the second version of Kant's ethics.

   These views violate the dictum that 'ought' implies 'can'. As the previous quotation from Nietzsche suggests (see above, p.119), human beings have only a limited capacity for love. In The Object of Morality (1971), Geoffrey J. Warnock (b. 1923) echoes the point, claiming

> that most human beings have some natural tendency
> to be more concerned about the satisfaction of
> their own wants, etc., than those of others. . . .
> Even if [a person] does care to some extent about
> others, it is likely to be only about some
> others—family, class, country, or "race."
> There is also, besides complete or comparative
> indifference, such a thing as active
> malevolence. . . .
>   [p.21]

   In short, if human nature is such that we cannot (psychologically) love everybody, much less love everybody equally, as agapism requires, then is it not absurd, as well as unfair, to insist that we are morally obligated to do so? The dictum that 'ought' implies 'can' says that you cannot be obligated to do more than you are capable of doing. In Civilization and Its Discontents (p.59), Freud himself asserts that "nothing else runs so strongly counter to the original nature of man" than the commandment to love your neighbor as youself.

   Notice that this criticism of agapism does not depend on endorsing the false doctrine of psychological egoism, which is the view that every voluntary act is determined solely by a desire of the agent to maximize his or her own welfare. All it asserts is that it is not humanly possible to love everybody equally, in the required manner. (No doubt we cannot hate everyone either.) Even the flower children of the 1960s, who saw love as the way out of our moral troubles, were hard put to cherish those who disliked them, and hardly distinguished themselves in helping those in distress or pain achieve happiness. Professed Christians and Jews no less conspicuously fail to love one another. Indeed, those who most claim to love their fellow human beings generally do not love them in their hearts, but only with their words. And what kind of love is that which only displays itself in talk? Genuine love—whether it be brotherly or romantic love—shows itself in loving acts, nonverbal as well as verbal. If you are unwilling to give up any of your comforts to help the poor and hungry in the world, you do not love them with love of the agape kind. It is significant that those who purport to be agapists generally seem unable to follow Emerson's advice of putting their "creed into [their] deed" ("Ode," Sung in the Town Hall, Concord, 4 July 1857). Thus the contrast Emerson notes between Stoics and Christians:

> For every Stoic was a Stoic, but in Christendom
> where is the Christian?
>
> [Essays: First Series, "Self-Reliance."]

Do we really care whether the house of a Lebanese or of a Salvadoran is on fire and they are starving? Terrible things are happening to people every day, all over the world, but we mostly pay no heed. "Do ye hear the children weeping. . .?" Elizabeth Barrett Browning asks (The Cry of the Children, 1844, st.1). I think most of us would have to reply "No." We do not hear the sobs; they are distant. More important, even if we did, we would probably not respond to them. Richard Le Gallienne sadly concludes:

> The Cry of the Little Peoples goes up to
> God in vain,
> For the world is given over to the cruel
> sons of Cain.
>
> ["The Cry of the Little Peoples."]

Admittedly, there are exceptions. Saint Francis of Assisi (1182-1226) and Mother Theresa of Calcutta are shining counter-examples to the claim that human beings cannot love their neighbors. Yet it may be wondered whether even they love everyone equally: the Pope and their immediate families no more than anyone else. But even if they do, they are both so exceptional and rare that I doubt whether they refute the general claim that the vast majority of us are psychologically incapable of being sincere, practicing agapists. That a few can love in the required way does not show that the rest of us can.

Perhaps the agapist will reply that being unwilling to act in a loving and caring manner towards others does not mean we cannot. It is possible to becomes kinder and to love more than we do. Not that we can directly choose to love everyone or anyone: obviously we cannot. But we can cultivate the emotion indirectly by becoming aware of people's desires, thoughts, sorrows, joys, and suffering, and, perhaps most important, by acting as if we love and respect them. In time we may actually come to. A religious agapist will no doubt add that we need divine help to achieve this aim. However, since "with God all things are possible" (Matthew 19:26), the ethical doctrine of agapism can be followed, and there is hope that, as Carl Sandburg says, "Brother may yet line up with brother" (The People Will Live On [1936]).

On the other hand, should the agapist agree with the criticism that it is psychologically impossible to love everyone, he or she may still insist that we can appreciate the doctrine as an ideal, if not as a tenable theory of right and wrong, as formulated here. Carl Schurz remarks that:

> Ideals are like stars; you will not succeed
> in touching them with your hands. But like the
> seafaring man on the desert waters, you choose
> them as your guides, and following them you
> will reach your destiny.
> [Address, Faneuil Hall, Boston, 18 April 1859]

So, however impossible it may be to love everyone, we can still try to love people as much as we can. And we can be guided by this ideal by doing our utmost to love one another. The more we do so, the closer we shall come to living a morally good life.

I conclude that agapism and the second version of Kant's ethics, despite their flaws, are still the best theories, or theory, we have examined. Certainly respect for people is a fundamental consideration, and its presence or absence is always morally relevant. Finally, we should not suppose that this general outlook is only of academic interest. For it has in fact given rise to a highly effective and realistic method of nonviolence to overcome certain forms of oppression and social injustice in the world, especially in India and the United States, the two largest democracies.[27] Martin Luther King himself says that "the foundation of such a method is love" (ibid.). Using this approach, Mahatma Gandhi and Martin Luther King stirred the conscience of their nations.

---

27. See Martin Luther King, Jr, Speech Accepting the Nobel Peace Prize (11 December 1964) and Mahatma Gandhi's Defense against the Charge of Sedition (23 March 1922).

CHAPTER VII

CONCLUSION

The only satisfactory normative position in ethics is a modified form of what John Rawls defines as intuitionism. In Chapters V and VI, we examined most of the major ethical theories: subjectivism, conventionalism, the golden rule, divine-command theory, different versions of egoism, utilitarianism, the appeal to nature, and Kant's ethics, and agapism. We found that not one of them gives us a single general basis or formula for deciding moral questions that we can and must accept or else be morally incompetent or irrational. It is reasonable to conclude that there is no true theory of morality consisting either (1) of a single principle—that is, a supreme moral principle—or (2) of a plurality of principles, including an explicit method, or "priority rules, for weighing these principles against one another."[1]

John Rawls (b. 1921), who is not himself an intuitionist but some sort of Kantian, believes that intuitionists endorse a plurality of first principles and deny that there is an explicit method for weighing these principles against one another. On their understanding, then, there is no decision making procedure to determine what is morally right and wrong. Rawls is mistaken, however, in contending that intuitionists all embrace a plurality of first principles: Prichard and Moore are clear counterexamples. Nor can we define an intuitionist as someone who makes Rawls's two negative claims that there is (1) no single moral principle and (2) no priority rules for a plurality of principles of the sort mentioned, for an emotivist (Ayer or Stevenson) and a prescriptivist (Hare) might also make both these last two claims. So, I propose a slight modification of Rawls's characterization of intuitionism. Let us drop his requirement that an intuitionist endorse a plurality of principles and add to his two negative conditions the positive one that an intuitionist be an objectivist, in the sense explained at the beginning of the last chapter. This seems to yield a more accurate account of intuitionism. Certainly most, if not all traditional intuitionists—for example, the "big three" Moore, Prichard, and Ross—do hold that moral judgments are true or false, and they reject the approbative viewpoint.[2] If you assert that having an

---

1. John Rawls, A Theory of Justice (Cambridge: Harvard Universtiy Press, 1971), p.34.

2. In his later work, A. C. Ewing (b. 1899), who is generally classified as an intuitionist, parts company from these philosophers. Moral judg-

abortion during the first three months of pregnancy is morally wrong and I counter that it is not, our moral judgments are flatly contradictory, according to Moore, Prichard, and Ross, and therefore they contend that both judgments cannot be true—at least one must be mistaken. Nor, in their view, can the true moral judgment be determined by simply appealing to the fact that someone (or some group) approves or has some sort of pro or con attitude about having an abortion during the first three months of pregnancy. Let us therefore characterize intuitionists as objectivists, but deny the converse. For we have seen in Chapter VI that there are many objectivists who are not intuitionists.

We should ourselves acknowledge that we are objectivists. Sidgwick rightly asserts that it is a "fundamental assumption on which [moral judgments] all proceed, that some such judgments are true and others false, and that when any two such judgments conflict, one or both must be erroneous."[3] Objectivism thus squares with our conviction that when we make a moral judgment, we imply that what we are saying is true. It also squares with the fact that we sometimes agree and sometimes disagree about moral matters; and when we disagree, we assume that our judgments are logically incompatible. Moreover, we believe that sometimes our moral judgments are correct and sometimes not, and when they are correct, we do not believe that this is so because someone, or some group, has certain pro or con attitudes about them. These are our honest convictions; so we should acknowledge them in our declared philosophical position. We do not want to be like the philosopher who lives in a humble shack but then builds next door a splendid but unrelated philosophical edifice (Kierkegaard's analogy). As Kierkegaard says, "Spiritually speaking a man's thought must be the building in which he lives—otherwise everything is topsy-turvy."[4] Enough of philosophical cathedrals devoted to empty intellectualism! Our moralities make real demands on us and most of us are able and willing to live by them. Our philosophy should recognize these facts, along with our fundamental conviction that there is truth in morality. At least those

---

ments are no longer characterized as descriptive, as true or false depending on whether they correctly ascribe certain non-natural properties to things. See Ewing's Ethics (Kent: Hodder and Stoughton, eleventh impression, 1976), pp.180–82; his Second Thoughts in Moral Philosophy (New York: Macmillan, 1959), pp.50–52; and The Morality of Punishment (Montclaire: Patterson Smith Publishing, 1970 (originally published in 1929), p.viii.

3. Henry Sidgwick, "Symposium—Is the Distinction between 'Is' and 'Ought' Ultimate and Irreducible?" Proceedings of the Aristolitian Society, vol.2, no.1, part I (1892), p.89.

4. Soren Kierkegaard, The Journal of Kierkegaard, tr., ed., Alexander Dru (New York: Harper Brothers, 1959), p.98.

moral judgments that are not too vague to be called true or false are either one or the other, though we may of course not know which they are.

We should be moderate deontologists. While the intuitionist Prichard is correct that consequential considerations are not the only moral reasons for or against performing an action, he is mistaken in supposing that this establishes that such considerations never constitute moral reasons for or against doing something. Prichard commits this non sequitur in his article "Does Moral Philosophy Rest on a Mistake?" when he tries to rebut the utilitarian answer to the question why ought you do something. Like Moore, Ross, Rawls, Frankena, and most other philosophers, then, I favor a mixed or moderate deontological position. As a deontologist I deny that the goodness of an act's consequences is the only relevant condition in determining that it is morally right. But being a moderate deontologist I grant that certain kinds of good or bad consequences of an act—for example, that it causes suffering or pain—are relevant to the question whether the act is morally right or wrong.

The intuitionism I espouse is not to be confused with the traditional intuitionism of either Prichard, Moore, or Ross. As we have just seen, I reject Prichard's extreme deontological position. Earlier I pointed out that Prichard fails to realize that ought-judgments rest on moral reasons, and that there are a great many moral reasons we appeal to (see pp.25-28). These reasons may support conflicting courses of action in particular cases, and there is no rule or principle that tells us how to weigh them against one another, or that can tell us, for example, when suffering or when honesty counts for more. That is why people can disagree on the weights they place on their moral values without being irrational, and why there is no decision making procedure for dealing with moral problems and moral disagreements.

My form of intuitionism also differs from Moore's. As we have seen, we part company over ideal utilitarianism, and especially because he allows any cognitions of intrinsic goodness to count as moral reasons in favor of doing something. If an act gives aesthetic enjoyment to someone (think of Rudolf Schwarzkogler, p.72)—remember that this is one of the most valuable things we can imagine, in Moore's view—this is alleged by him to be a moral reason for doing it. In short, his utilitarianism and intuitionism allow all sorts of things to be moral reasons which in fact are not.

My position is probably the most like Ross's, of the three traditional intuitionist views. According to him, we recognize that we have certain prima facie duties—for example, to keep promises, to produce good, to relieve distress, to refrain from lying and from harming others. "The [indefinable 'non-natural' property of rightness] (prima facie) of certain types of act is self-evident." This property that we can neither sense nor discover by scientific means (because it is non-natural) can "be apprehended directly by minds that have reached a certain degree of maturity," though not by every mind.[5] When we are in a situation in which several of these prima facie duties are incumbent on us, what we have to do, according to Ross, is to study the situation as fully as we can until we "form a considered opinion (it is never more) that in the circumstances one of them is more incumbent than any other"; this we then judge to be our actual duty (ibid., p.19).

There are several respects in which my approach clearly differs from Ross's. To begin with, I make no appeal either to a distinct intuitive faculty that tells us what is morally right or wrong or to "non-natural" properties of rightness, goodness, and the like. Nor do I say we know what is morally right or wrong "by intuition," for such a remark explains nothing, though it may look as if it does. Intuition is "an unnecessary shuffle," notes Wittgenstein (PI § 213). I also do not make use of the notion of prima facie duties or moral principles that are supposed to be directly evident to "mature" as opposed to immature minds. Indeed, I do not try to justify anything by appeal to the notion of self-evidence.

My appeal, instead, is to moral reasons, which I take to be factual statements or judgments of a special kind. In such judgments the factual consideration(s) is taken by the speaker, agent, or person making the judgment to be of ultimate or intrinsic importance, and he or she has a positive concern for its own sake for either justice, gratitude, charity, kindness, respect of others and self, generosity, honesty, integrity, loyalty, fortitude, courage, or the like. This sense of 'moral reason' was explained and defended above (pp. 40-48).

It is true that many of Ross's prima facie duties become my moral reasons, but some of them could never be so transformed. Consider, for example, his alleged prima facie duties of justice, which are to "upset or prevent [a] distribution [of pleasure or happinesss (or of the means thereto) which is not in accordance with the merit of the persons concerned]" (ibid., p.21). Here the conservative Ross shows himself to be a bit of a radical, for he is implying that we have a prima facie duty to make someone who is happy less happy, or someone who is enjoying himself enjoy himself less, if that someone does not deserve to be happy or to enjoy himself. I would never say that we have a moral reason to do this. Finally, where Ross appeals to "the main moral convictions of the plain [as well as the mature] man" (ibid., p.21n), or in effect to common sense, I am more likely to appeal, in my philosophizing about morality, to the correct everyday use of moral words. That is to say, he belongs, along with Moore, mainly in the camp of commonsense philosophers; I belong only partly

----

5. David Ross, The Right and the Good (Oxford: Clarendon Press, 1930), p.12.

there, my home being primarily with ordinary-language philosophers. The latter appeal to accepted linguistic practices, or to the way fluent, competent, and able users of the language use words and sentences in order to describe their meaning and to dissolve traditional philosophical problems. Thus, if you want to get clear about the expression 'moral reason', ordinary-language philosophers recommend that you consider how it is used by competent speakers of the language. Commonsense philosophers, in contrast, rely mainly on appeals to the opinions or beliefs accepted by people of "plain common sense," generally to refute erroneous philosophical views.

I hope this brief discussion suffices to show that, in spite of certain affinities, my form of intuitionism is not to be taken as merely a restatement of the intuitionism of either Prichard, Moore, or Ross. Still, objections can be leveled against my position as well as theirs. I shall therefore close this Chapter by trying to anticipate questions about, and objections to it, replying to them as well as I can.

Does my view fall into subjectionism or conventionalism? The short answer is no, because my position denies that beliefs about what is morally right of either an individual or a group are ever moral reasons for judging that something is morally right or wrong. Putting the point another way: we have seen that subjectivism and conventionalism are not even moral codes any more than are so-called ethical egoism, etiquette, or the law, in my view. Not every action-guide is a morality. Remember that my position is that of an objectivist, and hence nonapprobative. My concern with linguistic practices and conventions governing the use of words should not make us overlook this: it does not make me a conventionalist, in the sense in which that term has been used and explained here. For I do not believe that moral rightness rests on what some group or the majority thinks is morally right. Moral truth is not founded on public or group opinion. Nor, of course, am I recommending that we should (morally) follow the herd and conform to the prevailing customs of our society or group.

How do we determine that a moral judgment is true or tell what is morally right? In other words, how do we distinguish what is actually the case in morality from what is not, if there is no tenable theory of morality consisting of either a single or a plurality of principles? There is no general answer to this question. The best that we, as more or less moral people, can say is that we do it the way we do it. For example, Isabella (in the seventh moral problem) concludes that it is more important not to break her vows and to preserve her chastity than to save her brother's life by sleeping with the deputy. Could she be wrong? Of course. Probably most, certainly many, people today would agree with her brother Claudio that saving his life should have been a more important concern for her than her chastity, and that it would have been morally wrong--some would say an unspeakable offense--for her to have let her brother's

-131-

head be chopped off simply to preserve her virginity and to keep her vows. We can imagine Isabella herself changing her mind and concurring with us, especially after witnessing a beheading. She might then say she mistook a mere symbol of purity—chastity—for purity itself. The fact is, however, that in the play she and Claudio disagreed, and we have seen that there is no decison making procedure to resort to to establish whether Claudio's or her judgment is the correct one.

Still, both sides are convinced that one or the other is right, and both give their reasons for thinking as they do. Neither takes the relativistic position: "Well, its morally right for you, but its not morally right for me." Nor do they—or I—or I daresay you—believe, "Both views are actually correct." We recognize, however, that it is possible to disagree about the matter.

Must we not, then, be skeptics about morality, if we do not have a single standard or ethical theory? Not at all. There are many things that are beyond doubt in morality and that we clearly know to be true. My earlier emphasis on moral problems and moral disagreements should not obscure this fact. For example, we know that it is morally wrong to betray a friend the way Iago did Othello, to shoot down children with a high-powered rifle just for fun, to fire at moving cars just to improve your marksmanship, or to punt puppies for exercise.[6] The Nazis exterminating six million Jews because they were Jews is another example of something that we know to be morally wrong. The American philosopher and novelist William Gass (b. 1924) offers still a sixth illustration of a clear-cut moral wrong:

> Imagine I approach a stranger on the street
> and say to him, "If you please, sir, I desire
> to perform an experiment with your aid." The
> stranger is obliging, and I lead him away. In
> a dark place conveniently by, I strike him with
> the broad of an axe and cart him home. I place
> him, buttered and trussed, in an ample electric
> oven. The thermostat reads 450° F. Thereupon
> I go out to play poker with friends and forget
> all about the obliging stranger in my stove.
> When I return, I realize I have overbaked my
> specimen, and the experiment, alas, is ruined.
> Something has been done wrong. Or
> something wrong has been done.
> Any ethic that does not roundly condemn

------

6. This example comes from Samuel Gorovitz's fine book Doctors' Dilemmas: Moral Conflict and Medical Care (New York: Macmillan Publishing, 1982), p.82.

my action is vicious.

["The Case of the Obliging Stranger,"
Philosophical Review, vol.66, 1957, p.193]

By the same token, it is possible to know that particular actions are morally right. Renford Bambrough (b. 1926) gives the following example, which merely needs to be amplified a bit to serve its purpose:

> My proof that we have moral knowledge consists
> essentially in saying, "We know that this child,
> who is about to undergo what would otherwise be
> painful surgery, should be given an anaesthetic
> before the operation. Therefore we know at least
> one moral proposition to be true." I argue that
> no proposition that could plausibly be alleged
> as a reason in favor of doubting the truth of
> the proposition that the child should be given an
> anaesthetic can possibly be more certainly true
> than the proposition itself.[7]

This last remark, namely, that there is "no proposition that could plausibly be alleged as a reason [to doubt] the truth of the proposition that the child should be given an anaesthetic [that] can possibly be more certainly true than [that] proposition itself," seems to be a slip on Bambrough's part. For suppose we knew, or had reason to suspect, that the child was highly allergic to all known anaesthetics and that we might kill the child if we gave him an anaesthetic. Then we would certainly have reason to doubt the proposition, and we should therefore not claim that we know that the child should be given an anaesthetic before the operation. Bambrough's mistake here was not to give a full enough description of his example, anticipating, and thus forestalling, this and similar sorts of objection. Let us therefore add to the description of the case that the child is not allergic to all available anaesthetics; that giving an anaesthetic is the most effective way to minimize the pain; and that we have no reason to think that giving an anaesthetic will adversely affect the success of the surgery. Then Bambrough's example shows nicely that the lack of a normative theory of ethics of the sort philosophers have been looking for in no way precludes our having moral knowledge of right or wrong actions. There is a consensus about all of the actions mentioned. But I am not saying that they are morally right or wrong, or that we know they are morally right or wrong, when we know this, just because there is such a consensus. People who would say that, would, of course, be conventionalists.

------

7. Renford Bambrough, Moral Scepticism and Moral Knowledge (Atlantic Highlands: Humanities Press, 1979), p.15.

But can we not show that one morality, or moral code, is the right one, and thus establish with a knockdown argument all rational and moral people must accept that moral disputants who appeal to it are reasoning correctly, while those who do not are not? This can be called the question of "the right ethics" or, less flatteringly, of "the super-morality." Some doubt that the question even makes sense and wonder what someone who asks it is after.[8]

By reference to what beyond our values are we supposed to vindicate them? How could you possibly establish one morality, or set of moral values, to be better than another? It is true that we can judge moralities to be inadequate (for example, hedonistic utilitarianism, agapism, and the second formulation of Kant's ethics) because they fail to recognize that certain moral considerations are indeed moral ones. Furthermore, we can show that certain alleged moralities are not moralities, on the grounds that they confuse nonmoral with moral reasons (a flaw of ethical egoism, the golden rule when it is taken literally, the first formulation of Kant's ethics, as well as of subjectivism, and of conventionalism). But when neither of these criticisms can be made of a moral code, it is not clear how it is to be evaluated. Consider, for example, the second moral disagreement over birth control. Patricia has a Roman Catholic morality; her neighbor Jan does not. Suppose Jan is a member of the Society for Ethical Culture. Both Jan's and Patricia's moral codes are genuine moralities, and there is no reason to think that either fails to recognize any moral considerations as truly moral. Consequently, it is still not clear what criteria we are to use to choose between their moralities. We may, of course, simply affirm that Jan's or Patricia's is the right one because it fits in with the way we think about moral matters. But then we are merely showing that such a morality is our morality. This obviously settles nothing, since it begs the question—that is, assumes, without argument, the point originally at issue.

The attempt to justify a particular morality and morality in general—to provide a foundation for either--runs into a dilemma. On the one hand, we have just seen that if we try to justify them by appeal to moral considerations, we open ourselves to the charge of begging the question: we vindicate them by relying on moral judgments that presuppose what is to be vindicated. To justify morality on the basis of morality itself, then, is circular and hence is no justification of anything.

----

8. Rush Rhees reports Ludwig Wittgenstein as holding this opinion, in "Some Developments in Wittgenstein's View of Ethics," Discussions of Wittgenstein (New York: Schocken Books, 1970), p.100. D. Z. Phillips and H. O. Mounce express a similar view in Moral Practices (New York: Schocken Books, 1970) p.107.

On the other hand, if we make our justification consist only of nonmoral considerations, it fails to justify any morality as a morality. At best it will show that that morality is an effective means to achieve some nonmoral end. Thus this line of argument tends actually to undermine, instead of to support, morality in general by resting it on something alien to it. No doubt this is why the French philosopher, Voltaire (1694-1778), says, "Virtue debases itself in justifying itself" (Oedipe, act I, sc. 4). To illustrate, suppose that someone argues that a certain moral code should be adopted, or that you should be moral on the ground that it pays; that is, it gives a very high return on your investment. Indeed, the claim is often made that you will be rewarded with everlasting happiness or go to heaven if you adopt it. Then we are given egoistic or prudential reasons to be moral and to follow this code. There are two objections to this move. To begin with, it is often not to a particular person's advantage to be moral. But, secondly, even if it were advantageous, since this is not a moral reason, we must recognize that if we act on it, we shall not be acting morally; hence we shall not then be following any morality. Nonmoral considerations may at best be causally efficacious in getting us to act as if we were moral, which is not the same thing as to act morally. Doing the morally right thing for some nonmoral purpose, for example, giving a large amount of money to the needy to get a substantial tax break, is not to act as a moral person or to adopt a moral point of view. To quote Isaiah (64:6), such "righteousnesses are as filthy rags"; they merely consist of the rotten garments of morality. It is true that acting as if we were moral may eventually lead to our acting morally and thus to our becoming moral, but only if our reasons for acting in the prescribed ways both cease to be egoistic and are themselves moral reasons.

We confront the same difficulty if God's will is cited as the reason why we should be moral or follow a certain morality. If it is argued that God wills only what is morally right (recall the discussion of divine-command theory in Chapter V, pp.74-80), then we are in effect saying we should act as He says because it is morally right. This, obviously, does not justify the morality: it merely presupposes its legitimacy. On the other hand, if it is argued that we should adopt a particular code of behavior simply on the grounds that an all-powerful being commands us to—or because it is a way to maintain political power, to get rich, or to get the admiration of the community—we are back again with nonmoral reasons. We have already seen that if we act on them, we shall not be acting morally; hence we shall not be following any morality. So it seems that we cannot provide a foundation, or justification, for any morality, or morality generally, either in God, self-interest, in community approval, or in the achieving of political power.

Some may despair at this point, wring their hands, and cry "Alas!" over our inability to justify our morality. Yet if it makes no sense, or it is logically impossible, to do this—which more and more appears to be the case—then it should be questioned whether it is rational to react in such a despairing way over our not being able to do it. As Lady Macbeth counsels, "Things without all remedy should be without regard" (Macbeth, III, ii, 12). Certainly we should not begin our ethical inquiries with the dogmatic assumption that there must be such a foundation or justification to be discovered. The history of ethics itself suggests otherwise. Despite all their efforts, philosophers have been unable to agree on the foundation of ethics or on what the right morality might be, and they are no closer to achieving such an agreement now than they were when they first began doing ethics. The historical record, then, plus the kind of considerations mentioned here, provide us with ample reason to doubt that justifying our morality, or morality in general, is a clear and attainable goal.

I have no intention of maintaining, however, that people can never properly criticize their values. For example, Pip, the main character in Charles Dickens's novel Great Expectations, came to see the shallowness of his original goals, the falseness of the values he had as a younger man. He changed, though basically he had always been a good human being. Here we have a case of learning from your mistakes. Still, notice how different making a mistake is in this context from making scientific or purely factual mistakes. How we come to see our moral mistakes is also quite different. Often people change their values because of something concrete in their lives. For instance, a banker who once said he would never hire a woman executive later decided to do so. He had growing daughters, and his concern for them helped him to appreciate the need for sexual equality. So certainly it is possible for people to change their values, and in the light of this change to reassess their earlier ones. Sometimes the change happens gradually, sometimes suddenly. It may be expected or be surprising. When Americans changed their attitude toward the Vietnam War, many of them did so because they came to see that it involved far more suffering than they had imagined. But we may presume that avoiding suffering was always a fundamental consideration for these people; hence the change was not really a change in values but rather in their understanding of what the war meant. When a hedonist becomes an agapist, in contrast, we have a great moral change—so great it can be called a moral conversion. Nekhludox in Tolstoy's Resurrection experienced a moral conversion of this sort. In this case what he formerly "considered important and good [he afterwards found to be] actually repulsive or insignificant" (chap.28). But none of these examples of change in values or outlook in any way shows that a person's morality, or morality in general, can be justified.

It may seem at this point that I could be accused of making moral reasoning arbitrary. Yet I am merely reporting or describing how we reason morally, explaining what the logic of moral reasoning is. I do not wish to make it anything it is not, but merely to get the facts straight about what it is. If I am correct, my form of intuitionism, which recognizes that there are many different moral reasons, should have the virtue of implicitly acknowledging the many different ways in which people arrive at moral decisions. I want to emphasize that our moral opponents have a moral outlook no less than we. This is not humility on my part, but the recognition of reality. There is not exactly one moral point of view, but rather many moral points of view, or many different moralities, that overlap each other; none is entirely alien to us. We can see some of our own moral values in the other perspectives from which things look different. For people normally agree on what are moral reasons, even if they often give them different weights.

"But," you may ask, "is moral reasoning then itself arbitrary?" Again, the answer is no. To say that it is arbitrary is to say that it arises from will or caprice, or that it is random and without reason. But since moral reasoning is itself a species of reasoning, it obviously cannot be random and without reason. Nor is it wilful or capricious, for only certain sorts of things will be moral reasons. As was pointed out in Chapter III (pp.25-28, 37-40), there are moral and nonmoral approaches to problems, and not every consideration—not even every ultimate consideration—is a moral reason. You cannot make something a moral reason by willing that it be one, any more than you can make something a scientific or mathematical reason by mere fiat.

Another mistake to avoid here is to suppose that the word 'arbitrary' signifies 'not logically demonstrable'. If you make this error, you will naturally take moral conclusions and the moral life to be arbitrary. These contentions, however, are unfounded, since they rest on a simple misconception of what it is to be arbitrary. As noted in the previous paragraph, to say something is arbitrary is to say that it arises from will or caprice or that it is random and without reason. This is an altogether different statement from saying that it cannot be logically demonstrated or proved. Nor does the former imply the latter.

But how come there is this amazing agreement in the use of our moral language and about what we count as moral reasons? If there is nothing supporting this, should not we have chaos? Not necessarily. Much of life is like this. There is nothing supporting our mathematical and logical rules either and our agreeing on what following a particular rule is. For example, we agree on what it is to follow the rule "add the number four." We know if we add 4 to 200, we get 204. All who are competent in mathematics agree on this, yet it is arguable that mathematics has no more foundation than ethics. The basic thing we appeal to here is nothing but the accepted mathematical practice. The same is true of logic. Thus our logical or deductive rules of inference derive whatever validity they have from their conformity to inferences which we accept as logically valid. So logic in turn depends on logical practice. Consequently, if we are astonished at the amazing agreement in our linguistic practice in the one case—the moral one—we ought to be in the other as well. The fact is we do not need foundations for any of these practices to justify them. It is only a philosophical prejudice to think we do. As

Wittgenstein says, human beings "agree in the language they use. That is . . . agreement . . . in form of life" (PI, § 241). Later he adds that "what has to be accepted, the given, is . . . forms of life" (PI, p.226). This agreement in the use of our moral language and on what we count as moral reasons, then, is simply a basic fact to be accepted. Without it we might not have survived as a species. Yet we cannot say that this agreement is the product of our civilization, for having it is essential to there being any civilization at all.

But then why should we be moral if it is impossible to justify any single morality or morality in general? You might as well ask why be concerned about beauty, art, religion if these cannot be justified. The religious enthusiast, moral person, and art lover will answer, as does the French philosopher Victor Cousin (1792-1867), "We need religion for religion's sake, morality for morality's sake, art for art's sake" (Cours de philosophie). Moral goodness, like beauty, is its own justification to those who are moral, or, as the poet Matthew Prior says, "Virtue is its own reward" (Imitations of Horace, bk.III, ode 2). Emerson puts it even more strongly: "Virtue is the only reward of virtue" (Essays: First Series, "Friendship"). We should be moral, then, because from a moral point of view that is what we should be, which is not to answer the question but simply to reaffirm the claim. Acting morally, artistically, religiously are things people do, if they do them, for their own sake. It is futile to try to give someone who does not care about such things a reason to do so. In this sense, morality, art, and religion are autonomous or self-contained. None of these is merely of instrumental value or merely serves some external purpose. Each is taken to be an end in itself. Thus the moral person thinks justice, courage and the other moral values are important in themselves and not just because they are useful or sometimes help to achieve something else that is valued. Morality is autonomous in the sense of being an end in itself. Hence it cannot be justified by reference to anything outside itself.

But what is the source of morality? Where do we get it? This is like asking what the sources of art, music, and language are. Human beings seem always to have had art, music, morality, and language. Certainly it is not as if we have records of a time when human beings lacked one of these, and then of something happening that brought about one or the other. History and anthropology do not reveal any society in which there are no moral values. These values seem always to have been with us. This may be part of what Herbert Spencer is getting at when he writes, "Morality knows nothing of geographical boundaries or distinctions of race" (Social Statics, pt.iv, chap.30). It is to be found in all regions and among all the varieties of the human species. I would add that morality knows nothing of temporal boundaries either. So, the question, "What is the source of morality?" is misleading—perhaps even invalid. It seems to be quite different from the perfectly legitimate question, "What is the source of diamonds, or what caused diamonds to crystallize from pure carbon?" Here we can point to events that brought about the change.

Not that I am saying that being moral is a logical condition of being human. That would contradict my earlier discussion of amorality (see, for example, pp.37-40). We know, too, that children do not start out life as moral beings, even if they eventually become moral; they are generally brought up to be moral. Further, I grant that it is advantageous to a community if people are moral and hence act morally. Besides being its own reward, then, morality is of benefit to people: it improves life, helps to preserve the community and the social order. So we can admit that there is a sense in which morality "pays." But this does not mean, as we have seen, that it is always to the advantage of an individual to act morally. Indeed, we know that sometimes it definitely goes against a person's self-interest to be just, fair, honest, and courageous. Not that I wish to agree with Thrasymachus's cynical assertion that "the just man always come out at a disadvantage in his relation with the unjust . . . [that] he always has the worst of it" (Republic 343d) or with Leo Durocher's more recent comment along the same lines, that "nice guys finish last." They need not and in fact do not always. John F. Kennedy puts it correctly when he writes: "a man does what he must--in spite of personal consequences, in spite of obstacles and dangers and pressures--and that is the basis of all human morality" (Profiles in Courage, 1956, chap.11). Morality can thus be a burden, a disadvantage. That is why it can be to a person's advantage to be without moral scruples, which obviously does not imply that it always is advantageous.

Edward Westermarck (1862-1939) seems to address himself to the question of the source of morality when he asks, on the first page of his book, The Origin and Developement of Moral Ideas (vol.1, 1906), "Nay, why are there any moral ideas at all?" And why is there such wide agreement, as well as disagreement, in moral opinions? He gives the Humean reply--that is, the sort of reply David Hume would be likely to give--that our moral views derive primarily from our sentiments. This looks like a possible explanation, but I believe it is not. Consider the question, "What is the source of sexual love?" along with the answer: "It originates from our sentiments or passions." This is unenlightening, since the sentiment or passion it originates from is the sentiment or passion of sexual love. As someone with a robust sense of reality once observed, I do not remember who: "There has always been . . . the love of young men for fair maidens" and vice versa. We may add that there has always been respect and compassion for others, concern for honesty, admiration of courage, and the like. This fact does not explain the source of moral values. It merely shows that people have always had them.[9]

Before I leave this question let me briefly mention, and give reasons for rejecting, another possible answer to it—namely, that experience is the source of morality. This could mean at least two different things. First, it might be thought that experience is the source of morality in that we learn from it that if we are moral, we shall get along better. But, again, we have seen that this is not always true. Sometimes we get along worse if we are moral and act accordingly—that is, if we do the just, courageous, or compassionate thing. Moreover, if such a belief motivates us to "act morally," we shall not really be acting morally, for our motivation will be egoistic or prudential. Secondly, it won't do to say that experience, in a broad sense, somehow makes us moral. For it seems to make people both moral and nonmoral as well as immoral. In other words, it apparently makes some people be motivated largely by moral considerations; others, exclusively by nonmoral ones. Finally, it seems to make some people develop a tendency to act immorally—that is, to do the morally wrong thing. Thus, experiences which often change people dramatically—being in a concentration camp, in jail, in the army, and the like—seem to improve the character of some people, while they make others less moral. Hence it seems implausible, or unilluminating, to say that experience is the basis of morality in this way as well.

In conclusion, I would like to consider the question of what does and should happen when moral and nonmoral reasons come into conflict. Will the moral considerations always prevail? Should they? The fact is they do not always predominate. For some, what is prudent, vulgar, or indecorous, or in violation of either etiquette, convention, or the law may be worse than what is morally wicked. Another will be carried away by love, beauty, art, or the pursuit of truth. For example, C. Day Lewis says that he knows that he "would in the last resort sacrifice any human relationship, any way of living to the search for truth which produces my poem"[10] Morality is not our only concern. It is merely one thing people appeal to to make decisions and to settle—or to get into—conflicts. Etiquette,

---

9. Peter Singer offers a different and competing answer to the question what is the source of moral values in his recent book The Expanding Circle: Ethics and Sociobiology (New York: Farrar, Straus and Giroux, 1981). He contends that ethics has a biological basis. We get it from our genes. He thinks that sociobiologists have explained "the existence of genuinely altruistic motivation" by showing how altruistic behavior has survival value (see p.45f). It is not clear that this view really conflicts with mine, although at first sight it appears to.

10. C. Day Lewis, "I Wish I Could Believe," from This I Believe, ed. Edward R. Murrow (New York: Simon and Schuster, 1952), p.101.

convention, the law, religion, self-interest, romantic and sexual love, and aesthetic considerations may on occasion each play a more decisive role. To know yourself and others it is essential to understand when people are dealing with a problem or a dispute in primarily a moral or a nonmoral way. This means that we must be cognizant of our own and other people's motivation, recognize when moral reasons are involved, when they are not, and, if both are, which considerations prevail for an individual in a given case. We find out such things by looking long and hard at ourselves and others in the mirror of our and their behavior. It is also necessary to examine the way people—including ourselves—talk and think about their and our actions, feelings, and aims, using the previously outlined criteria (see especially p.43) to distinguish those concerns that are moral from those that are not. That is how we determine when we and others are acting morally or nonmorally.

Granted that moral reasons do not always override nonmoral ones, it still may be asked whether moral considerations should not prevail over nonmoral ones. Is there any point of view transcending the moral, prudential, legal, aesthetic, and other points of view from which we could judge which of these should prevail? Perhaps it is possible to adopt a purely rational and logical perspective, and ask what considerations should prevail from that point of view. In his Carus Lectures, Frankena implies that this is possible (The Monist, January 1980, p.66). Accordingly, we can ask whether we should (rationally) be moral. Frankena holds that the answer is yes, because it is a postulate of his that "being moral is part of the life one would choose to live if one were truly rational in the sense of being clearheaded, logical, informed about oneself and the world, and in Butler's sense, 'cool' " (ibid., pp.45-46; see also p.66). "To choose a way of life rationally is to choose it freely, impartially, and in full knowledge of all that is involved, that is, one chooses from the rational point of view" (ibid., p.63).

I am not sure whether we can make sense of, and if so, wheth- er there can exist, this simple rational point of view, which Frankena describes as a "nonmoral, overall, ultimate, or 'period' point of view" (ibid., p.44). Still more doubtful is his assumption that it is intelligible to talk of choosing to live morally. Waiving these objections, however, there is still a third one raised by Alan Gewirth. It is this: "may not an egoist or an amoralist, who by definition rejects the moral point of view, be 'clear-headed, logical, fully cognizant of himself and the world'?" (ibid., p.77). It is not apparent why such people cannot have these intellectual qualities. Egoists and other amoralists—subjectivists, conventionalists, and the like—can be as clear-headed and logical as anyone else, as well as rational in the additional sense of taking effective means to achieve their ends. Finally, there is no obvious reason why they cannot also be well-informed both about themselves and the world. So when we chastise people for letting nonmoral considerations override moral ones and, in particular, for not being sufficiently motivated by moral reasons, we must recognize that this does not mean that these people can fairly be accused of any rational or logical deficiencies or improprieties.

My conclusion is that we cannot refute amoralists or people acting for nonmoral reasons when they ought (morally) to be acting on moral ones, though we would certainly criticize and condemn them, and rightly so. We are not indifferent to morality. Moreover, we do have criteria for finding out when people are acting morally or nonmorally. We do this by coming to know their motivating reasons. In this way we can find out how moral (as opposed to nonmoral) we and others are, which is hardly a trifling matter.

Some multiple-choice review questions to help you check your understanding of the text. For each question choose exactly one answer--the best one. The answer key is given on pages 224-25.

Chapter II

1. What account does <u>Are You Moral?</u> want to derive from the descriptions of eight moral problems and of eight moral disputes?

    a. An account of an extreme form of moral individualism.
    b. An account of moral problems and of moral disputes that clarifies the nature of each.
    c. An account of moral skepticism along with a demonstration that it is impossible to have moral knowledge.
    d. An account and defense of the view that there is really no right or wrong.
    e. An account that shows that everybody must occasionally be involved in moral problems and in moral disagreements.

2. According to <u>Are You Moral?</u>,

    a. there can be a moral problem without those involved perceiving it as a problem.
    b. there is a moral problem only if whoever has it is bothered by the problem.
    c. moral problems are a recent phenomenon; for example, there were not any in ancient Greece.
    d. the conflict experience in a moral problem is between or among people.
    e. two of the above.

3. A moral problem, unlike a moral disagreement,

    a. involves at least two people.
    b. involves at least one person.
    c. does not require at least two people.
    d. b and c.
    e. is usually concerned with actions.

4. According to Are You Moral?, a moral problem

    a. is just any serious problem.
    b. is basically an external conflict.
    c. can only exist if it is perceived as a problem.
    d. is best solved by others who can view the matter
       objectively.
    e. is not something Christians have.

5. According to Are You Moral?, people with moral problems are

    a. generally unstable.
    b. bewildered.
    c. perplexed.
    d. b and c.
    e. generally confident types.

6. In what respects does Are You Moral? claim that moral problems
   resemble headaches?

    a. They both cause physical pain.
    b. Each must be experienced by at least and at most one person
    c. Both are hard to get rid of and leave you with a feeling
       of regret.
    d. They both require at least one, but both do not require
       more than one person to have or feel them.
    e. none of the above.

7. Which one of the following is not a characteristic of a moral
   disagreement?

    a. It requires at least two people.
    b. People who have a moral disagreement with each other must
       be aware that they disagree on that issue.
    c. Moral disputants need not be in a state of bewilderment.
    d. The characteristic of facing a dilemma need not apply
       individually to the people who disagree with one another
       morally.
    e. People in moral disagreements need not be perplexed in
       the special way of confronting a moral dilemma.

8. According to Are You Moral?, a moral disagreement differs from
   a moral problem in that

a. it can exist without those involved perceiving it as a disagreement.
b. a moral problem requires at least two people, a moral disagreement only one.
c. the moral disagreement is generally about actions, the moral problem about beliefs.
d. we can sometimes solve moral problems, but there is no way to resolve moral disagreements.
e. a and c.

9. Which of the following is incorrect? Moral problems are like moral disagreements, according to Are You Moral?, in that they both

a. are based on deeply held moral values and beliefs.
b. involve being perplexed.
c. usually concern actions.
d. involve some sort of conflict.
e. require either at least one person or at least two people.

10. To have a moral problem a dilemma must be

a. solved by another person, preferably by someone who has studied it objectively.
b. associated with some religion.
c. communicated to at least one other person.
d. a moral one.
e. none of the above.

11. Which of the following is incorrect: moral problems are like moral disagreements, according to Are You Moral?, in that they both

a. involve dilemmas.
b. are based on deeply held moral values and beliefs.
c. usually concern actions.
d. involve some sort of conflict.
e. require at least one or at least two persons.

12. According to Are You Moral?, a moral dilemma involves

a. one or more moral values.
b. one or more nonmoral values.
c. both moral and nonmoral values.

-145-

d.   neither moral nor nonmoral values.
e.   none of the above.

13.   What is the difference between a nonmoral and a moral dilemma?

a.   A moral dilemma involves beliefs and values, whereas a
     nonmoral dilemma merely involves logic and concrete
     matters of fact.
b.   You can solve a nonmoral dilemma without going against
     your values, but you cannot solve a moral dilemma without
     going against your values.
c.   A moral dilemma is perplexing, unlike a nonmoral dilemma.
d.   A nonmoral dilemma involves conflicting values that are
     nonmoral; a moral dilemma, conflicting values at least
     one of which is moral in nature.
e.   A nonmoral dilemma has a legal aspect, unlike a moral
     dilemma.

14.   If your action is motivated by moral considerations,

a.   your action is a moral (as opposed to a nonmoral) action.
b.   your action must be morally right.
c.   a and b.
d.   we can infer that you believe in the existence of God.
e.   we can infer that you follow the golden rule, interpreted
     literally.

15.   Which of the following is an example of a pure moral action?

a.   A coal mining company's stripping mines for greater profit.
b.   A husband's beating his wife because her father did and
     feeling that that is what she expects from the man of
     the house.
c.   A widow's adhering to her late husband's will even though
     he left most of his estate to his children.
d.   A soldier's shooting down some children as target practice.
e.   A student's plagiarizing in hope of getting a higher grade
     in the course.

16.   According to Are You Moral?, when a person has a pure moral
      problem,

a.   he or she is a morally pure person.
b.   moral considerations tug the person in opposite directions.

c. a and b.
d. a nonmoral value competes with a moral one, but the moral one wins out in the end.
e. a, b, and d.

17. People with moral problems experience within themselves

a. a conflict between themselves and someone else they are close to.
b. a dilemma, which may be either a moral or a nonmoral dilemma.
c. a conflict of rights or obligations, of values or reasons, some or all of which are moral.
d. a and c.
e. at least two of the above.

18. An impure moral disagreement

a. includes moral values.
b. includes nonmoral values.
c. is an intrapersonal conflict.
d. a and b.
e. a, b, and c.

19. A person with a moral problem

a. is generally a happy person.
b. always puts other people before himself or herself.
c. must be personally perplexed.
d. is an unhappy person.
e. only thinks of himself or herself.

20. One characteristic of a pure moral problem is that

a. the person who has it does not always know that he or she has it.
b. it requires at least two people.
c. somebody else can solve the problem for you.
d. moral considerations tug a person in opposite directions.
e. it is not a dilemma.

21. The dispute between the humane society and the commercial hunters of baby seals in Canada is best characterized as

a. a pure moral problem.
b. an economic disagreement and a power struggle.
c. an impure moral disagreement.
d. a moral problem shared by more than one person.
e. a pure moral disagreement.

22. Michelle cannot decide whether to go to the movies or to stay
at home and get drunk. She is not sure which will give her
more pleasure. According to Are You Moral?, Michelle's problem
is

a. a moral problem.
b. not a moral problem.
c. a nonhedonistic problem.
d. an aesthetic problem.
e. a difficult philosophical problem.

23. Sally knows it would be to her advantage to go out with her
boss: he would give her a raise if she did. But she does not
care for him, and she feels she would be dishonest--somewhat of
a fake--if she did go out with him. Her dilemma seems to be

a. a nonmoral dilemma.
b. an impure moral problem.
c. a pure moral problem.
d. at least one of the above.
e. b and d.

24. Two friends are in disagreement about smoking. Ray opposes it
because he thinks you have a moral obligation to preserve your
health. Jim favors it because it makes him feel cool and
worldly. Their disagreement seems to be

a. an impure moral disagreement.
b. a pure moral disagreement.
c. an impure nonmoral disagreement.
d. a pure nonmoral disagreement.
e. an impure moral problem.

25. Jan's daughter has been comatose for six months. She is unable
to move, to speak, or to think. She has no mental functions and
her doctors describe her condition as a "persistent vegetative
state." Jan has been advised that she is without hope of a full
recovery. Yet she is undeniably alive. Jan must choose to let

her "live" indefinitely on the machine, causing great financial hardship and suffering for her family, or to take her off the machine, which she thinks would be murder, morally speaking. Jan

a. is involved in a moral disagreement.
b. has a moral-aesthetic problem.
c. has a pure moral problem.
d. faces an impure legal-aesthetic problem.
e. none of the above.

26. If your action is motivated by moral considerations, what you have done, according to Are You Moral?, is

a. morally right.
b. a moral action as opposed to a nonmoral one.
c. a and b.
d. based on judgment(s) that involve a positive concern for its own sake for either justice, gratitude, charity, kindness, respect of others and self, generosity, honesty, integrity, loyalty, fortitude, courage, or the like.
e. b and d.

27. According to Are You Moral? a moral disagreement

a. exists if you are in opposition with yourself.
b. generally involves actions.
c. is an impure moral disagreement if both disputants support themselves with moral reasons.
d. at least two of the above.
e. none of the above.

28. In a moral problem the conflict is

a. intrapersonal.
b. political.
c. economic.
d. interpersonal.
e. not to be taken too seriously.

29. Which of the following is a characteristic of a moral disagreement?

a. It is interpersonal.
b. The disputants must be perplexed.

c. It can never be dissolved.
d. It requires exactly one person.
e. It is intrapersonal.

30. Moral problems and moral disagreements both presuppose

    a. that we have values and beliefs.
    b. that the individuals involved know what is morally
       right and wrong.
    c. that the individuals involved are highly moral.
    d. that the individual who has the problem and the individuals
       that have the moral disagreement all have within themselves
       moral values that push each individual in different
       directions.
    e. that the individuals involved all face a dilemma.

31. People would cease to have certain moral problems if they
    changed their

    a. hair color.
    b. factual beliefs, their values, and/or their understanding
       of those values.
    c. looks.
    d. reading habits.
    e. religion.

32. Dick and Jane had been going out for a year. After they had
    been having sex for a few months Jane became pregnant. Dick
    wanted her to get an abortion; she thought this would be morally
    wrong. But she was torn between keeping the baby or giving it
    up for adoption. What statement below best summarizes the
    situation?

    a. Dick and Jane had a moral disagreement about abortion.
    b. Dick was probably a Roman Catholic.
    c. Jane had a moral problem whether she should marry Dick.
    d. Jane may well have had a moral problem about whether she
       should put her child up for adoption or keep it.
    e. a and d.

33. What four things play a decisive role in moral disagreements,
    according to Are You Moral?

-150-

a. Your factual beliefs, values, including your ordering of priorities and the importance you assign to your values, as well as your understanding of them.
b. Your factual beliefs, religious upbringing, values, and desires.
c. Your factual beliefs, the situation you are in, your values, and priorities.
d. Your factual beliefs, sex, values, and priorities.
e. none of the above.

34. If two parties had the same values and ordering of priorities, assigned the same importance to them, understood them in the same way, and nevertheless disagreed with each other, their disagreement would be

a. most unusual.
b. purely factual.
c. moral in nature.
d. mathematical.
e. religious in nature.

35. Suppose there are two people who have the same values and the same ordering of priorities, they assign the same importance to their values, and they understand them in the same way. These two people

a. could never disagree with each other.
b. could disagree with each other.
c. would have a purely factual disagreement if they did disagree with each other.
d. b and c.
e. none of the above.

36. According to Are You Moral?, the resolution of a moral disagreement is the parties'

a. agreeing on something.
b. finding a compromise.
c. coming to an agreement about the actions that are in dispute.
d. agreeing on some course of action.
e. dissolving their disagreement by thinking of another alternative action that squares with their values.

37. When a person solves his or her moral problem, he or she
_____. What is the incorrect answer,
according to Are You Moral?

   a. feels pleased and relieved.
   b. suffers heartache.
   c. feels regret.
   d. feels despair.
   e. feels anguish.

38. According to Are You Moral? why does a person feel remorse,
or at least regret, when he or she solves a moral problem?

   a. Because in doing so the person goes against one or more
      of his or her values.
   b. Because the person naturally worries whether he or she
      is making the right decision.
   c. Because in doing so, the person completely gives up, or
      rejects, one of his or her moral values.
   d. Because people cannot help but feel a certain ambivalence
      when dealing with moral questions.
   e. Because the person fears that he or she may have chosen
      the wrong value.

39. Neurotic guilt is characterized in the text as guilt that you
feel

   a. no matter what you do.
   b. when you do something that you think is wrong.
   c. only when you do things for yourself.
   d. when you are overcome by fear.
   e. when you go against one of your own values.

40. A person with a moral problem

   a. is moral to some extent, since he or she has one or more
      moral values.
   b. is immoral.
   c. could be quite an immoral person.
   d. a and c
   e. moves in the direction of becoming a moral expert when
      he or she solves that moral problem.

41. According to <u>Are You Moral?</u>, people who have moral disagreements are

a. subnormal types, psychologically speaking.
b. usually fanatics.
c. not aware that they are in disagreement with someone.
d. aware that they are in disagreement with someone.
e. none of the above.

42. When a moral problem is dissolved,

a. you go against one of your own values.
b. only your pure moral values remain intact.
c. you decide, on the basis of a moral reason, to do one of the things you initially found unacceptable, or acceptable but mutually incompatible.
d. a particular dilemma vanishes.
e. c and d.

43. Which of the following would <u>not</u> be a way of dissolving a moral problem, according to <u>Are You Moral?</u>

a. You decide to do one of the unacceptable, or acceptable but mutually incompatible, things on the basis of moral or other deeply cherished values and beliefs.
b. You discover an alternative course of action that does not conflict with your values.
c. New developments change the situation in such a way that the problem ceases to pose itself.
d. You either change your factual beliefs, values, and/or your understanding of those values.
e. b and d.

44. How might a moral problem be dissolved?

a. By simply choosing what you take to be the lesser of the two evils.
b. By discovering an alternative course of action that does not conflict with your values.
c. By deciding to do one of the actions you are torn between on the basis of your moral or other deeply cherished values and beliefs.
d. Two of the above.
e. None of the above.

45. What is one way a moral problem may be dissolved?

    a. A third party may solve the problem by deciding the matter for you.
    b. You may simply decide to change what you care about.
    c. You may find another alternative action that is not in conflict with your values.
    d. You may choose one of the alternative courses of action that you are torn between.
    e. You may find a natural solution to the problem.

46. A 14-year old boy's parents decide to separate. He loves them both and has moral reasons for staying with each of them. He would dissolve his moral problem if

    a. he finally decided to stay with his father for many good reasons.
    b. he finally decided to stay with his mother for several excellent reasons.
    c. he set up a meeting with a marriage counselor for them and it resulted in their reconciliation.
    d. two of the above.
    e. none of the above.

47. Jane is pregnant. The trouble is that she does not know who the father is, and she must finish college to support herself. If she has the child, she won't be able, for financial reasons, to finish college. She thinks having an abortion is morally wrong. How could her moral problem be dissolved?

    a. Jane miscarries.
    b. A friend of Jane's identifies himself as the father and demands that she have an abortion.
    c. Jane meets her long lost and wealthy mother, who offers to support Jane as long as she likes.
    d. Jane, after much thought, decides simply to have the child and to quit school.
    e. a and c.

48. Jan's dilemma concerning her comatose daughter would be solved (as opposed to dissolved) if

    a. her daughter died of pneumonia.
    b. she got a court ruling saying it would not be murder, legally speaking, if she took her daughter off the machine.

c. someone discovered a way to restore her daughter to a perfectly normal state.
d. all of the above.
e. none of the above.

49. According to Are You Moral?, what does a person who has a moral problem usually prefer, a solution or a dissolution, and why?

a. A solution, because then the moral problem is solved and over with.
b. A dissolution, because a solution always entails feeling neurotic or irrational guilt.
c. A dissolution, because then you no longer have to choose between alternatives that seem to involve going against some of your deepest values.
d. A dissolution, because you may later have doubts about your solution.
e. A solution because moral problems are hard to dissolve.

50. Which statement below is _incorrect_ regarding the dissolution of a moral disagreement?

a. When two people disagree about two incompatible actions, they dissolve their disagreement when they come to agree about which of these two actions they should do, on the basis of their moral or other deeply cherished values.
b. Outside forces or new developments so change the situation that the disagreement vanishes.
c. The disagreeing parties find an alternative course of action that does not conflict with the values of either person.
d. Their disagreement is dissolved if it vanishes, but not by either or both of the parties' agreeing to either of the two actions they originally disagreed about.
e. One of the disputants dies.

CHAPTER III

51. Prichard is a(n)

    a. ethical skeptic.
    b. subjectivist.
    c. emotivist.
    d. intuitionist.
    e. utilitarian.

52. Who wrote "Does Moral Philosophy Rest on a Mistake?" and maintains
    that you cannot give justificatory reasons why a person is morally
    obligated to do something?

    a. A. J. Ayer.
    b. R. M. Hare.
    c. H. A. Prichard.
    d. G. E. Moore.
    e. Charles Stevenson.

53. A cognitive judgment

    a. has a truth-value.
    b. is meaningful.
    c. a and b.
    d. is a true judgment.
    e. a, b, and d.

54. In A. J. Ayer's view, moral judgments

    a. lack cognitive significance.
    b. cannot be used to express a thought or to say something true
        or false.
    c. a and b.
    d. function merely to express our pro-attitude towards things.
    e. c and d.

55. Ayer,

    a. unlike Prichard, denies that it is even theoretically possible
        to have any knowledge of what is morally right or wrong.
    b. unlike Moore, thinks that moral judgments are noncognitive.
    c. a and b.
    d. unlike T. H. Huxley, believes in moral experts.
    e. unlike Stevenson, rejects emotivism.

56. According to the noncognitive and emotive theory of ethics, moral judgments

    a. lack cognitive significance.
    b. lack truth-value.
    c. function merely to express or to evince the speaker's feelings about some object or action.
    d. a and b.
    e. a, b, and c.

57. Which of the following is not a moral reason for doing something, according to Are You Moral??

    a. The Ouija board said I should.
    b. I promised I would do it.
    c. I might get caught.
    d. a and c.
    e. It would cause a lot of suffering if I didn't do it.

58. According to Are You Moral?, whenever considerations of courage, respect for persons and for human life, whenever concern for suffering, whenever promise-keeping enter a discussion as something of ultimate value, we know we are up against

    a. logical reasons for or against doing something.
    b. powerful maxims or principles in support of different courses of action.
    c. scientific considerations that should be taken seriously.
    d. moral reasons for or against doing something.
    e. some sort of religious point of view.

59. Which philosopher believes that veracity is the heart of morality?

    a. A.J. Ayer.
    b. Charles Stevenson.
    c. a and b.
    d. T. H. Huxley.
    e. none of the above.

60. Which of the following statements is incorrect?

    a. Prichard is an intuitionist and holds that you just know-- if you know, immediately, by intuition--what your obligations are and what actions are morally right.
    b. Ayer is an emotivist and denies that it is even theoretically possible to have knowledge of what is morally right or wrong.
    c. Stevenson is an intuitionist and thinks that moral judgments can be supported logically by reasons.
    d. Hare thinks moral reasoning takes a syllogistic form.

e. Suter thinks that three conditions have to be satisfied for something to be a moral reason for somebody.

61. Which of the following best explains the sense in which Stevenson thinks there can be moral reasons?

   a. Our Declaration of Independence implies that there are moral reasons.
   b. He thinks moral judgments can be supported logically and that whatever supports them logically is a moral reason.
   c. He believes that moral judgments can be supported psychologically.
   d. He thinks Americans act in a moral way and that when they do so, their actions are based on moral reasons.
   e. c and d.

62. According to Stevenson, moral judgments can only be supported

   a. psychologically.
   b. religiously.
   c. logically.
   d. with inductive evidence.
   e. deductively.

63. Which of the following best explains the sense in which Stevenson thinks there cannot be moral reasons?

   a. He thinks there cannot be such reasons because he can see no similarity at all between factual and moral judgments.
   b. He simply doubts that logical statements can be adduced as factual statements.
   c. He thinks there cannot be any moral reasons for doing things because people merely act on their emotions.
   d. He believes there cannot be any moral reasons in the sense that it is impossible to rationally explain our emotions.
   e. He thinks there is nothing--no evidential statements--which inductively or deductively support moral judgments.

64. Which best explains the sense in which Stevenson thinks there can be moral reasons?

   a. He believes there are moral reasons because this is a traditional philosophical view which comes from the British empiricists.
   b. Certain things are adduced as, or count as, moral reasons.
   c. He is convinced that a factual statement can be a moral reason if it is coupled with a major premise.
   d. He believes we can understand psychologically why something is right or wrong.

e. He thinks there can be moral reasons in the sense that some things stand in logical relations to moral judgments. ·

65. Which of the following statements is true?
   a. Emotivists believe it is possible, but not easy, to have knowledge of what is morally right or wrong.
   b. H. A. Prichard believes that it is impossible to have any kind of moral knowledge.
   c. a and b.
   d. Ayer and Stevenson think that moral judgments cannot be logically supported by reasons.
   e. Stevenson thinks that factual statements have moral status only if they are backed up by general principles.

66. According to Charles Stevenson, moral judgments can only be supported

   a. hedonistically.
   b. honestly.
   c. philosophically.
   d. religiously.
   e. none of the above.

67. Something may count as a moral reason for or against a moral judgment, according to Stevenson, if

   a. it is a true statement or judgment connected with some ultimate value of the speaker.
   b. it is a factual statement or judgment that the speaker believes is likely to alter the attitude(s) of another person.
   c. the speaker bases his or her decisions on it and believes it may alter the views of another person.
   d. the speaker sincerely believes his factual statement is a moral reason and it in fact does alter someone's attitude toward some action.
   e. none of the above.

68. According to Stevenson, for something to be a moral reason, it must be

   a. an analytical statement that the speaker believes is likely to change someone's attitude.
   b. a factual statement that changes the attitude(s) of someone else.
   c. any kind of statement or judgment that actually changes the attitude(s) of another person.
   d. a factual statement or judgment that the speaker believes is likely to change the attitude(s) of another person.

e. a statement or judgment that can be universalized without contradiction.

69. According to Stevenson, moral reasons are_____, but merely being this is not enough to make something a moral reason.

   a. tautologies
   b. analytic statements
   c. factual statements or judgments
   d. categorical statements or judgments
   e. c and d

70. Which of the following nonmoral reasons becomes a moral reason for Tex to leave his wife if we accept Stevenson's analysis of moral reasons?

   a. Jones remarks to Tex that Tex's wife's lover often picks her teeth and nose in public; Jones believes this remark will probably alter Tex's attitude towards leaving his wife.
   b. Smith remarks to Tex that it will probably cause Tex's wife a lot of pain if Tex leaves her; but Smith thinks his remark is unlikely to have any effect on Tex's attitude(s).
   c. Someone says to Tex that it would not be morally right for him to leave his wife.
   d. a and c.
   e. none of the above.

71. According to Are You Moral?, the basic objection to Charles Stevenson's analysis of moral reasons is that

   a. it fails to tell us what is morally right and what is morally wrong.
   b. it disregards the norms of the society.
   c. it is too obscure.
   d. his conditions are together neither necessary nor sufficient for a moral reason.
   e. his analysis is much too complex, since he makes use of four different criteria for being a moral reason.

72. The statement "The motive of an action is either moral or non-moral" is an example of

   a. moral reasoning.
   b. a syllogistic argument.
   c. a tautology.
   d. an empirical judgment.
   e. none of the above.

73. Factual statements or judgments

    a. attempt to say something about the way things are in "the world."
    b. are true.
    c. a and b.
    d. may be false.
    e. a and d.

74. Something may count as a moral reason for or against a moral judgment, according to Stevenson,

    a. if it is a true statement connected with some ultimate value of the speaker.
    b. if the speaker bases his or her decisions on it and believes that it may alter the views of another person.
    c. if it is a statement that is connected to a major premise and the speaker is willing to universalize his or her judgment.
    d. if the speaker sincerely believes his factual statement is a moral reason and it in fact alters someone's attitude towards some action.
    e. none of the above.

75. 'Contradiction' is closest in meaning to:

    a. something that is false.
    b. something that is false no matter what state the world is in.
    c. an analytic statement.
    d. a false tautology.
    e. a false factual statement.

76. According to Stevenson, a factual statement may count as a moral reason if

    a. the speaker believes his hearer will agree with it.
    b. the speaker believes he or she will gain something from the other person by making the statement to him or her.
    c. the speaker believes it is true.
    d. the speaker believes it is in conflict with the views of the other person.
    e. none of the above.

77. According to Hare, a moral argument or moral reason consists of

    a. a principle and a major premise; it concludes that a minor premise is true.

b. a major premise and an ought-statement; it concludes that a certain principle is true.
c. a principle and a minor premise; the conclusion is a categorical ought-statement.
d. a factual judgment; the conclusion is a categorical statement.
e. none of the above.

78. According to Are You Moral?, Hare's analysis of moral reasons

a. implies that every statement is a moral reason.
b. overlooks the fact that people can be moral as well as rational.
c. makes the mistake of thinking that an ultimate or intrinsic value can be a moral reason.
d. two of the above.
e. requires that moral reasons logically imply a categorical ought-statement and that they take a syllogistic form.

79. Hare thinks that

a. all ultimate values consistently adhered to and universalized by rational people are nonmoral values.
b. any factual statement could count as a moral reason providing that the speaker believes that it is likely to alter the attitude of someone.
c. moral reasons must take a syllogistic form in which the conclusion is a categorical ought-statement.
d. you know what a moral reason is, if you know it at all, immediately, by intuition.
e. b and d.

80. According to R. M. Hare's analysis of moral reasons,

a. any statement about any matter of fact that any speaker considers likely to alter attitudes may be adduced as a moral reason for or against an ethical judgment.
b. moral judgments can only be supported psychologically, not logically.
c. moral judgments are meaningless.
d. a factual statement alone is never a complete moral reason.
e. none of the above.

81. Are You Moral? objects to the syllogistic representation of Carmen's moral reasoning, because

a. it notes that the conclusion drawn from the syllogism does not follow from the major and minor premises.
b. the reasons people give for or against doing something are generally sincere.
c. Carmen may well assert the minor premise as her reason without believing in any substantive nonvacuous moral principle.
d. b and c.
e. none of the above.

82. Are You Moral? objects to Hare's representation of moral reasoning because

a. it notes that the reasons people give for or against performing actions are usually sincere.
b. in many moral syllogisms the conclusion does not actually follow from the major and minor premises.
c. someone may well assert the minor premise of one of Hare's syllogisms as his or her moral reason without believing in any substantive nonvacuous moral principle that could play the role of the major premise.
d. a and c.
e. b and c.

83. Moral principles that are nonvacuous

a. have content.
b. may play a part in a person's moral reasoning.
c. a and b.
d. everyone judges to be false.
e. all of the above.

84. According to Are You Moral?, moral principles that are non-vacuous, such as, "You must never lie, break promises, cause suffering," etc., all seem to

a. be truncated syllogisms in which one of the premises is understood but not stated.
b. be understood and accepted by almost everyone.
c. have exceptions and not to hold universally.
d. be assigned a truth-value by Charles Stevenson.
e. be minor premises in what R. M. Hare would call a moral argument.

85. Are You Moral? claims

a. that Hare mistakenly thinks that merely supporting a judgment with a principle is sufficient to make the judgment a moral one.

b. that Hare's analysis of moral reasons does not seem to allow for people acting out of nonmoral reasons.
c. that it seems that we cannot formulate any true exceptionless, nonvacuous moral principles.
d. that Hare wrongly thinks that simply placing an 'ought' in a predicate creates a moral judgment.
e. that people reason morally so long as they think that their actions are moral.

86. Are You Moral? objects to Hare's analysis of moral reasons on the grounds

a. that it allows anything to be a moral reason.
b. that it allows too many things to be moral reasons.
c. that it is too broad.
d. b and c.
e. a, b, and c.

87. Are You Moral? objects to Hare's analysis of moral reasons on the grounds that

a. it is too broad.
b. Hare gives a general account of moral reasons.
c. a and b.
d. it fails to recognize that people can be amoral.
e. a, b, and d.

88. Are You Moral? criticizes Hare's analysis of moral reasons for

a. wrongly assuming that what is right for one person must be right for all.
b. being a disguised form of emotivism.
c. overlooking the fact that rational people who universalize their ultimate values may be amoral.
d. two of the above.
e. none of the above.

89. According to Are You Moral?, Hare

a. fails to recognize that people can be amoral.
b. allows too many things to be moral reasons.
c. overlooks the fact that rational people who universalize their ultimate values may be amoral.
d. b and c.
e. a, b, and c.

90. One objection to Hare's account of moral reasons, according to
    Are You Moral?, is that it

    a. makes every syllogism a moral argument.
    b. rules out the possibility of there being a rational person
       who is ever prepared to universalize being amoral.
    c. requires people to give absurd arguments in support of their
       moral beliefs.
    d. b and c.
    e. a, b, and c.

91. What is the definition of an amoralist?

    a. A person who holds that moral considerations are the only
       considerations.
    b. A person who holds that everything is lawful, morally
       speaking.
    c. A person who holds that moral considerations are really
       emotional considerations.
    d. Anyone who acts immorally.
    e. Someone who fails to recognize that there are moral people
       in the world.

92. Amoralists are people who

    a. are single-minded.
    b. are motivated solely by nonmoral considerations.
    c. play baseball for Detroit.
    d. think pleasure is intrinsically valuable.
    e. b and d.

93. An example of someone holding something to be of intrinsic
    value is

    a. Bill's being honest so that he can collect on the reward
       money offered for turning in the lost wallet.
    b. Jill's donating a kidney to her sister so that she will
       be able to get a good reputation in her community.
    c. Jennifer's being motivated by philanthropic reasons that
       are directed solely to the recipient.
    d. John's visiting his invlaid father in an old folks home
       so that his father will be sure to remember him in his will.
    e. Craig's going on a low-salt diet to remain healthy.

94. According to Are You Moral?, moral reasons

    a. must be factual judgments, but merely being this kind of
       judgment is not enough to make something a moral reason.

-165-

b. purport to say or judge something true about the world.
c. can be either true or false, but are neither tautologies, nor analytic nor mathematical statements.
d. must involve a positive concern for either justice, gratitude, charity, kindness, respect of others and self, generosity, honesty, integrity, loyalty, fortitude, courage, or the like on the part of the person who has the reason.
e. all of the above.

95. According to Are You Moral?, moral reasons are

a. nothing but ultimate values.
b. whatever a person sincerely gives as his or her reason(s) for doing something.
c. factual judgments, but not all factual judgments are moral reasons.
d. generally aesthetic judgments.
e. c and d.

96. According to Are You Moral?, moral reasons must be

a factual statements or judgments.
b. true or false simply in virtue of the meanings of the words used in making such statements or judgments.
c. true no matter what state the world is in.
d. either true or false.
e. a and d.

97. According to Are You Moral?, something is a moral reason for somebody if and only if

a. the person making the statement expresses a consideration that connects up with one of his or her ultimate values.
b. the speaker is willing to universalize his or her judgment.
c. it is a factual statement that the speaker believes is likely to alter the attitude(s) of another person.
d. some combination of the above.
e. none of the above.

98. According to Are You Moral?, moral reasons are

a. whatever a person sincerely gives as his or her reason for doing something.
b. factual judgments, though not all factual judgments are moral reasons.
c. not to be equated with ultimate values.

d. judgments that involve a positive concern for its own sake for either justice, gratitude, charity, kindness, respect of others and self, generosity, honesty, integrity, loyalty, fortitude, courage, or the like.
e. b, c, and d.

99. In Suter's account of moral reasons a restriction is put on ultimate values. This is the restriction that

a. the person has a positive concern for either justice, gratitude, charity, kindness, respect of others and self, generosity, honesty, integrity, loyalty, fortitude, courage, or the like for its own sake.
b. the speaker, agent, or person making the judgment takes the factual consideration(s) to be of ultimate or intrinsic importance.
c. the speaker, agent, or person making the judgment regards the fact in question as a fundamental terminating consideration.
d. the values in question must be universalized.
e. the values in question must be empirically verifiable.

100. Which of the following are cases of moral change, according to Are You Moral?

a. A person ceases to have, or acquires new, ultimate moral values.
b. A person changes his or her order of moral priorities or preferences.
c. A person changes his or her understanding of what it is to have respect for a human being or of what courage consists in.
d. a, b, and c.
e. A person is greatly changed after reading Tolstoy's novel Resurrection.

101. According to Are You Moral?, moral change may occur if

a. people cease to have, or they acquire, new, ultimate moral values.
b. people change their order of priorities or preferences.
c. certain considerations gain or lose in importance for them, but not necessarily in relation to other values.
d. people change their understanding of their values.
e. all of the above.

CHAPTER IV

102. Which of the following is _not_ an empirical science?

   a. Physics.
   b. Mathematics.
   c. Astronomy.
   d. Geology.
   e. Biology.

103. In the empirical sciences, the best available reasons or evidence are

   a. logically conclusive.
   b. inductive.
   c. purely deductive.
   d. a and c.
   e. none of the above.

104. In moral reasoning,

   a. there is the same general acceptance of procedures, methods, or criteria for settling problems and disputes as in scientific reasoning.
   b. there is not the same general acceptance of procedures, methods, or criteria for settling problems and disputes as in scientific reasoning.
   c. rational and morally competent people give the same solutions to moral problems.
   d. rational and morally competent people weigh considerations the same way.
   e. at least one person in a disagreement about the way to settle a moral question must lack moral competence and/or rationality.

105. In moral reasoning,

   a. as in scientific reasoning, those who are competent and rational generally accept the same procedures, methods, or criteria for settling questions.
   b. there is not the same general acceptance of procedures, methods, or criteria for settling moral questions by those who are morally competent and rational as there is in scientific reasoning for settling scientific questions.
   c. disputants share a notion of common evidence.

d.　the best available reasons or evidence are conclusive and purely deductive in the way in which mathematical and logical arguments are.

e.　a and c.

106.　Which of the following is true?

　　a.　Chemistry is an empirical and purely deductive science.
　　b.　Mathematics is nonempirical and deductive.
　　c.　Physics is nonempirical and the evidence it appeals to inductive.
　　d.　Mathematics is nonempirical and its best evidence always inductive.
　　e.　none of the above.

107.　Which of the following is <u>not</u> true of rational and morally competent people?

　　a.　They may give different solutions to moral problems.
　　b.　They never agree when it comes to moral questions.
　　c.　They may weigh considerations differently.
　　d.　They may take different sides on a moral issue.
　　e.　none of the above.

108.　In moral reasoning,

　　a.　there is a general acceptance of procedures, methods, or criteria for settling moral questions by those who are morally competent and rational, but they are different from the procedures and methods used in science for settling scientific questions.
　　b.　everything is a matter of deduction.
　　c.　rational and morally competent people may weigh considerations quite differently and take different sides on a moral issue.
　　d.　the best available reasons or evidence are inductive, and hence never conclusive and purely deductive in the way in which scientific arguments are.
　　e.　a and c.

109.　Nonformal scientific problems differ from moral problems in that

　　a.　generally there are procedures or methods accepted by those competent in such sciences for settling problems that arise in them, but no comparable agreement in problem-solving methodology exists in morality.
　　b.　there are conclusive reasons or proofs in all these sciences, but not in morality.

-169-

c.   no factual evidence supports moral conclusions, but
there is such evidence in support of scientific conclusions.
d.   there are points that all such scientists agree on, but
no points all who are competent in morals agree on.
e.   a and b.

110.   According to <u>Are You Moral?</u>, which of the following is a good
argument for concluding that there are no moral experts?

a.   No one can solve another person's moral problem for him
or her.   Therefore, there cannot be any moral experts.
b.   Experts agree with each other and understand their fields.
So-called experts disagree with each other about premarital sex and other things.   Therefore, there are no
moral experts.
c.   Moral reasoning is inductive; therefore, there are no
moral experts.
d.   It is generally agreed that there are no experts in the
sciences, but morality is not a science.   Hence there
are no experts in morality.
e.   none of the above.

111.   According to <u>Are You Moral?</u>, which of the following is a good
argument for concluding that there are no moral experts?

a.   Moral reasoning is inductive, in the sense of falling
short of being deductive; therefore, there are no moral
experts.
b.   There are no tests or criteria that enable us to tell who
are experts in philosophy at a given time, who are not,
and what a person's level of competence is.   Therefore,
there are no moral experts.
c.   a and b.
d.   none of the above.
e.   Morality is not a science and there are experts in the
sciences; therefore, there are no moral experts.

112.   According to <u>Are You Moral?</u>, who are moral experts?

a.   Priests, ministers, and rabbis.
b.   Anthropologists.
c.   Philosophers.
d.   Nobody is a moral expert.
e.   a, b, and c.

113.   Experts

a.   in a field know everything about it.

b. are extremely knowledgeable in the sciences.
c. have a special skill, technique, competence, or
knowledge in a field, trade, study, or activity.
d. always agree with other experts in the same area.
e. b and c.

114. Are You Moral? contends there are no moral experts because

a. morality is not a science and never will be.
b. when a person confronts a moral problem, there is a
sense in which he or she alone can decide what to do;
no one can come to a conclusion for him or her.
c. no two people ever have exactly the same total set of
values and beliefs.
d. there are no formulae that give either necessary and/or
sufficient conditions of what is morally right or wrong
or what we ought to do.
e. none of the above.

115. Which of the following is not a bad argument for concluding
that there are no moral experts, according to Are You Moral?

a. There are no commonly accepted criteria or tests to
distinguish between experts and nonexperts in morality.
b. There are no formulae that give either necessary and/or
sufficient conditions of what is morally right or wrong.
c. When a person confronts a moral problem, there is a sense
in which he or she alone can decide what to do.
d. Experts always agree with each other, but we know that
the alleged moral experts--Ann, Abby, the Playboy Advisor,
priests, ministers, rabbis--often disagree with each
other.
e. none of the above.

116. If morality, like cooking, presupposed an end external to
itself, we could judge people to be moral experts on the
basis of

a. how well their advice contributed to attaining that end.
b. how effective they are in achieving their own goals.
c. how well they reason logically.
d. the soundness of their moral values.
e. none of the above.

117. Are You Moral? is committed to the view

a. that Ann Landers is a genuine moral expert.
b. that there are a few, but not as many moral experts as
most people seem to believe.

        c. a and b.
        d. that the Playboy Adviser is not a moral expert.
        e. none of the above.

118. According to Are You Moral?,

        a. almost everybody is a moral expert.
        b. there are only a few moral experts.
        c. there must be at least one moral expert.
        d. b and c.
        e. there are no moral experts and never could (logically)
            be any.

119. Since there are tests to find out whether someone understands
      various moral notions, why not call those who pass these
      tests moral experts? According to Are You Moral?,

        a. all normal people would pass such tests; so calling these
            people moral experts would undermine the contrast between
            experts and nonexperts.
        b. expertise can only be acquired by going to school; so
            those who do not go to school should not be called
            experts no matter how many tests they pass.
        c. if we called everyone who demonstrates an understanding
            of moral notions a moral expert, we would misuse the
            notion of an expert.
        d. a and c.
        e. a, b, and c.

120. According to Are You Moral?,

        a. it cannot be assumed that people who have moral authority
            over other people have moral authority over them that
            rests on moral expertise.
        b. there are different kinds of authority.
        c. a and b.
        d. no one has any kind of moral authority.
        e. a, b, and d.

121. The following is an (or are) objection(s) to the view that
      there are no moral experts that is (or are) discussed in the
      text:

        a. If that view is correct, the advice of others should be
            worthless to people with moral problems, but clearly it
            often is not.

-172-

b. The fact is that there are people with special knowledge of moral concepts, of ethical theories, and of moralities.
c. a and b.
d. The view that there are no moral experts seems to deny that anyone has any kind of moral authority. But what about papal authority, parental authority, and the like?
e. a, b, and d.

CHAPTER V

122. "There is nothing either good or bad, but thinking makes it so."

a. This is from Hamlet, by Shakespeare.
b. This reflects the point of view of ethical egoists.
c. This reflects the point of view of utilitarians.
d. a and b.
e. none of the above.

123. According to Are You Moral?,

a. all approbative theories say "Do your own thing."
b. an approbative theory determines what is morally right (wrong) solely on the basis of someone's, or a group's, approving (or disapproving) or having a pro (or con) attitude towards it.
c. conventionalists are really disguised subjectivists.
d. most people are general or universal conventionalists, but very few are individual or specific conventionalists.
e. a and b.

124. Which of the following groups holds a subjectivist or a conventionalist position in ethical theory?

a. Platonists.
b. Sophists.
c. Kantians.
d. Aristotelians.
e. none of the above.

125. Sue is fifteen years old, pregnant, and wonders whether she should have an abortion. She consults a right-to-life group. She thinks whatever that group believes is morally right is, by definition, morally right. It is reasonable to conclude that Sue is

a. a divine-command theorist.
b. a conventionalist.
c. a golden ruler.
d. a subjectivist.
e. inner-directed.

126. Subjectivism is

a. an intuitionist view.
b. the view that it is the thinking of some group that makes something morally right or wrong.
c. the view of G. E. Moore.
d. the view that a particular action's being morally right is to be equated with some individual's thinking that it is morally right.
e. c and d.

127. Suppose Emily is an ethical conventionalist. How would she decide what is the morally right thing to do?

a. She would simply do what the group believes morally right.
b. She would get the advice of her friends in the dorm.
c. She would try to determine what the group believes to be the morally right thing to do.
d. She would base her decision on what everybody else thought was morally right.
e. a and d.

128. If a Frenchman asked a group of Nazi SS troopers for advice,

a. he would be an ethical conventionalist.
b. he would be an ethical subjectivist.
c. he would be a divine-command theorist.
d. he would be some sort of Kantian.
e. we cannot say for sure whether he would be any of the above.

129. The statement "Action A (any particular action) is morally right (wrong) if and only if some individual thinks or believes that A is morally right (wrong)" is a formulation of

a. ethical conventionalism.
b. ethical subjectivism.
c. "other-directed" reasoning.
d. "inner-directed" reasoning.
e. none of the above.

130. "Hitler thought he was morally right to do what he did; therefore what he did was morally right"

   a. is an example of subjectivist thinking.
   b. is something all ethical subjectivists would agree with.
   c. is a relativistic subjectivist argument, according to
      Are You Moral?
   d. is a general ethical subjectivist statement.
   e. is the correct way to define the individual or specific
      (as opposed to general) variant of ethical subjectivism.

131. Ethical subjectivists contend that

   a. nothing is either good or bad, or morally right or wrong,
      but thinking makes it so.
   b. A (a particular action) is morally right if and only if
      A is actually or probably in my overall self-interest.
   c. it is the beliefs of individuals that make things right
      or wrong.
   d. a and c.
   e. a, b, and c.

132. Ethical subjectivism

   a. is a nonapprobative theory.
   b. is assumed to be true by Hare.
   c. is another term for ethical conventionalism.
   d. is nothing but an emotivist theory of ethics.
   e. none of the above.

133. A theory is approbative if

   a. an individual thinks or believes it is morally right
      to believe the theory.
   b. a group thinks or believes that it is morally right
      to believe in the theory.
   c. a and b.
   d. it implies that moral judgments can be true or false.
   e. none of the above.

134. David Riesman's "inner-directed" people

   a. are concerned simply to do what is morally right.
   b. look to what other people think is morally right or
      what is morally wrong.
   c. tend to be peer-oriented.
   d. do not look to what other people think is right or what
      is wrong to determine what is right or what is wrong.
   e. a and d.

135. Ethical subjectivists

    a. are people who think on a very deep level about moral questions.
    b. always adopt someone else's point of view.
    c. are people who are lonely.
    d. are "inner-directed" people, in David Riesman's sense of that expression.
    e. none of the above.

136. According to Are You Moral?, the following criticism seems to apply to all forms of ethical subjectivism and conventionalism:

    a. the theories are too self-centered.
    b. they are all self-contradictory.
    c. they all contain an apparent circularity, at least if they are taken to define what is morally right (wrong).
    d. they all raise the question of what is in someone's self-interest or benefit and how self-interest and benefit are to be measured.
    e. a and d.

137. In Are You Moral?, the circularity objection is raised. This objection is raised in connection with what theory or theories?

    a. Ethical conventionalism.
    b. Agapism.
    c. One of the variants of ethical egoism.
    d. a and b.
    e. The golden rule.

138. Which of the following appears to be circular, at least if it is taken as a definition?

    a. An action is morally right if, and only if, Jones believes it is morally right.
    b. An action is morally wrong if, and only if, the group believes it is morally wrong.
    c. a and b.
    d. "Let's go to the store," said John. "Yes, let's," agreed Betty.
    e. "Do you have the time, sir?" "No, I do not have the time."

139. According to Are You Moral?, Emily should

a. Follow the general or universal variants of ethical subjectivism because that way she could protect her own identity and not have to make a moral decision.
b. not even consider following the general or universal variants of ethical subjectivism because they imply that "anything goes," and such a view easily leads to a contradiction.
c. follow the general or universal variants of ethical subjectivism because, although they are not perfect, they do a good job accounting for moral agreement and disagreement.
d. not follow the general variants of ethical subjectivism, but instead follow a relativistic variant of ethical subjectivism.
e. none of the above.

140. According to Are You Moral?, the general or universal variants of ethical subjectivism must be rejected because

a. such theories lead to a contradiction if one person believes that a certain act is morally right or permissible and another person believes that that act is morally wrong.
b. evidence indicates that the majority is sometimes wrong.
c. such theories raise the difficult question how we are to select the key individual.
d. a and b.
e. a, b, and c.

141. Which of the following statements would be endorsed by a consistent general or universal subjectivist?

a. There is nothing either good or bad, right or wrong, but thinking makes it so.
b. If Sandra believes prostitution is morally right, it is.
c. a and b.
d. Abortion is morally wrong for the Moral Majority if and only if the Moral Majority thinks abortion is morally wrong.
e. a, b, and d.

142. Suppose Kathy is a general conventionalist. She is pregnant and does not know whether she should or should not have an abortion. One group of people tells her she should have an abortion; another group tells her she should not. Being a logical person Kathy infers

a. she should have an abortion.
b. she should not have an abortion.
c. she should commit suicide.
d. a and b.
e. she'd better consult Ann Landers quickly!

143. Which theory states that A is morally right (wrong) for a certain individual (group) if and only if that individual (group) believes that A is morally right (wrong)?

a. Personal ethical egoism.
b. Impersonal ethical egoism.
c. Individual or specific variants of subjectivism and conventionalism.
d. General or universal variants of subjectivism and conventionalism.
e. Relativistic variants of subjectivism and conventionalism.

144. If Emily decided what she should do simply by asking anyone at random what he or she thought she (Emily) should do, she would be

a. a general or universal subjectivist.
b. an individual subjectivist.
c. an individual conventionalist.
d. a no preference student at the University of Texas.
e. a general or universal conventionalist.

145. According to Are You Moral?,

a. the intensionality of belief is a characteristic of belief.
b. King Oedipus in Oedipus Rex contradicts himself if he believes that it is right to marry Jocasta but not to marry his mother, since Jocasta is his mother.
c. a and b.
d. the intensionality of belief relies on ignorance.
e. none of the above.

146. The intensionality of belief

a. relies on ignorance.
b. depends on there being moral disagreement.
c. claims that it is a contradiction to say that Oedipus believes his sleeping with Jocasta, his wife, is all right, but that his sleeping with his mother is not all right.
d. is a characteristic of belief.
e. none of the above.

147. Objects of beliefs seem to be

a. flesh-and-blood entities.
b. nonsentential.
c. nonpropositional.

d. propositions or sentences.
e. none of the above.

148. Which of the following does <u>not</u> display the characteristic of **intensionality**?

a. Belief.
b. Hunting.
c. Desire.
d. Shooting.
e. Looking for.

149. Something believed under one description may not be believed under another description of one and the same thing, because

a. believing is an extensional relation.
b. believing is nonintensional.
c. objects believed are different from objects shot.
d. beliving is an intensional relation.
e. two of the above.

150. Believing is intensional because

a. someone may believe that Adam is Eve's husband without believing that Adam is the man without a navel, even though Adam is in fact the man without a navel.
b. Jones's daughter should not have an abortion.
c. either I'm standing or I'm not.
d. what we believe we intend to believe.
e. a and d.

151. Belief is said to be intensional because

a. what one person believes may be different from what someone else believes.
b. what we believe depends on what our intentions are.
c. hunting is intensional.
d. something believed under one description may not be believed under another description of one and the same thing.
e. it is something psychological.

152. Which of the following is (or are) <u>not</u> (an) intensional relation(s)?

a. Shooting.
b. Wounding.
c. Touching.

d. a, b, and c.
e. Hunting

153. Relativistic variants of ethical subjectivism and
conventionalism

a. can lead to contradictory conclusions, given human
fallibility and the intensionality of belief.
b. have a problem accounting for moral agreement and moral
disagreement.
c. seem to ignore, or to dismiss as irrelevant, a major
portion of our moral discourse and deliberations.
d. a and b.
e. a, b, and c.

154. Which of the following criticisms is not made of relativistic
variants of subjectivism and conventionalism in Are You Moral?

a. These theories reveal themselves to be only pseudo-ethical
views.
b. These theories imply that any and all of us do right if
and only if we further our own self-interest; such a view
can lead to our disregarding the interests of others.
c. These theories have a problem accounting for moral
agreement and moral disagreement.
d. These theories leave no room for any nonrelative sense of
'right' and 'wrong'.
e. a and c.

155. The theories of ethical subjectivism and ethical conventionalism
imply that the only reason for saying something is morally
right (or wrong) is

a. that Jim Jones thinks it is.
b. that the action has passed the test of trial and error.
c. that some individual or group believes that it is
morally right (or wrong).
d. that there is evidence for thinking that it will help
pacify a troubled society.
e. that the person who has the moral problem thinks it is
morally right (or wrong).

156. According to Are You Moral?, subjectivism and conventionalism

a. in the end reveal themselves to be only pseudo-ethical
views.
b. are different versions of Getting on the Bandwagon.

c. a and b.
d. are objectivist theories.
e. are disguised forms of emotivism.

157. "All things whatsoever ye would that men should do to you, do ye even so to them"

    a. is a quotation from <u>The Confucian Analects</u>.
    b. is a quotation from Matthew.
    c. is a positive formulation of the golden rule.
    d. b and c.
    e. a and c.

158. Consider a male obstetrician who finds no need to burden new mothers of defective infants with the issue of euthanasia, since he thinks there is only one question: "What would <u>I</u> want if this in fact were <u>mine</u>?" Such an obstetrician is best classified as

    a. a utilitarian.
    b. a Kantian.
    c. a golden ruler.
    d. an emotivist.
    e. one who accepts the Protestant mode of moral reasoning.

159. According to <u>Are You Moral?</u>, the golden rule, interpreted literally, must be rejected, because

    a. if you follow this doctrine, you will in effect be deciding moral issues on the basis of what the Michigan State University Fencing Team believes to be morally right (or wrong).
    b. you will be some sort of an agapist.
    c. it can be used to justify immoral acts.
    d. it commits you to being a specific or individual subjectivist.
    e. none of the above.

160. How would Francois, a Frenchman young during the Second World War, go about solving his moral problem whether he should stay with his dependent mother or go off to fight with the Free French if he accepted the golden rule in its literal interpretation? He would try

    a. to determine what his mother would do if she were in his situation, and do the same thing himself.

b. to determine what he would want done, or not done, to himself if the roles were reversed and he were in his mother's position.
c. to do the other people before they do him.
d. a and b.
e. none of the above.

161. Which of the following does <u>Are You Moral?</u> cite as a positive formulation of the golden rule?

a. "What you do not want done to yourself, do not do to others."
b. "All things whatsoever ye would that men should do to you, do ye even so to them: for this is the law and the prophets." Matthew 7:12.
c. "The one who has the gold rules."
d. "Do unto the other feller the way he'd like to do unto you an' do it fust." (From <u>David Harum</u>, by Edward Noyes Westcott, chap. 20.)
e. "'Do other men for they would do you.' That's the true business precept" (from <u>Martin Chuzzlewit</u>, chap. 11, by Charles Dickens).

162. The golden rule, interpreted literally, is

a. an approbative theory.
b. a form of subjectivism.
c. a form of disguised conventionalism in ethics.
d. a form of agapism.
e. none of the above.

163. Agapism is

a. an ethics of love.
b. equivalent to one nonliteral interpretation of the golden rule that makes the golden rule a moral (as opposed to a nonmoral) doctrine.
c. the golden rule, in its literal form.
d. a and b.
e. none of the above.

164. According to <u>Are You Moral?</u>, if the golden rule is given a plausible nonliteral interpretation, it may express

a. some sort of Kantian doctrine of universalizability.
b. Prichard's intuitionist philosophy.
c. a form of agapism.
d. a and c.
e. a, b, and c.

165. According to <u>Are You Moral?</u>, the golden rule can be taken as
a moral doctrine by

a. giving it a literal interpretation.
b. interpreting it nonliterally.
c. interpreting it as an egoistic doctrine of a special kind.
d. interpreting it as a form of agapism.
e. b and d.

166. Divine-command theory says

a. that all things whatsoever ye would that men should do
to you, do ye even so to them. It is the divine path.
b. that those, and only those, actions God commands are
morally right and those He forbids are morally wrong.
c. that the thing to do is look out for number one--take
part in the divine cult of the Self.
d. that the moral rightness or wrongness of particular
actions or sorts of actions is determined by the amount
of goodness or badness they bring about.
e. that an action is morally right if, and only if, the
New Testament says it is.

167. Divine-command theorists believe that

a. if an atheist thinks something is morally right, it is
unlikely to be morally right.
b. those, and only those, actions that God commands are
morally right.
c. a voice in his or her mind will tell him or her what is
morally right and this will be the voice of God.
d. b and c.
e. a. b. and c.

168. Suppose Jones were a divine-command theorist and his moral
problem was to choose between doing A or B. How should he
go about deciding whether A or B was morally right?

a. He should consult the Bible.
b. If he is a Moslem, he should ask Ayatollah Khomeini.
c. He should try to determine what God predicts or knows
he will do.
d. He should try to determine what God commands or wills
him to do.
e. a and d.

169. The divine-command theory is an approbative theory
because

   a. it is pious.
   b. it refuses to equate an act's seeming to be morally
      right with its actually being so.
   c. God in fact approves of what is morally right.
   d. it determines what is morally right solely on the basis
      of someone's, or a group's, approving of it or having
      a pro attitude towards it.
   e. b and d.

170. The Euthyphro objection

   a. states that there is no God.
   b. neither presupposes the existence nor the nonexistence
      of God.
   c. assumes that God does exist.
   d. bypasses the question of God's existence altogether.
   e. b and d.

171. What is the famous question that Socrates asked that is
relevant to the divine-command theory?

   a. Does the government have a divine right to legally
      enforce whatever is morally right?
   b. Should we equate what is morally right with what is
      religious?
   c. Is what is morally right followed by God and His believers,
      or is it made right by His believers by their acting in
      certain ways?
   d. Is what is loved by God morally right just because He
      loves it, or is it loved by God because it is morally
      right?
   e. What makes things the kind of things they are?

172. What does Socrates finally conclude from his discussion with
Euthyphro, according to <u>Are You Moral?</u>

   a. That Euthyphro has only given us an inessential
      characteristic of what is morally right, whereas what
      we wanted to know was its essential nature.
   b. That the phrases 'morally right' and 'loved by God'
      may have the same extension, but they cannot have the
      same intension.
   c. a and b.
   d. That William of Ockham was on the right track in his
      examination of the notion of moral rightness.
   e. That without God there can be no morality.

173. The divine-command theory

    a. exemplifies a divine form of ethical conventionalism.
    b. is an approbative theory if God's will or command
       is taken to define morality.
    c. is accepted by most agnostics.
    d. is accepted by most philosophers, providing it is
       taken as a definitional claim.
    e. b and d.

174. In the dialogue Euthyphro, Socrates concludes from Euthyphro's
response: "Thus you appear to me, Euthyphro, when I ask you
what is the nature of holiness, to offer a(n)_____
only..."

    a. opinion
    b. idea
    c. attribute or inessential characteristic
    d. essence or true nature
    e. cause

175. In the dialogue Euthyphro, Socrates concludes from Euthyphro's
response: "Thus you appear to me, Euthyphro, when I ask you
what is the nature of holiness, to offer an attribute or
inessential characteristic only, and not the_____."

    a. truth
    b. effect
    c. attribute
    d. essence
    e. reality

176. (I) God commands or wills what is morally right because those
things are morally right. (II) What is morally right is
morally right just because God commands or wills it.
According to Are You Moral?,

    a. Thomas Aquinas would favor interpretation (I) over (II).
    b. Thomas Aquinas would favor interpretation (II) over (I).
    c. William of Ockham would favor interpretation (I) over (II).
    d. Most theologians think that God's will defines morality.
    e. at least two of the above.

177. What are the two interpretations of divine-command theory
that are distinguished in Are Your Moral?

    a. God's will is inscrutable/God is silent.

b. What God commands is morally right simply because God commands it/and God commands what is morally right because it is morally right.
c. Things that God commands are morally right/things God commands are not morally right.
d. The word of God is morally right simply because it is the word of God/and when God says something is right, it is right.
e. What is morally right is what is commanded or willed by God/whatever God commands or wills is morally right.

178. What criticism is given in Are You Moral? of the view that what God commands is morally right simply because God commands it?

a. If God commanded what was wrong, people would act immorally, according to this interpretation.
b. People who do not believe in God can refute it.
c. God often commands immoral things.
d. If God had commanded that we rape or murder, such acts would be morally right, according to this interpretation.
e. It is possible for God to command immoral things, for He is completely free.

179. To determine whether there is an extensional equivalence between what God commands and what is morally right, you must

a. be able to determine what God commands.
b. be able to determine what is morally right.
c. see whether all the acts that God commands are morally right.
d. see whether all the acts that are morally right are actually commanded by God.
e. all of the above.

180. What criticism is given in Are You Moral? of the view that there is an extensional, but only an extensional, equivalence between God's commands and what is morally right?

a. It is logically possible that God might make a mistake and command something evil.
b. This view makes morality independent of God.
c. There are serious problems determing what God commands.
d. b and c.
e. none of the above.

181. According to Are You Moral?, some philosophers are unsure whether there is an extensional equivalence between God's commands and what is morally right because

   a. they doubt that we can ever really know God's will.
   b. they say the Bible and Koran themselves give us reason to doubt whether God's commands are always morally sound.
   c. they maintain we are mere pip-squeaks in comparison to God.
   d. a and b.
   e. a, b, and c.

182. Chico, the leader of the gang "The Jets," killed Gomez, the leader of "The Sharks." Chico rejects all of the approbative theories discussed in Are You Moral? Which of the following would be a consistent thing for Chico to say in answer to the question, why did you kill Gomez?

   a. The Lord ordered me to kill him; so I knew, by definition, that this was the right thing to do.
   b. The people in my community believed it was my duty to dispose of Gomez; I always carry out my duties.
   c. He lied to my parents; so I knew it was my duty to kill him.
   d. My father said I ought to get rid of him; by that alone I knew it was my duty to do it.
   e. I didn't want him to kill me; so I reasoned I shouldn't kill him. But, unfortunately, he ran in front of the car and I couldn't stop in time.

183. Which of the following are approbative theories?

   a. Subjectivism.
   b. Conventionalism.
   c. The golden rule, interpreted literally.
   d. the divine-command theory.
   e. all of the above.

184. 'Extension' is closest in meaning to

   a. the meaning of a term.
   b. all the things to which a term truly applies.
   c. the connotation of a word or expression.
   d. intensionality.
   e. none of the above.

185. Begging the question is

   a. a form of the definist fallacy.

b. another name for the naturalistic fallacy.
c. the fallacy of assuming the conclusion of an argument
    by using the conclusion as a premise.
d. something bag ladies do.
e. an enthymeme.

CHAPTER VI

186. According to Are You Moral?, a theory is objectivist if

a. it refuses to equate either an act's seeming to be morally
    right (wrong), or someone's (or a group's) thinking that
    it is right (wrong), with its actually being so.
b. it determines what is morally right solely on the basis
    of someone's approving of it.
c. it holds that moral judgments are true or false.
d. a and c.
e. b and c.

187. An objectivist theory, in ethics, is

a. an emotivist theory.
b. a normative theory.
c. an approbative theory.
d. b and c.
e. a form of platonism.

188. Which of the following theorists are usually or always
     objectivists?

a. Ethical intuitionists.
b. Emotivists.
c. Divine-command theorists who make the definitional claim.
d. Ethical egoists.
e. a and d.

189. Ethical egoism is

a. an objectivist theory.
b. an approbative theory.
c. a subjectivist viewpoint.
d. a form of emotivism.
e. an intuitionist theory.

190. According to <u>Are You Moral?</u>, ethical objectivists believe

    a. that there are criteria to appeal to in determining what
       is morally right.
    b. that there is moral knowledge.
    c. that there is a distinction between what is morally
       right and what is believed to be morally right.
    d. that consequences are to be considered when determining
       what is morally right.
    e. three of the above.

191. Ethical egoism could be called

    a. "me-ism."
    b. the I-me-mine approach.
    c. looking out for number one.
    d. all of the above.
    e. only two of the above.

192. An ethical consequentialist is

    a. someone who focuses on the consequences of actions to
       other people rather than to himself or to herself.
    b. someone who accepts a deterministic perspective which
       holds that the physical aspects of reality are predicated
       upon an irreducible set of laws and structures.
    c. someone who believes that the goodness (badness) of
       the consequences of an act determines its moral rightness
       (wrongness).
    d. b and c.
    e. a hedonistic utilitarian.

193. In the definition of personal ethical egoism given in
    <u>Are You Moral?</u> the word 'me'

    a. functions as a variable.
    b. functions as a constant.
    c. sometimes functions as a constant, sometimes as a variable.
    d. always refers to God.
    e. refers to Anne McGill Burford, who resigned as EPA
       administrator during the winter of 1983.

194. "A (a particular action) is morally right if and only if A
    is actually or probably in my overall self-interest, that is, it
    actually or probably benefits me in the long run, where 'me' is
    to be replaced in all of its occurrences with a proper name or
    a definite description" is a formulation of

a. ethical subjectivism.
b. impersonal ethical egoism.
c. personal ethical egoism.
d. universal or general ethical egoism.
e. Ayn Rand's version of ethical egoism.

195. Suppose Prince Andrew is an ethical egoist. What could he give as a moral reason for leaving his former soft-core porno star girlfriend?

a. He read in the National Enquirer that the Queen was shocked at his behavior.
b. He felt the bad press might damage the Royal Family's image.
c. The former porno star was not as naughty as he expected.
d. He believes the bad press might hurt him by damaging his image.
e. He thinks God would not want him to have such a relationship.

196. If John were a consistent and practicing ethical egoist--personal or impersonal--he would encourage Pete to steal an exam for him because

a. he (John) believed Pete would benefit in the long run by memorizing the correct answers the night before the exam.
b. he (John) wanted to impress Rocco, the President of the Cheaters Club, whom he greatly admired.
c. he (John) believed he (John) would benefit in the long run from Pete's stealing the exam for him.
d. a and c.
e. two of the above.

197. Suppose Francois were an impersonal ethical egoist. How should he go about solving his moral problem of whether he should stay with his mother or go off to war?

a. He should consult a key individual and find out what most benefited him or her.
b. He should consider what probably would benefit his mother most.
c. He should simply do what he is most inclined to do or what he spontaneously wants to do.
d. He should consider which course of action would best prove his manhood.
e. none of the above.

198. Suppose Francois were a personal ethical egoist. He would then go about solving his moral problem by trying

   a. to determine what God wanted him to do.
   b. to determine what would maximize his mother's welfare.
   c. to do what his countrymen wanted him to do.
   d. to consider what would do the greatest damage to the enemy.
   e. none of the above.

199. Suppose Emily were a believer in personal ethical egoism and that she had to decide whether it is morally right to do A, a particular action. What criteria would she use to decide whether A was morally right?

   a. She would try to find out whether A most benefited her.
   b. She would consider whether the person performing A most benefited from performing it.
   c. She would try to determine whether A most benefited the specific individual referred to in the theory.
   d. She would consider whether A most benefits anyone else.
   e. none of the above.

200. If a person is an ethical egoist, he or she

   a. believes other people are of no value.
   b. believes it is important to consider the long-run consequences of his or her acts.
   c. puts his or her own self-interest first.
   d. b and c.
   e. a, b, and c.

201. A person who follows God's teaching, and only God's teaching, simply because he or she thinks it will benefit him or her in the long run to do so is

   a. a divine-command theorist.
   b. an ethical egoist.
   c. a golden ruler.
   d. an individual subjectivist.
   e. a utilitarian.

202. Impersonal ethical egoism

   a. implicitly encourages everyone to be an egoist.
   b. implies that we must act to further our self-interest if we are to do what is morally right.
   c. implies that we must oppose the interests of others.
   d. a and b.
   e. a, b, and c.

203. Impersonal ethical egoism

 a. contains no implicit proper names or definite descriptions.
 b. gives no one any special normative role.
 c. allows everyone to be an egoist.
 d. a and b.
 e. a, b, and c.

204. Eudaemonia is

 a. pleasure.
 b. the absence of pain.
 c. a and b.
 d. happiness or well-being.
 e. a form of eros.

205. Eudaemonistic egoists

 a. believe that we should try to maximize the general happiness
 b. say that it is personal self-realization that is the only thing that is truly in our overall self-interest.
 c. believe that happiness and the avoidance of unhappiness are the only things that are truly in our overall self-interest.
 d. a and c.
 e. maintain that pleasure and the avoidance of pain are, ultimately, the only two things in our self-interest.

206. Hedonistic ethical egoists say that

 a. happiness and the avoidance of unhappiness are the only things that are truly in our overall self-interest, where happiness is something different from mere pleasure and the avoidance of pain.
 b. money is the only thing in our overall self-interest.
 c. personal self-realization is the only thing in our overall self-interest.
 d. what contributes to the survival of man qua man--that is, as a human being--is the only thing in our overall self-interest.
 e. none of the above.

207. Which of the following statements is (or are) false?

 a. You can be a personal and an impersonal ethical egoist simultaneously and without contradicting yourself.
 b. Ethical egoists only consider their own pleasure, nothing else, when deciding what they ought to do.
 c. a and b.

d. Neither personal nor impersonal ethical egoism is a
    logically self-contradictory position.
e. Agapism is an ethical doctrine.

208. According to Are You Moral?, Ayn Rand

a. advocates impersonal ethical egoism.
b. advocates personal ethical egoism.
c. believes that ethical egoism is axiomatic.
d. believes that what contributes to the survival of man
    qua man is the only thing that is truly in our overall
    self-interest and benefit.
e. a and d.

209. If Emily could solve her problem without any hesitation,

a. she would be a personal ethical egoist.
b. she would be an impersonal ethical egoist.
c. she would be immoral.
d. she would be amoral.
e. none of the above.

210. What is one of the reasons given by Are You Moral? for
      rejecting personal ethical egoism?

a. It provides no guidance, even when coupled with a clear
    theory of value.
b. We have to neglect our own self-interest if we adopt it.
c. The problem of who is to be the specific individual is
    insurmountable.
d. The theory is too hedonistic.
e. two of the above.

211. A consistent, knowledgeable, and practicing ethical egoist
      would value others

a. only to the extent to which they furthered his or her
    own long-term self-interest.
b. only if they made the egoist happy.
c. a and b.
d. only if they contributed to the long-term well being
    of the key individual picked out by the theory.
e. a, b, and d.

212. One reason Are You Moral? gives for rejecting ethical egoism
      is that it

a. provides no guidelines.
b. is not a normative theory.
c. is a self-destructive doctrine.
d. legitimates immoral behavior.
e. none of the above.

213. According to <u>Are You Moral?</u> both variants of ethical egoism are immoral doctrines because

   a. they are normative doctrines.
   b. their moral right-making conditions are at bottom pornographic.
   c. they can be used to justify performing acts that are morally wrong.
   d. more than one of the above.
   e. none of the above.

214. Why is it alleged to be a misnomer to call ethical egoism an ethical doctrine?

   a. Sometimes there are real conflicts of interest between people.
   b. Fluent and competent speakers of the language would deny that someone who acts solely out of self-interest acts morally.
   c. It is not in our self-interest to espouse the doctrine of ethical egoism.
   d. Considerations of self-interest are never moral reasons, much less the only morally relevant considerations.
   e. b and d.

215. According to <u>Are You Moral?</u>, ethical egoism

   a. is not an ethical doctrine.
   b. is a nonmoral normative doctrine.
   c. never offers any substantive guidance as to how we should act, even if we know what benefits us.
   d. a and b.
   e. a, b, and c.

216. <u>Are You Moral?</u> implies that impersonal ethical egoism

   a. is an immoral doctrine, because it can be used to
      justify morally wrong actions.
   b. is not even an ethical doctrine.
   c. is a nonmoral, normative theory.
   d. exactly two of the above.
   e. a, b, and c.

217. <u>Are You Moral?</u> argues that it is a misnomer to even call
   <u>ethical egoism</u> an ethical doctrine on the grounds

   a. that ethical egoism is not a normative doctrine; hence
      it cannot be an ethical doctrine.
   b. that ethical egoism recognizes only one kind of morally
      relevant consideration--is the action in my overall self-
      interest in the long run--and this consideration is never
      a moral reason; therefore the doctrine is not an ethical
      doctrine.
   c. that ethical egoism is an approbative theory and as
      such cannot be an ethical doctrine.
   d. that ethical egoism is practiced by very few people and
      no doctrine that has so little popular support can be an
      ethical doctrine.
   e. that ethical egoism does not consider what most benefits
      the group; hence it is not properly called an ethical
      doctrine.

218. According to <u>Are You Moral?</u>, the main reason impersonal ethical
   egoism is not a moral (as opposed to a nonmoral) doctrine
   is that

   a. no one would think that it is to his or her interest to
      burn down someone's house just to roast some eggs.
   b. it implies that the only morally relevant consideration is
      what benefits the agent performing the act.
   c. it is too broad.
   d. it would give the agent a massive ego.
   e. a, b, and d.

219. Why is it a misnomer, according to <u>Are You Moral?</u>, to call
   ethical egoism an ethical doctrine?

   a. The ethical egoist recognizes only one kind of morally
      relevant consideration: Is the action actually or
      probably in my overall self-interest.
   b. The consideration mentioned in a. is never a moral reason.

c. Fluent and competent speakers of the language--at least those who are not in the grip of some philosophical or normative theory--would deny that someone who acts solely out of self-interest acts morally (as opposed to non-morally).
d. a, b, and c.
e. none of the above.

220. Utilitarianism is the view that the moral rightness or wrongness of particular actions or sorts of actions is determined by

a. the amount of goodness or badness they bring about.
b. what has the greatest utility to the individual.
c. what most people think will benefit them the most.
d. our existentialist ideas of what is right and wrong.
e. whatever brings about the greatest amount of pleasure.

221. Which of the following is a correct definition of "ideal" act utilitarianism? A particular act A is morally right if and only if

a. A actually or probably produces at least as great a total balance of pleasure over pain as any alternative action open to the agent.
b. A is actually or probably in the overall self-interest of the agent performing it.
c. A actually or probably produces at least as much intrinsic good as any other action open to the agent.
d. of all the actions open to us, A is likely to maximize the probable happiness of the greatest number.
e. none of the above.

222. According to G. E. Moore, a particular act is morally right provided

a. it will not cause less good than any possible alternative.
b. it pleases God.
c. it will help a lot of people lead a better life.
d. it will benefit the agent in the long run.
e. it will cause more good for the agent than any possible alternative action.

223. Which of the following is an influential ideal utilitarian?

a. Immanuel Kant.
b. John Stuart Mill.

c. Jeremy Bentham.
d. G. E. Moore.
e. Henry Sidgwick.

224. Ken saw a lion pacing back and forth in a lion's cage at the zoo. He wondered whether he should let it go free or leave it locked in the cage. If Ken were an ideal utilitarian, what would he do?

a. He would ask the humane society what to do.
b. He would try to find out what God wanted him to do.
c. He would ask himself how he (Ken) would want to be locked up and decide accordingly.
d. He would ask himself whether he would actually or probably produce more good freeing the lion or leaving it locked in its cage.
e. He would consider whether it would make the lion happier to be free or not.

225. Utilitarianism

a. is an approbative theory.
b. is the ethical view of agapism.
c. focuses on the motive of the act in determing its rightness.
d. logically implies that we must reject all deontological views.
e. none of the above.

226. Who is one of the most influential ideal utilitarians?

a. Ayn Rand
b. G. E. Moore
c. John J. C. Smart
d. John Donne
e. Joseph Butler

227. Which of the following statements in false?

a. The basic aim of ideal utilitarianism is to promote the good.
b. Ideal utilitarians deny that the good is confined to either happiness or pleasure.
c. The basic aim of ideal utilitarianism is to promote your own good.
d. In its "ideal" form, the normative theory of act utilitarianism is the view that a particular act is morally right if and only if it produces quite a lot of intrinsic good.
e. c and d.

228. A person who argues that it was morally right for Truman to drop the atomic bomb on Hiroshima because it shortened the war and thus saved the lives of many people on both sides seems to be thinking like

a. an ethical subjectivist.
b. a divine-command theorist.
c. an extreme deontologist.
d. a utilitarian.
e. a general ethical egoist.

229. Which of the following statements is not held to be true by G. E. Moore?

a. Judgments of intrinsic value are neither provable nor disprovable.
b. Intrinsic goodness is indefinable.
c. We cannot hope to discover which is the best possible alternative in any given circumstances.
d. It is not the actual, but the probable, production of good that counts.
e. You must consider both the action's value and its consequences in determining whether the action is morally right or a duty.

230. Ethical hedonists hold that the only intrinsic goods are

a. law and order.
b. sex and drugs.
c. pleasure and the absence of pain.
d. religion and celibacy.
e. self-realization and happiness.

231. Which of the following philosophers is closest to Mill's philosophy of ethics?

a. Plato.
b. Aquinas.
c. Protagoras.
d. Bentham.
e. Kant.

232. "That action is best which procures the greatest happiness or pleasure for the greatest number of people," is best classified as the view of
a. hedonistic utilitarianism.
b. ideal utilitarianism.
c. agapism.

d. a and b.
e. one version of ethical egoism.

233. Hedonistic utilitarians think actions are right if and only if they

    a. increase the amount of pleasure in the world.
    b. produce more happiness than unhappiness.
    c. produce more good than bad, where 'good' does not mean 'pleasure'.
    d. a and b.
    e. none of the above.

234. How would a hedonistic utilitarian deal with Gauguin's moral problem of whether he should leave his wife and family for his art?

    a. The utilitarian would talk with Gauguin's priest and be guided by his advice.
    b. Decide what is morally right by seeing what the majority of Gauguin's fellow artists think is morally right.
    c. Check to see which act maximizes his wife's and children's pleasure.
    d. Find out what Gauguin would want done to him if he were in his wife's position.
    e. none of the above.

235. Which of the following philosophers is not a hedonistic utilitarian?

    a. James Mill
    b. John Stuart Mill
    c. H. A. Prichard
    d. Jeremy Bentham
    e. Henry Sidgwick

236. _____, the important English moral philosopher who died in 1900, says that "all or most men in whom moral consciousness is strongly developed find themselves from time to time in conflict with the commonly received morality of the society to which they belong." Extra information: this philosopher is generally grouped among the classical hedonistic utilitarians, and he seems to be equally drawn to egoistic hedonism.

    a. John J. C. Smart
    b. William James
    c. Henry Sidgwick

d. Jeremy Bentham
e. Ralph Barton Perry

237. Which philosopher seems to be equally drawn to hedonistic utilitarianism and to egoistic hedonism?

a. Immanuel Kant
b. Henry Sidgwick
c. James Mill
d. Aristotle
e. Jeremy Bentham

238. Hedonistic act-utilitarians believe that a particular act A is morally right if and only if

a. A is generally thought to be highly beneficial.
b. A actually or probably produces at least as great a total balance of pleasure over pain as any alternative action open to the agent.
c. A actually or probably gives the agent more pleasure than pain in the long run.
d. b and c.
e. A gives the agent little or no pleasure, but produces a great deal of pleasure for others.

239. Which one of the following utilitarians opposes the hedonist view that pleasure alone is good or the only thing that makes life worth living?

a. James Mill
b. Jeremy Bentham
c. John J. C. Smart
d. J. S. Mill
e. Henry Sidgwick

240. Hedonistic and eudaemonistic utilitarians

a. agree that any action is morally right so long as it actually or probably produces the most pleasure.
b. both apply morality to animals and to human beings.
c. are approbative theorists.
d. both give no preference to one human being over another.
e. b and d.

241. "An action A is morally right if and only if of all the actions open to us (including the null-action of doing nothing) A is likely to, or better, it in fact, maximizes the probable happiness of all sentient beings, where happiness is not equated with pleasure," is the view known as

a. ideal utilitarianism.
b. hedonistic act utilitarianism.
c. eudaemonistic act utilitarianism.
d. explicit rule utilitarianism.
e. b and c.

242. Which of the following statements is _false_? Hedonistic utilitarians believe

a. that we should try to maximize pleasure, but not necessarily our own pleasure.
b. that the greatest happiness of the greatest number is the foundation of morals and legislation, where 'happiness' is taken to be another name of 'pleasure'.
c. that an action A is morally right if and only if of all the actions open to us A is likely to maximize the total balance of happiness over unhappiness, where 'happiness' is taken to be something different from 'pleasure and the absence of pain'.
d. that that action is best which procures the greatest happiness for the greatest numbers, where happiness is thought to be nothing but pleasure and the avoidance of pain.
e. that we should consider the pleasures and pains of animals as well as of human beings when we decide what we ought to do.

243. G. E. Moore believes that the predicate 'good'

a. can be defined in terms of pleasure and pain.
b. has only meaning in the sense 'good for me'.
c. may be reduced to the predicates of psychology.
d. is indefinable.
e. is meaningless.

244. _Are You Moral?_ considers the objection to "ideal" utilitarianism

a. that it is a self-contradictory doctrine.
b. that it only involves considerations of pleasure and pain.
c. that it does not allow you to admit to others that an act that you judge to be morally right is morally right.
d. that it is beyond our human capacity, because we can never know all of the consequences of our actions.
e. that it implies that there are no moral problems.

245. Which one of the following characteristics of pleasure
would Bentham <u>not</u> include in calculating the moral value
of the action which produces the pleasure?

    a. Intensity.
    b. Quality.
    c. The number of people affected.
    d. Duration.
    e. The likelihood that it will bring about a certain
       amount of pain.

246. <u>Are You Moral?</u> discusses several objections to act utilitiarian-
ism. These include the objection(s)

    a. that we can never know what is morally right if we
       accept either ideal, hedonistic, or eudaemonistic
       act utilitarianism.
    b. that ideal, hedonistic, and eudaemonistic utilitarianiam
       justify unjust or inhuman behavion and other immoral
       acts.
    c. a and b.
    d. that it is a misnomer to even call act utilitarianism,
       in any of its forms, an ethical doctrine.
    e. a, b, and d.

247. Ideal utilitarianism is a(n)_____theory.

    a. approbative
    b. noncognitive
    c. axiological
    d. emotivist
    e. selfish

248. Which of the following statements is false?

    a. Hedonistic and eudaemonistic utilitarians cannot contend
       with any plausibility that it is morally wrong to murder.
    b. According to Bentham, the fact that an act produces
       pleasure is a moral consideration in favor of doing it.
    c. Bentham and Mill are British.
    d. Act utilitarianism remains today among the dominant
       and most popular ethical theories.
    e. Exactly one of the above is false.

249. Which of the following objections to hedonistic
utilitarianism are discussed in <u>Are You Moral?</u>

a. It has too narrow a conception of what is good in itself and what is bad in itself.
b. It oversimplifies moral reasoning.
c. a and b.
d. The theory has the curious consequence that if an action is morally right, it cannot be morally right to say that it is morally right.
e. a, b, and d.

250. Ideal utilitarianism is said to be incomplete and unclear because

a. it fails to tell us who the key individual is.
b. it is psychologically unacceptable to most people.
c. it is often unclear what the group believes to be morally right.
d. it does not tell us what intrinsic goodness is.
e. two of the above.

251. Are You Moral? discusses several criticisms of ideal utilitarianism. Which is thought to be the most powerful criticism?

a. Ideal utilitarianism employs a double standard.
b. Ideal utilitarianism justifies immoral acts.
c. Ideal utilitarianism is unclear and incomplete.
d. Ideal utilitarianism fails to realize that not every ultimate or intrinsic value is a moral reason or a moral value.
e. c and d.

252. The following philosophers are natural-law theorists:

a. Thomas Aquinas
b. John Locke
c. H. A. Prichard
d. a, b, and c.
e. a and b.

253. Many different thinkers make an appeal to nature for moral guidance. Which of the following does not make such an appeal?

a. Thomas Aquinas
b. J. S. Mill
c. Marcus Aurelius
d. Lecomte du Noüy
e. Aristotle

254. The doctrine that we should appeal to nature for moral
     guidance may be interpreted as a(n)

     a. emotivist point of view.
     b. approbative theory.
     c. hedonistic theory.
     d. nonapprobative theory.
     e. b and d.

255. The Euthyphro objection can be used as a criticism of what
     theory or theories?

     a. The divine-command theory.
     b. The appeal-to-nature doctrine interpreted as an
        approbative theory.
     c. a and b.
     d. Ethical egoism.
     e. a, b, and d.

256. Aristotle believes that it is our essence or nature to be

     a. creators of things.
     b. manipulators of our environment.
     c. artists.
     d. rational animals.
     e. tellers of jokes.

257. Are You Moral? makes the following criticism(s) of the
     "natural" doctrine which says that morally right actions
     are those that are natural or that conform to, or are in
     harmony with, nature, including your own and/or human nature:

     a. the doctrine can be interpreted as either an approbative
        or a nonapprobative theory, neither variety of which
        will do.
     b. it is at bottom a self-contradictory doctrine.
     c. it provides no moral guidance.
     d. a and b.
     e. the people who follow this theory are rather low types,
        morally speaking.

258. According to Are You Moral?, the appeal-to-nature doctrine

     a. when interpreted as an approbative theory, seems to give
        us guidance about how we should act.
     b. provides no substantive moral guidance.
     c. provides no substantive moral guidance unless it is
        interpreted as a nonapprobative doctrine.

d. when interpreted in a reasonable way, would be a doctrine
   that Euthyphro would probably approve of, given what
   we know about him.
e. when interpreted correctly, requires that we live in
   wilderness areas and live as one with nature.

259. Are You Moral? concludes that the appeal-to-nature doctrine

a. cannot give us moral guidance.
b. can give us moral guidance if we combine it with
   intuitionism.
c. can give us moral guidance because we can find in nature
   examples of morally correct behavior.
d. can give us moral guidance because we can clearly
   recognize what is naturally morally right or wrong.
e. is the only truly American view examined in the text.

260. According to Are You Moral?,

a. understanding nature, including human nature, helps
   provide needed constraints on our moral judgments.
b. the appeal-to-nature doctrine give positive moral
   guidance about what we should do.
c. understanding nature helps provide information that
   is morally relevant.
d. a and c.
e. a, b, and c.

261. Kant believes that when you are considering performing any
particular action, A, you must always

a. ask yourself what maxim or principle you would be
   acting on if you did A.
b. ask yourself whether A would benefit you more in the
   long run than any other action you could perform at
   that time.
c. consider what God wants you to do.
d. decide the question on the basis of what your group
   believes to be morally right.
e. determine by intuition, that is, directly, what you
   morally ought to do.

262. The supreme principle of morality, according to Kant's
first formulation of the Categorical Imperative, is that

a. we are to act on maxims that are generally compatible
   with other people's maxims.

b. we should act on maxims Kant approves of.
c. a maxim is moral if most people act on it; otherwise it is immoral.
d. we are to act on maxims that we can will to become universal laws.
e. none of the above.

263. Immanuel Kant is considered to be a(n)

a. ethical egoist.
b. golden ruler.
c. general subjectivist.
d. extreme deontologist.
e. conventionalist.

264. According to Kant,

a. we should show true humanity to all human beings, including ourselves, because people should always be treated as means to some end.
b. whenever you consider performing an action, A, you should always ask yourself what principle or maxim would I be acting on if I did it, and then perform the action without fear.
c. when considering what to do you should always consider the effects of your actions; if they are good, the action is morally right.
d. your actions are morally right if and only if you can consistently will that the maxim you are acting on be acted on by everyone in similar circumstances.
e. your actions are morally right if and only if they are similar to the actions of others, performed in the same circumstances.

265. Kant's Categorical Imperative

a. is a conditional command.
b. provides a general rule for judging maxims.
c. is held by him to be the supreme principle of morality.
d. b and c.
e. a, b. and c.

266. Kant is mainly concerned

a. with the motives of actions.
b. with the consequences of actions.
c. with preventing faculty unionization.

d. with establishing rule utilitarianism.
e. none of the above.

267. Are You Moral? objects to Kant's application of his first
formulation of the Categorical Imperative to lying

a. because it questions whether the results of acting on a
maxim that permits some lying would actually be as Kant
imagines.
b. because it contends that lying would become universally
accepted under the principle of self-love or personal
advantage and this would be morally undesirable.
c. by noting that Kant's argument against lying runs
counter to his own theory, which is deontological.
d. because it shows that Kant does not adequately appreciate
the approbative point of view in ethics.
e. a and c.

268. Sometimes it seems as if Kant is arguing that the results
of everyone always acting on the egoistic maxim of making promises
with no intention of keeping them, unless you think it is
to your own advantage to do so, are bad, and this is the
reason you should not act on that maxim. This leads to
the possible criticism

a. that Kant is inconsistent, since he is then making the
moral rightness of actions depend on the value of their
consequences.
b. that he is not a consistent deontologist.
c. a and b.
d. that Kant misunderstood the nature of lying.
e. none of the above.

269. 'Deontologist' is closest in meaning to

a. a person who thinks that good intentions are all that
count in determining the moral rightness of an act.
b. a person who denies that the moral rightness of an
action is determined solely on the basis of the goodness
of its consequences.
c. a person who believes that the consequences of an action
are morally irrelevant.
d. a person who thinks that obligations are dependent on
values.
e. a person who thinks it is a mistake to try to define
ethical terms by nonethical ones.

270. On a second interpretation of Kant's argument, the claim is, not that the results of everyone's always acting on the deceitful promise-maxim are bad, but that they are self-defeating since if that maxim were universally acted on, we could not even have the institution of promise making which that maxim pre-supposes. In _Are You Moral?_ the following counter is considered:

a. this fails to take into account the possibility of sadomasochists, but they really exist.
b. this is a highly implausible interpretation of Kant's argument.
c. this shows that Kant inconsistently accepts the golden rule.
d. the results of universally acting on this principle need not be self-defeating; hence it does not follow that universalizing the maxim would be to engage in something self-defeating.
e. none of the above.

271. Suppose Kant argues that there is a kind of inconsistency in the lying cases he considers that has nothing to do with the consequences of everyone acting on the maxim nor with the claim that the results would be self-defeating if everyone acted on such a maxim. Suppose his point instead is that it would be logically self-contradictory to will that no one should be obligated who makes a promise since it is analytic that promises entail the obligation to keep the promise. _Are You Moral?_ replies that if this is Kant's point,

a. his theory has still not been shown to rule out all lying.
b. at best he has merely shown that what purports to be an action, namely promising without incurring an obligation to keep your promises, is not an action, since it is logically impossible.
c. it does not show that you cannot consistently universalize the principle of promising without intending to keep your promises.
d. a, b, and c.
e. exactly two of the above.

272. Which of the following is (or are) given as an objection (or objections) to Kant's first formulation of the Categorical Imperative in _Are You Moral?_

a. It is far too wordy.
b. It provides no moral guidance.
c. It seems to convert nonmoral acts into moral ones.
d. b and c.
e. It suggests that it would be morally all right to
   cannibalize our dead relatives at a party in their
   honor.

273. "So act as to treat humanity whether in thine own person
     or in that of any other, in every case as an end withal, never
     as means only." This is a statement of

    a. the golden rule.
    b. the golden mean.
    c. the categorical imperative.
    d. utilitarianism.
    e. ethical conventionalism.

274. Kant claims

    a. that it is all right to commit suicide if it is to end
       a miserable life.
    b. that you may neglect to develop your natural talents
       if developing them interferes with your having a
       pleasant and enjoyable life.
    c. that it is immoral to help others in distress if you do
       not really feel like doing it.
    d. two of the above.
    e. none of the above.

275. 'Agapism' is synonymous with

    a. 'ethical objectivism'.
    b. 'utilitarianism'.
    c. 'the ethics of love'.
    d. 'intuitive ethics'.
    e. 'the golden rule, interpreted literally'.

276. Kant implies

    a. that you should treat people as ends and never merely
       as means.
    b. that you should follow the golden rule, taken literally.
    c. a and b.
    d. that morality depends on God.
    e. a and d.

277. Kant's conclusion that lying is always morally wrong

    a. can be established beyond a shadow of a doubt by everyday experience, according to most empiricists.
    b. does not seem to follow from either his first or his second main formulation of the Categorical Imperative, according to Are You Moral?
    c. has nothing to do with morals.
    d. is also accepted by Ross.
    e. is also accepted by Prichard.

278. Kant believes that when you consider performing any particular act, A, you must always ask yourself

    a. what moderate deontologists would say about what you should do.
    b. whether it will produce more good than any other act you could perform.
    c. whether the Bible says you should do such things.
    d. whether it is rational and in your long-term self-interest.
    e. none of the above.

279. Agapism says that what is morally right is to

    a. love your neighbor more than yourself.
    b. love all your neighbors equally and as much as yourself.
    c. love yourself somewhat more than others since you can hardly do otherwise: 'ought' implies 'can'.
    d. love your family most, since charity begins at home.
    e. love the unlovable more than the lovable.

280. Agape is

    a. love expressed freely and without calculation of cost or gain to the giver or the merit of the loved one.
    b. personal affection or fondness.
    c. possessive love.
    d. a form of the naturalistic fallacy.
    e. a and b.

281. How would Francois go about solving his moral problem if he were an agapist?

    a. He would concentrate on maximizing his mother's welfare. Love of his mother would be his top priority.
    b. He would try to determine which course of action was the more loving, respectful, compassionate, charitable.

c. He would try to do what his mother most wanted him to do.
d. He would try to put his love ahead of his own better judgment of what it was morally right to do.
e. at least two of the above.

282. Explain briefly what Judaeo-Christian love or human agape is (not what agapism is).

a. It is appealing to a higher being and giving all your love to that higher being.
b. It is the belief that the Bible is the best textbook of morals; hence you find out what is morally right by consulting it.
c. It is reciprocal love among all people.
d. It is loving your neighbor as much as yourself, where 'your neighbor' means 'everyone'.
e. It is unconditional, charitable, brotherly and sisterly love, not to be confused with erotic or romantic love; when you love someone in this way, you cherish, care about, and deeply respect the person.

283. Which of the following criticisms of agapism is definitely rejected by Are You Moral?

a. Some people do not deserve to be loved, because they are unlovable (Nietzsche).
b. Agapism provides no moral guidance.
c. Suppose you hate yourself. Then you follow the precept if you hate others no more than you hate yourself.
d. There may be a conflict between love of one person and love of another.
e. There are other moral values, for example, fortitude, besides caring about and respecting other people.

284. Kant believes that ethics does or at least would apply to

a. certain extragalactic beings or beings who come from outside the Milky Way.
b. human beings.
c. all rational beings.
d. exactly two of the above.
e. a, b, and c.

285. Which of the following is given as a criticism of Kant's second version of ethics and of agapism in Are You Moral?

a. The theory is too vague.

b. People do not know what is meant by the word 'good'.
c. The theory fails to recognize that there is a difference between 'ought' and 'can'.
d. The theory is circular.
e. The theory disregards the moral relevance of our standing in certain relationships to one another.

286. Are You Moral? makes the following criticism of agapism.

a. Most human beings do not seem to be able to love everyone in the required way.
b. It allows too many considerations to count as moral reasons.
c. We have no idea what is meant by 'neighbor' here.
d. It is not at all clear in what sense of the word 'love' we should love others according to this doctrine.
e. The theory is too broad, it lets in too much.

287. 'Philia' is closest in meaning to

a. brotherly or sisterly love.
b. personal affection, fondness.
c. possessive love.
d. a female who comes from Finland.
e. someone who lived in ancient Greece.

CHAPTER VII

288. According to Are You Moral?, the only satisfactory normative position in ethics is

a. a form of emotivism.
b. one or another form of traditional intuitionism.
c. a modified form of what John Rawls defines as intuitionism.
d. some sort of extreme deontological position.
e. c and d.

289. Are You Moral? implies

a. that universal moral principles which are qualified lose their rigor and are undermined.
b. that the best normative position in ethics is a form of moderate deontological objectivism.

c. that it is Hare's view that all arguments of a
    syllogistic form are moral ones.
d. that Hare makes no room for amorality.
e. that an argument form that includes a universal
    principle as a premise can never correctly represent
    someone's actual process of moral reasoning.

290. According to _Are You Moral?_, it is reasonable to conclude

a. that there is no true theory of morality consisting of
    a single supreme moral principle.
b. that there are no genuine moral reasons.
c. that moral problems are just a special variety of
    scientific problems.
d. that there is no true theory of morality consisting of a
    plurality of principles, including an explicit method for
    weighing these principles against one another.
e. a and d.

291. In John Rawls's _A Theory of Justice_, he maintains

a. that intuitionists endorse a plurality of first
    principles.
b. that intuitionists deny that there is an explicit
    method for weighing first principles against one another.
c. that intuitionists think that there is one and only one
    supreme ethical rule, though they cannot agree on
    what that rule is.
d. that ethical intuitionism is the only correct position
    in ethics.
e. a and b.

292. According to _Are You Moral?_, John Rawls is

a. an intuitionist.
b. a Kantian.
c. a subjectivist.
d. a golden ruler.
e. none of the above.

293. According to the modified form of Rawlsian intuitionism
advocated by _Are You Moral?_,

a. moral disputants must dissolve their moral disagreements
    by deciding which of their moral views are morally
    correct.

b. there is no decision making procedure for dealing with moral problems and moral disagreements.

c. moral disputants must compare and contrast all of their moral values and then try to come up with a set of mutual "priority rules" to decide what is the morally right thing to do.

d. moral disputants should determine which of their positions is morally right by considering only the consequences of their respective contemplated actions.

e. objectivism is a kind of intuitionism.

294. What is the only satisfactory normative position in ethics, according to John Rawls?

a. Intuitionism.
b. Subjectivism.
c. Conventionalism.
d. The golden rule.
e. none of the above.

295. According to Are You Moral?, which of the following theories gives a single general basis or formula for deciding moral questions that we can and must accept or be morally incompetent or irrational?

a. Conventionalism.
b. Divine-command theory.
c. Kant's ethics.
d. Utilitarianism in its "ideal" form.
e. none of the above.

296. According to Are You Moral?, traditional intuitionists

a. believe in a plurality of first principles and deny that there is an explicit method for weighing these principles against each other.
b. are really disguised emotivists.
c. need not endorse a plurality of first principles.
d. imply that there is no decision procedure to determine what is morally right (wrong).
e. c and d.

297. Which of the following is true?

a. Intuitionists are usually objectivists.
b. Objectivists are usually intuitionists.

c. Golden rulers who follow the theory, in its literal sense, are intuitionists.
d. a and b.
e. a and c.

298. <u>Are You Moral?</u> modifies Rawls's characterization of intuitionism by_____ his requirement that an intuitionist endorse a plurality of principles.

a. dropping
b. adding
c. retaining but modifying
d. strongly endorsing
e. b and d

299. The slight modification of Rawls's characterization of intuitionism proposed in the last chapter of <u>Are You Moral?</u> includes

a. adding the negative claim that there is no single moral principle.
b. adding the point that an intuitionist may be an emotivist.
c. adding the negative claim that there are no priority rules for weighing ethical principles against one another and there never will be such rules.
d. dropping his requirement that an intuitionist endorse a plurality of principles.
e. dropping his requirement that an intuitionist be an objectivist.

300. <u>Are You Moral?</u> modifies Rawls's characterization of intuitionism by adding the requirement that an intuitionist be

a. an emotivist.
b. an extreme deontologist.
c. a prescriptivist.
d. an objectivist.
e. a moderate deontologist.

301. Most, if not all, traditional ethical intuitionists are

a. objectivists.
b. emotivists.
c. objectivists and all objectivists are intuitionists.
d. approbative theorists.
e. extreme deontologists.

302. According to <u>Are You Moral?</u>, it is a point in favor of objectivism that it squares with our conviction that when we make a moral judgment we imply that what we are saying is

    a. the word of God.
    b. in accord with the Ten Commandments.
    c. true.
    d. a and b.
    e. in accord with the basic views of others.

303. According to <u>Are You Moral?</u>, objectivism squares with our conviction that when we make a moral judgment

    a. we imply that what we are saying is true.
    b. and someone else disagrees with us, we assume that our judgments are logically incompatible.
    c. other people only rarely agree with us.
    d. a and b.
    e. we expect others to agree with us if they are at all rational.

304. Objectivists in morality think

    a. that if a person (or group) believes that an act is morally right, then it must be.
    b. that an act is morally wrong if and only if someone (or some group) believes that it is morally wrong.
    c. that moral judgments have a truth-value.
    d. that it is not possible to have a mistaken belief about what is morally right or good.
    e. that the truth-value of a moral judgment depends on whether anyone (or any group) believes that this judgment is true (or false).

305. <u>Are You Moral?</u> says that we should acknowledge that we are

    a. objectivists.
    b. golden rulers.
    c. subjectivists.
    d. Kantians.
    e. none of the above.

306. According to the modified form of Rawlsian intuitionism advocated in the conclusion of <u>Are You Moral?</u>,

    a. moral judgments lack both cognitive significance and truth-value.

b. the only tenable theory in ethics is some sort of sophisticated approbative theory.
c. moral judgments are true or false and the approbative viewpoint must be rejected.
d. there is a plurality of true moral principles, but no explicit method for weighing these principles against one another.
e. c and d.

307. Are You Moral? advocates a(n)_____view.

a. deontological
b. agapist
c. egoist
d. objectivist
e. a and d.

308. According to Are You Moral?,

a. Prichard is correct that consequential considerations are not the only moral reasons for or against performing actions.
b. Pritchard is mistaken in supposing that consequential considerations never constitute moral reasons for or against doing something.
c. a and b.
d. Prichard fails to realize that our ought-judgments rest on moral reasons.
e. a, b, and d.

309. Are You Moral? _____the extreme deontological position.

a. accepts
b. rejects
c. argues in favor of
d. a and c.
e. is neither in favor of nor against.

310. A deontologist is

a. a person who thinks that good intentions are all that count.
b. one who denies that the moral rightness of an action is determined solely on the basis of the goodness of its consequences.
c. one who rejects consequentialism.

-217-

d. one who believes that the consequences of an action
   are morally irrelevant.
e. b and c.

311. According to <u>Are You Moral?</u>, Moore, Ross, Rawls, and Frankena
     are all

     a. intuitionists of one sort or another.
     b. moderate deontologists.
     c. hedonistic utilitarians.
     d. ideal utilitarians.
     e. none of the above.

312. The intuitionism espoused by <u>Are You Moral?</u>

     a. is just a restatement of the traditional intuitionism
        of Prichard, Moore, or Ross.
     b. is not a restatement of Prichard, Moore, or Ross.
     c. denies that beliefs about what is morally right of
        either an individual or a group constitute moral reasons
        for judging that something is morally right or wrong.
     d. a and c.
     e. b and c.

313. Being (a) moderate deontologist(s)_____grant(s)
     that certain kinds of good and bad consequences of an act are
     relevant to the question whether—the act is morally right
     or wrong.

     a. Kant
     b. Ross and Frankena
     c. Ayer
     d. Prichard
     e. Prichard and Ayer

314. Moore's utilitarianism and intuitionism

     a. allows all sorts of things to be moral reasons which in
        fact are not.
     b. gives a hedonistic account of moral reasons.
     c. a and b.
     d. reduces to a kind of emotivist theory.
     e. none of the above.

315. The intuitionism of <u>Are You Moral?</u> probably resembles most
     closely the intuitionism of which of the following
     philosophers?

a. Ross
b. Moore
c. Prichard
d. Rashdall
e. Urmson

316. According to Are You Moral?,

    a. all objectivists are intuitionists, but not all
       intuitionists are objectivists.
    b. Moore could never be accused of allowing any cognitions
       of intrinsic goodness to count as moral reasons in favor
       of doing something.
    c. ordinary-language philosophers appeal to accepted
       linguistic practices, or to the way fluent, competent,
       and able users of the language use words and sentences
       in order to clarify what they mean.
    d. philosophers have finally been able to agree during
       our century on the foundation of ethics.
    e. a and c.

317. Ordinary-language philosophers

    a. contend that their writings are not very heavy in
       meaning and thought--they are just ordinary.
    b. think of themselves as commonsense philosophers.
    c. appeal to accepted linguistic practices or the way
       fluent, competent, and able users of the language
       use words and sentences, in order to describe their
       meaning.
    d. a and c.
    e. would not be caught dead using a technical or non-
       ordinary word.

318. The following philosophers are ethical intuitionists:

    a. Ayer and Prichard.
    b. Stevenson, Ayer, and Moore.
    c. Prichard, Ross, and Ayer.
    d. Moore, Prichard, and Ross.
    e. c and d.

319. Are You Moral? tries to show that we need not be skeptics about
morality if there is no single standard or ethical theory

    a. by mentioning things that are beyond doubt in morality
       and that we clearly know to be true.

b. by claiming that no one does, or ever would, disagree with the extreme examples of moral wrong doing cited in the last chapter.
c. a and b.
d. by conceding that if someone were to disagree with the examples of moral wrong doing given in the last chapter, we would have to embrace moral skepticism.
e. b and d.

320. It is the view of Are You Moral?

a. that it can be established that one morality, or moral code is the right one.
b. that the right morality is the one which is the most rational.
c. a and b.
d. that it is not clear what criteria we should use to choose between different genuine moralities.
e. that the right morality is the morality of its author.

321. According to Are You Moral?, which of the following statements is not correct?

a. A deontologist denies that the moral rightness (or wrongness) of an act is entirely dependent on the goodness (or badness) of its consequences.
b. Moral considerations do not always predominate over nonmoral ones when moral and nonmoral reasons come into conflict.
c. Moral reasoning is not arbitrary.
d. If we make our justification of a particular morality consist only of nonmoral considerations, it will indeed justify that morality as a morality.
e. Nonmoral considerations do not always predominate over moral ones when moral and nonmoral reasons come into conflict.

322. What is wrong with justifying morality on the basis of morality itself?

a. This only succeeds in justifying it in a few rare cases.
b. Such a "justification" is circular.
c. This sort of justification only works if it is approved of by a certain group of people.
d. It would be more convincing to develop a justification consisting only of nonmoral considerations.
e. Many eminent philosophers oppose such a move.

323. Are You Moral? agrees with the statement that

    a. "Virtue debases itself in justifying itself."
    b. experience is the source of morality.
    c. the best morality is the one you would choose to live
       by if you were fully rational in the sense of being
       clearheaded and logical.
    d. if we try to justify morality by appeal to moral
       considerations, we open ourselves to the charge of
       begging the question.
    e. a and d.

324. According to Are You Moral?,

    a. philosophers are no closer to achieving an agreement
       on the foundation of ethics now than when they first
       began doing ethics.
    b. it is a good working assumption to suppose that we can
       justify our morality.
    c. philosophers are nearly unanimous in believing that it
       is logically possible to justify our morality.
    d. a and c.
    e. a and b.

325. According to Are You Moral?,

    a. it seems that we cannot provide a foundation, or
       justification, for any morality, or morality generally.
    b. moral reasoning is unfortunately arbitrary--we just have
       to accept it for what it is.
    c. a and b.
    d. the only satisfactory normative position in ethics is an
       extreme form of deontological objectivism.
    e. a and d.

326. According to Are You Moral?, can we show that one morality,
or moral code, is the right one?

    a. Yes, by employing the right ethics.
    b. Yes, by appealing to a super morality.
    c. No.
    d. a and b.
    e. Yes, by considering the right nonmoral considerations.

327. According to Are You Moral? 'arbitrary' means

    a. 'not logically demonstrable'.

b.   'arising from will or caprice or being random and without
     reason'.
c.   a and b.
d.   'not scientific'.
e.   a and d.

328. According to Are You Moral?,

a.   it is always to the advantage of an individual to act
     morally.
b.   in a sense, morality does "pay."
c.   acting morally can be a disadvantage to the agent.
d.   b and c.
e.   none of the above.

329. According to Are You Moral?,

a.   morality is of benefit to people.
b.   morality improves life.
c.   morality helps to preserve the community and social order.
d.   morality is to be found in all regions and among all
     the varieties of the human species.
e.   a, b, c, and d.

330. John F. Kennedy writes: "a man does what he must--in spite
      of personal consequences, in spite of obstacles and dangers
      and pressures--and that is the basis of all human morality."
      His statement implies that

a.   morality can be a burden to someone.
b.   no matter which path you take in life, you will always
     be in contact with dangers and obstacles.
c.   morality sometimes requires you to hurt other people.
d.   man must have free will if he is to be moral.
e.   a and b.

331. According to Are You Moral?, will moral considerations always
      prevail over nonmoral ones, when moral and nonmoral reasons
      come into conflict?

a.   We find that in actual practice moral considerations
     do not always prevail.
b.   The truth is that nonmoral considerations generally
     prevail over moral ones.
c.   The truth is that nonmoral considerations always
     prevail over moral ones.
d.   a, b, and c.
e.   Yes.

332. According to <u>Are You Moral?</u>, we do have criteria for finding out when people are acting morally or nonmorally. We do this by examining

a. the mores of a given society.
b. their motivating reasons.
c. the end results of their actions.
d. whether their actions are in accord with the Bible.
e. a, b, c, and d.

333. Knowing the extent to which you are moral as opposed to nonmoral

a. is to have some knowledge of yourself.
b. requires that you know something about your motivation.
c. is something you learn in formal logic.
d. a and b.
e. a and c.

The Answer Key for the Multiple-Choice Review Questions

1. b	41. e	81. c	121. e
2. b	42. d	82. c	122. a
3. c	43. a	83. c	123. b
4. c	44. b	84. c	124. b
5. d	45. c	85. c	125. b
6. d	46. c	86. d	126. d
7. b	47. e	87. a	127. c
8. a	48. e	88. c	128. e
9. b	49. c	89. d	129. b
10. d	50. a	90. b	130. a
11. a	51. d	91. b	131. d
12. a	52. c	92. b	132. e
13. d	53. c	93. c	133. e
14. a	54. c	94. e	134. e
15. c	55. c	95. c	135. e
16. b	56. e	96. e	136. c
17. c	57. d	97. e	137. a
18. d	58. d	98. e	138. c
19. c	59. d	99. a	139. b
20. d	60. c	100. d	140. a
21. c	61. c	101. e	141. c
22. b	62. a	102. b	142. d
23. e	63. e	103. b	143. e
24. a	64. b	104. b	144. a
25. c	65. d	105. b	145. a
26. e	66. e	106. b	146. d
27. b	67. b	107. b	147. d
28. a	68. d	108. c	148. d
29. a	69. c	109. a	149. d
30. a	70. a	110. e	150. a
31. b	71. d	111. d	151. d
32. e	72. c	112. d	152. d
33. a	73. e	113. c	153. e
34. b	74. e	114. e	154. b
35. d	75. b	115. a	155. c
36. c	76. e	116. a	156. a
37. a	77. c	117. d	157. d
38. a	78. e	118. e	158. c
39. a	79. c	119. d	159. c
40. d	80. d	120. c	160. b

161.	b	204.	d	247.	c	290.	e
162.	a	205.	c	248.	a	291.	e
163.	d	206.	e	249.	c	292.	b
164.	d	207.	c	250.	d	293.	b
165.	e	208.	e	251.	e	294.	e
166.	b	209.	e	252.	e	295.	e
167.	b	210.	c	253.	b	296.	e
168.	d	211.	a	254.	e	297.	a
169.	d	212.	d	255.	c	298.	a
170.	e	213.	c	256.	d	299.	d
171.	d	214.	e	257.	c	300.	d
172.	c	215.	d	258.	b	301.	a
173.	b	216.	e	259.	a	302.	c
174.	c	217.	b	260.	d	303.	d
175.	d	218.	b	261.	a	304.	c
176.	a	219.	d	262.	d	305.	a
177.	b	220.	a	263.	d	306.	c
178.	d	221.	c	264.	d	307.	e
179.	e	222.	a	265.	d	308.	e
180.	c	223.	d	266.	a	309.	b
181.	d	224.	d	267.	e	310.	e
182.	c	225.	e	268.	c	311.	b
183.	e	226.	b	269.	b	312.	e
184.	b	227.	e	270.	d	313.	b
185.	c	228.	d	271.	d	314.	a
186.	d	229.	d	272.	d	315.	a
187.	b	230.	c	273.	c	316.	c
188.	e	231.	d	274.	e	317.	c
189.	a	232.	a	275.	c	318.	d
190.	c	233.	e	276.	a	319.	a
191.	d	234.	e	277.	b	320.	d
192.	c	235.	c	278.	e	321.	d
193.	b	236.	c	279.	b	322.	b
194.	c	237.	b	280.	a	323.	e
195.	d	238.	b	281.	b	324.	a
196.	c	239.	c	282.	e	325.	a
197.	e	240.	e	283.	b	326.	c
198.	e	241.	c	284.	e	327.	b
199.	c	242.	c	285.	e	328.	d
200.	d	243.	d	286.	a	329.	e
201.	b	244.	d	287.	b	330.	a
202.	d	245.	b	288.	c	331.	a
203.	e	246.	c	289.	b	332.	b
						333.	d

B I B L I O G R A P H Y[1]

ABBREVIATIONS

Mark of Special Recommendation

u   Especially useful for undergraduates.

Collections

A:LP   Ayer, Alfred J., ed. _Logical Positivism_. New York: Free Press, 1959.

A:PE   Ayer, Alfred J. _Philosophical Essays_. New York: St. Martin's Press, 1954.

A:PPUN   Acton, H.B., ed. _The Philosophy of Punishment_. New York: St. Martin's Press, 1969.

A:RC   Aiken, Henry D. _Reason and Conduct: New Bearings in Moral Philosophy_. New York: Knopf, 1962.

AL:GEMER   Ambrose, Alice, and Lazerowitz, Morris, eds. _G.E. Moore: Essays in Retrospect_. Atlantic Highlands: Humanities Press, 1970.

B:CU   Bayles, Michael D., ed. _Contemporary Utilitarians_. Garden City: Doubleday, 1968.

---

[1]This bibliography roughly corresponds to the Table of Contents.

BIBLIOGRAPHY

F:PM   Frankena, William K. Perspectives on Morality. Edited
       by Kenneth Goodpaster. Notre Dame: Notre Dame Uni-
       versity Press, 1976.

F:RR   Feinberg, Joel, ed. Reason and Responsibility: Read-
       ings in Some Basic Problems of Philosophy. Encino:
       Dickenson Publishing Co., 1965.

F:TE   Foot, Philippa, ed. Theories of Ethics. London:
       Oxford University Press, 1967.

FUW:SET French, Peter A.; Uehling, Theodore E., Jr.; and
       Wettstein, Howard K., eds. Studies in Ethical Theory:
       Midwest Studies in Philosophy. Vol. 3 (1978).
       Minneapolis: University of Minnesota Press, 1980.

G:MRSI   Gauthier, David, ed. Morality and Rational Self-Interest.
       Englewood Cliffs: Prentice-Hall, 1970.

H:EMC   Hare, Richard M. Essays on the Moral Concepts.
       Berkeley: University of California Press, 1972.

H:EPM   Hare, Richard M. Essays on Philosophical Method.
       Berkeley: University of California Press, 1971.

H:IOQ   Hudson, William D., ed. The Is/Ought Question. New
       York: St. Martin's Press, 1969.

H:NSE   Hudson, William D., ed. New Studies in Ethics. 2 vols.
       London: Macmillan & Co., 1971.

H:PI   Hare, Richard M. Practical Inferences. Berkeley: 1971.

BIBLIOGRAPHY

B:FM   Bricke, John, ed. Freedom and Morality. Lindley
              Lectures at the University of Kansas. Lawrence: Uni-
              versity of Kansas, 1976.

B:MRPC   Brody, Baruch A., ed. Moral Rules and Particular Cir-
              cumstances. Englewood Cliffs: Prentice-Hall, 1970.

B:VO   Brandt, Richard B., ed. Value and Obligation. New
              York: Harcourt Brace & World, 1961.

C:MMR   Casey, John, ed. Morality and Moral Reasoning. Lon-
              don: Methuen & Co., 1971.

C:OL   Chappell, V.C., ed. Ordinary Language: Essays in Philo-
              sophical Method. Englewood Cliffs: Prentice-Hall, 1964.

C:SMP   Carter, Curtis L., ed. Skepticism and Moral Principles.
              Evanston: New University Press, 1973.

CN:MLC   Castañeda [Calderon], Hector-Neri, and Naknikian, George,
              eds. Morality and the Language of Conduct. Detroit:
              Wayne State University Press, 1963.

E:EP   Edwards, Paul, ed. Encyclopedia of Philosophy. 8 vols.
              New York: Macmillan Co. & Free Press, 1967.

F:ICR   French, Peter A., ed. Individual and Collective Respon-
              sibility: The Massacre at My Lai. Cambridge:
              Schenkman, 1972.

F:MC   Feinberg, Joel, ed. Moral Concepts. London: Oxford
              University Press, 1969.

BIBLIOGRAPHY

University of California Press, 1971.

H:SU   Hearn, Thomas K., Jr., ed. Studies in Utilitarianism. New York: Appleton-Century-Crofts, 1971.

HL:WFR   Holtzman, Steven H., and Leich, Christopher M. Wittgenstein: to Follow a Rule. Boston: Routledge & Kegan Paul, 1981.

L:CBP   Lewis, Hywel D., ed. Contemporary British Philosophy. 4th series. London: Allen & Unwin, 1976.

L:PL   Lyas, Colin, ed. Philosophy and Linguistics. London: Macmillan & Co., 1971.

M:CET   Margolis, Joseph, ed. Contemporary Ethical Theory. New York: Random House, 1966.

M:EMP   Meldon, Abraham I., ed. Essays in Moral Philosophy. Seattle: Washington University Press, 1958.

M:MIE   Munitz, Milton K., ed. A Modern Introduction to Ethics: Readings from Classical and Contemporary Sources. Glencoe: Free Press, 1958.

MC:BR   MacIntosh, John J., and Coval, Samuel C., eds. The Business of Reason. New York: Humanities Press, 1969.

O:JSP   Olafson, Frederick A., ed. Justice and Social Policy. Englewood Cliffs: Prentice-Hall, 1961.

P:EJ   Phelps, Edmund S., ed. Economic Justice. Harmondsworth: Penguin, 1973.

BIBLIOGRAPHY

P:MO   Prichard, Harold A. _Moral Obligation and Duty and_
Interest: Essays and Lectures by H.A. Prichard.
New York: Oxford University Press, 1968.

P:NC   Peters, R.S., ed. _Nature and Conduct: Royal Institute_
of Philosophy Lectures. Vol. 8 (1973/74). New York:
Macmillan Press, 1975.

PS:RCET   Pahel, Kenneth, and Schiller, Marvin, eds. _Readings in_
Contemporary Ethical Theory. Englewood Cliffs:
Prentice-Hall, 1970.

R:SE   Rescher, Nicholas, ed. _Studies in Ethics_. American
Philosophical Quarterly Monograph Series, no. 7.
Oxford: Basil Blackwell, 1973.

R:SMP   Rescher, Nicholas, ed. _Studies in Moral Philosophy_.
American Philosophical Quarterly Monograph Series,
no. 1. Oxford: Basil Blackwell, 1968.

R:UMP   Rachels, James, ed. _Understanding Moral Philosophy_.
Encino: Dickenson Publishing Co., 1976.

RT:PICI   Rachels, James, and Tillman, Frank A., eds. _Philosophi-_
cal Issues: A Contemporary Introduction. New York:
Harper & Row, 1972.

S:FV   Stevenson, Charles L. _Facts and Values_. New Haven:
Yale University Press, 1963.

S:M..   Schneewind, Jerome B., ed. _Mill: A Collection of Cri-_

BIBLIOGRAPHY

tical Essays. Notre Dame: University of Notre Dame
Press, 1968.

S:PGEM   Schilpp, Paul A., ed. The Philosophy of G.E. Moore.
Evanston: Northwestern University, 1942.

SH:RET   Sellars, Wilfrid, and Hospers, John, eds. Readings in
Ethical Theory. 1st edition 1952. 2nd edition 1970,
altered. New York: Appleton-Century-Crofts, 1952 and
1970. If no date is given, then the item appears in
both editions.

SS:MU   Smith, James M., and Sosa, Ernest, eds. Mill's Utilitarianism: Text and Criticism. Belmont: Wadsworth
Publishing Co., 1969.

T:PMP   Taylor, Paul W., ed. Problems of Moral Philosophy: An
Introduction to Ethics. 3rd ed. Encino: Dickenson
Publishing Co., 1978.

TD:E   Thomson, Judith J[arvis], and Dworkin, Gerald, eds.
Ethics. New York: Harper & Row, 1968.

TW:TW   Timms, Noel N., and Watson, David, eds. Talking about
Welfare: Readings in Philosophy and Social Policy.
Boston: Routledge & Kegan Paul, 1976.

W:K   Wolff, Robert Paul, ed. Kant: A Collection of Critical
Essays. Garden City: Doubleday & Co., 1967.

WS:AE   Walsh, James J., and Shapiro, Henry L., eds. Aristotle's

BIBLIOGRAPHY

Ethics: Issues and Interpretations. Belmont:
Wadsworth Publishing Co., 1967.

WW:DM   Wallace, Gerald, and Walker, A.D.M., eds. The Definition of Morality. London: Methuen & Co., 1970.

Moral Problems and Moral Disagreements

Baier, K[urt]. "Guilt and Responsibility." Appears in F:ICR,
pp. 37-61.

Falk, Werner. "Moral Perplexity." Ethics 66(1956):123-31.

Guttenplan, Samuel. "Moral Realism and Moral Dilemmas."
Proceedings of the Aristotelian Society 80(1979/80):61-80.

Hall, Everett W. "Practical Reason(s) and the Deadlock in
Ethics." Mind 64(1955):319-32.

Johnson, Oliver A. "On Moral Disagreements." Mind 68(1959):
482-91.

Kavka, Gregory S. "Wrongdoing and Guilt." Journal of Philosophy
71(1974):663-64.

Ladd, John. "Remarks on the Conflict of Obligations." Journal
of Philosophy 55(1958):811-19.

u   Lemmon, E.J. "Moral Dilemmas." Philosophical Review 71(1962):
139-58.

Mallock, David. "Moral Dilemmas and Moral Failure."

BIBLIOGRAPHY

Australasian Journal of Philosophy 45(1967):159-78.

Norman, R. "On Seeing Things Differently." Radical Philosophy
1(1972):6-14.

Rundle, B[ede] B. "Disputes and Values." Appears in MC:BR,
pp. 207-27.

Squires, J.E.R. "Blame." Philosophical Quarterly 18(1968):54-
60. Also in A:PPUN.

Steiner, Hillel. "Moral Conflict and Prescriptivism." Mind
82(1973):586-91.

u   Stevenson, Charles L. "The Nature of Ethical Disagreement."
Appears in B:VO, pp. 368-76; M:MIE, pp. 547-52; S:FV, pp.
1-9.

Trigg, Roger. "Moral Conflict." Mind 80(1971):41-55.

Moral Reasons and Moral Reasoning

u   Ayer, A[lfred] J. Language, Truth and Logic. London: Victor
Gollancz Ltd., 1954. See the preface and chap. 6.

u   ————. "On the Analysis of Moral Judgments." Horizon
20(1949):171-84. Also in A:PE.

Baier, Kurt. "Good Reasons: A Reply to Mr. Terrell and Mr.
Sachs." Philosophical Studies 5(1954):53-58.

u   ————. "Good Reasons." Philosophical Studies 4(1953):1-15.
Also in PS:RCET, TD:E.

BIBLIOGRAPHY

————. "Moral Reasons." Appears in FUW:SET, pp. 62-74.

u   ————. "The Point of View of Morality." Australasian
Journal of Philosophy 32(1954):104-35.

Beardsmore, R[ichard] W. Moral Reasoning. New York: Schocken
Books, 1969.

Becker, Lawrence C. On Justifying Moral Judgments. New York:
Humanities Press, 1973.

Blackburn, S[imon] W. "Moral Realism." Appears in C:MMR,
pp. 101-24.

Brandt, R[ichard] B. "The Emotive Theory of Ethics."
Philosophical Review 59(1950):305-18.

————. "Stevenson's Defense of the Emotive Theory."
Philosophical Review 59(1950):535-40.

Brennan, J.M. The Open-Texture of Moral Concepts. New York:
Harper & Row, 1977.

Cavell, Stanley. The Claim of Reason: Wittgenstein, Skepticism,
Morality, and Tragedy. New York: Oxford University Press,
1979. See Part Three ("Knowledge and the Concept of
Morality"), pp. 247-326.

Cohen, L.J. "Are Moral Arguments Always Liable to Break Down?"
Mind 68(1959):530-32.

Cooper, N[eil]. "Rules and Morality." Proceedings of the

BIBLIOGRAPHY

Aristotelian Society, Supplementary Volume 33(1959):159-72.
Part of a symposium. See also R.J. Edgley on the same
topic.

Cross, R.C. "Ethical Disagreement." Philosophy 25(1950):301-
15.

Edel, Abraham. "Ethical Reasoning." Academic Freedom, Logic,
and Religion. Edited by Morton White. Philadelphia:
University of Pennsylvania Press, 1953.
Papers for the Symposia held at the annual meeting, 1953,
of the American Philosophical Association, Eastern Division.
See pp. 127-42.

Edgley, R.J. "Rules and Morality." Proceedings of the
Aristotelian Society, Supplementary Volume 33(1959):173-94.
Part of a symposium. See also N[eil] Cooper on the same
topic.

Emmet, Dorothy. The Moral Prism. New York: St. Martin's
Press, 1979.

u   Flynn, James R. "The Realm of the Moral." American Philosophical Quarterly 13(1976):273-86.

u   Foot, P[hilippa] R. "Moral Arguments." Mind 67(1958):502-13.
Also in M:CET, PS:RCET, TD:E.
An attack on some modern forms of nonnaturalism.

u   Frankena, William K. "On Saying the Ethical Thing."

BIBLIOGRAPHY

Proceedings of the American Philosophical Association
39(1965/66):21-42. Also in F:PM.

——————. _Thinking about Morality_. Ann Arbor: The University
of Michigan Press, 1980.

Garnett, A. Campbell. "Virtues, Rules, and Good Reasons."
Monist 47(1962/63):545-62.

u   Geach, P[eter] T. "Good and Evil." _Analysis_ 17(1956/57):33-42.
Also in F:TE.

u   Gewirth, Alan. "Meanings and Criteria in Ethics." _Philosophy_
38(1963):329-45.

Ginsberg, M[orris]. "The Functions of Reason in Morals."
Proceedings of the Aristotelian Society 39(1938/39):249-70.

Grice, Geoffrey R. _The Grounds of Moral Judgement_. Cambridge:
Cambridge University Press, 1967. See chap. 4, pp. 24-26,
120-26, 173-74.

u   Hare, R[ichard] M. "Ethical Theory and Utilitarianism."
Appears in L:CBP, pp. 113-31.

——————. _Freedom and Reason_. London: Oxford University
Press, 1963.

u   ——————. "Freedom of the Will." _Proceedings of the
Aristotelian Society, Supplementary Volume_ 25(1951):201-16.

u   ——————. "Geach: Good and Evil." _Analysis_ 17(1956/57):
103-11. Also in F:TE.

BIBLIOGRAPHY

u   ————. The Language of Morals. London: Oxford University
Press, 1952.

u   ————. "Meaning and Speech Acts." Philosophical Review
79(1970):3-24. Also in H:PI.

————. Moral Thinking: Its Levels, Method and Point.
London: Oxford University Press, 1981.

Harman, Gilbert H. "R.M. Hare and Moral Reasoning." Mind 77
(1968):427-28.

Harrison, J[onathan]. "Moral Talking and Moral Living: Solace
for Obsessionals." Philosophy 38(1963):314-28.

Hay, W[illiam] H. "C.L. Stevenson and Ethical Analysis."
Philosophical Review 56(1947):422-30.

Hudson, William D. "Moral Arguments." Mind 68(1959):533-34.

Kerner, George C. "Approvals, Reasons and Moral Argument."
Mind 71(1962):474-86.

Lesser, A.H. "Aesthetic Reasons for Acting." Philosophical
Quarterly 22(1972):19-28.

MacIntyre, Alasdair. "Imperatives, Reason for Action and
Morals." With comments by David S. Shwayder and Joseph
Margolis. Journal of Philosophy 62(1965):513-24.

McCloskey, H.J. "Hare's Ethical Subjectivism." Australasian
Journal of Philosophy 37(1959):187-200.

McIver, A.M. "Good and Evil and Mr. Geach." Analysis 18(1957/

BIBLIOGRAPHY

58):7-13.

u   Nielsen, Kai. "Good Reasons in Ethics: An Examination of the
Toulmin-Hare Controversy." Theoria 24(1958):9-28.

Perry, T[homas] D. "Moral and Judicial Reasoning: A Structural
Analogy." Buffalo Law Review 22(1972/73):769-96.

————. Moral Reasoning and Truth: An Essay in Philosophy
and Jurisprudence. Oxford: Clarendon Press, 1976.
His view of moral judgment resembles Hare's. See chap. 4
and app. 3, pp. 115-21, 197-208.

Phillips, D[ewi] Z., and Mounce, H.O. Moral Practices. New
York: Schocken Books, 1969.

Pincoffs, E[dmund]. "Quandary Ethics." Mind 80(1971):552-71.

u   Prichard, H[arold] A. "Duty and Interest." Appears in
G:MRSI, pp. 111-30; P:MO, pp. 203-38; and excerpts in
SH:RET, pp. 469-86.

Quine, Willard van Orman. Theories and Things. Cambridge:
Harvard University Press, 1981. See chap. 6 ("On the
Nature of Moral Values"), pp. 55-66.

Rhees, Rush. Without Answers. New York: Schocken Books,
1969.

Robinson, R[ichard]. "Argument and Moral Argument." Mind 70
(1961):426-29.

Sachs, David. "On Mr. Baier's 'Good Reasons.'" Philosophical

Studies 4(1953):65-69.

u   Scruton, Roger. "Attitudes, Beliefs, and Reasons." Appears in
C:MMR, pp. 25-100.

Stevenson, Charles L. "Brandt's Questions about Emotive
Ethics." _Philosophical Review_ 59(1950):528-34.

—————. "The Emotive Conception of Ethics and Its Cognitive
Implications." _Philosophical Review_ 59(1950):291-304.
Also in _S:FV_, _SH:RET_ (1970).

u   —————. "The Emotive Meaning of Ethical Terms." _Mind_ 46
(1937):14-31. Also in _A:LP_, _M:CET_, _S:FV_, _SH:RET_.

—————. "Ethical Judgments and Avoidability." _Mind_ 47
(1938):45-57. Also in _S:FV_.

—————. _Ethics and Language_. New Haven: Yale University
Press, 1944.

u   —————. "Persuasive Definitions." _Mind_ 47(1938):331-50.
Also in _S:FV_.

Stigen, Anfinn. "Mrs. Foot on Moral Arguments." _Mind_ 69
(1960):76-79.

Terrell, D.B. "A Remark on Good Reasons." _Philosophical
Studies_ 4(1953)58-63.

u   Toulmin, Stephen E. _An Examination of the Place of Reason in
Ethics_. Cambridge: Cambridge University Press, 1980.
An ethical view strongly influenced by Wittgenstein. See

chaps. 11, 12. This book is reviewed by Hare in
Philosophical Quarterly 1(1951), Mackie in Australasian
Journal of Philosophy 29(1951), Sacksteder in Ethics 62
(1951/52), Paton in Philosophy 27(1952).

Wasserstrom, Richard. "On the Breakdown of Moral Arguments:
A Reply to Philippa Foot." Philosophical Quarterly 10
(1960):79-81.

Whiteley, C.H. "Rationality in Morals." Proceedings of the
Aristotelian Society 50(1949/50):1-14.

Moral Virtues and Moral Vices

Aristotle. Nicomachean Ethics. Translated by H. Rackham.
Cambridge: Harvard University Press, 1975. See bks.
2, 3 (1113b 2 - end), 4, 5.

u   Brandt, R[ichard] B. "Traits of Character: A Conceptual
Analysis." American Philosophical Quarterly 7(1970):23-
37.

u   Dreher, J[ohn] H. "Who's at Fault?" Analysis 35(1974/75):145-
47.

u   Foot, Philippa. "Moral Beliefs." Proceedings of the
Aristotelian Society 59(1958/59):83-104. Also in F:TE,
H:IOQ, T:PMP, TD:E, WW:DM.
An attack on some modern forms of nonnaturalism. See

BIBLIOGRAPHY

esp. pp. 94-104.

————. Virtues and Vices and Other Essays in Moral Philosophy. Berkeley: University of California Press, 1978.

Frankena, W[illiam] K. "Prichard and the Ethics of Virtue;
Notes on a Footnote." Monist 54(1970):1-17. Also in
F:PM.

Geach, Peter. The Virtues. Cambridge: Cambridge University
Press, 1977.

u Hare, R[ichard] M. Freedom and Reason. New York: Oxford
University Press, 1963.

In chap. 2 and on pp. 164, 187-89, Hare discusses Foot's
"Moral Beliefs."

————. "Wrongness and Harm." Appears in H:EMC, pp. 92-109.
Hare discusses Foot's "Moral Beliefs."

Kant, Immanuel. The Metaphysic of Morals. Translated by
Mary J. Gregor. Philadelphia: University of Pennsylvania
Press, 1964. See Part II: "The Doctrine of Virtue."

MacIntyre, Alasdair. After Virtue: A Study in Moral Theory.
Notre Dame: University of Notre Dame Press, 1981.

————. "How Virtues Become Vices," with a reply by Samuel
Gorovitz. In Evaluation and Explanation in the Biomedi-
cal Sciences. Edited by H. Tristram Engelhardt and Stuart
F. Spicker. Boston: D. Reidel Publishing Co., 1975.

BIBLIOGRAPHY

See pp. 97-121.

McPherson, T., and Harrison, J[onathan]. Symposium: "Christian
Virtues." Proceedings of the Aristotelian Society, Supplementary Volume 37(1963):51-82.

Mounce, H.O. "Virtue and the Understanding." Analysis 28
(1967/68):11-17.

Paton, H[erbert] J. "Kant on Friendship." Proceedings of the
British Academy 42(1956):45-66.
On Kant's "The Doctrine of Virtue," which is Part II of
Kant's The Metaphysic of Morals.

u   Savile, A[nthony]. "Mr. Wheatley on Virtue." Analysis 23
(1962/63):93-95.

Sparshott, F[rancis] E. "Five Virtues in Plato and Aristotle."
Monist 54(1970):40-65.

u   Taylor, G[abriele], and Wolfram, S[ybil]. "Virtues and
Passions." Analysis 31(1970/71):76-83.

Teichmann, J[enny]. "Mrs. P. Foot on Morality and Virtue."
Mind 69(1960):244-48.

Urmson, J.O. "Aristotle's Doctrine of the Mean." American
Philosophical Quarterly 10(1973):223-30.

u   Wheatley, Jon. "Virtue: An Analysis and a Speculation."
Analysis 22(1961/62):15-18.

u   Wright, George Henrik von. The Varieties of Goodness. New

York: Humanities Press, 1963. See chaps. 6-7.

Moral Experts

Szabados, Bela. "On 'Moral Expertise.'" Canadian Journal of
  Philosophy 8(1978):117-29.

Noble, Cheryl N. "Ethics and Experts." Hastings Center Report
  12(1982):7-15. With comments by Peter Singer, Jerry Avorn,
  Daniel Wikler, and Tom L. Beauchamp.

Phillips, D[ewi] Z. "The Possibilities of Moral Advice."
  Analysis 25(1964/65):37-41. Reprinted in Moral Practices,
  D[ewi] Z. Phillips and H.O. Mounce. New York: Schocken
  Books, 1970. Also in H:IOQ.

Ethical Subjectivism and Conventionalism

Acton, H[arry] W.B. "Moral Subjectivism." Analysis 9(1948):1-8.
  Makes some critical comments on Ewing's attempted reductio
  ad absurdum of a simple form of ethical subjectivism.

Becker, L[awrence] C. "The Finality of Moral Judgments: A
  Reply to Mrs. Foot." Philosophical Review 82(1973):364-70.

Benedict, Ruth. "Anthropology and the Abnormal." Journal of
  General Psychology 10(1934):59-82.
  Uses ethnological data in support of an extreme type of
  relativism.

Blanshard, Brand. "Subjectivism in Ethics, a Criticism."

BIBLIOGRAPHY

<u>Philosophical Quarterly</u> 1(1950/51):127-39.

u   Brandt, Richard B. "Ethical Relativism." Appears in <u>E:EP</u>,
vol. 3, pp. 75-78.

Coburn, Robert. "Relativism and the Basis of Morality."
<u>Philosophical Review</u> 85(1976):87-93.

Dilman, Ilham. <u>Morality and the Inner Life: A Study in</u>
<u>Plato's Gorgias</u>. Totowa: Barnes & Noble Books, 1979.
See chap. 7 ("Morality and Convention"), pp. 105-28.

Ewing, Alfred C. "Subjectivism and Naturalism in Ethics."
<u>Mind</u> 53(1944):120-41. Also in <u>SH:RET</u>(1952).

Findlay, J[ohn] N. "Morality by Convention." <u>Mind</u> 53(1944):
142-69.

Foot, P[hilippa] R. "In Defence of the Hypothetical Imperative." <u>Philosophic Exchange</u> 1(1970/74):137-45.

————. "'Is Morality a System of Hypothetical Imperatives?': A Reply to Mr. Holmes." <u>Analysis</u> 35(1974/75):
53-56.

————. "Morality as a System of Hypothetical Imperatives." <u>Philosophical Review</u> 81(1972):305-16.

Garnett, A. C[ampbell]. "The Interest Theory of Value."
<u>Philosophy</u> 11(1936):163-75.

Hare, R[ichard]M. "Some Confusions about Subjectivity."
Appears in <u>B:FM</u>, pp. 191-208.

BIBLIOGRAPHY

u   Harman, Gilbert. "Moral Relativism Defended." Philosophical
       Review 84(1975):3-22.

Harrison, Jonathan. "Ethical Subjectivism." Appears in
       E:EP, vol. 3, pp. 78-81.

Harsanyi, J[ohn] C. "Ethics in Terms of Hypothetical Impera-
       tives." Mind 67(1958):305-16.

Hobbes, Thomas. Leviathan: Or the Matter, Forme and Power
       of a Commonwealth, Ecclesiasticall and Civil. Edited
       by Michael Oakeshott. Oxford: Basil Blackwell, 1955.

Holmes, R[obert] L. "Is Morality a System of Hypothetical
       Imperatives?" Analysis 34(1973/74):96-100.

James, William. "The Essence of Good is to Satisfy Demand,"
       in The Will to Believe and Other Essays in Popular
       Philosophy. New York: Longmans, Green, 1919.

Kluckhohn, C[lyde]. "Ethical Relativity: Sic Et Non."
       Journal of Philosophy 52(1955):663-77.
       Stresses the uniformities of value systems.

McClintock, T[homas] L. "The Argument for Ethical Relativism
       from the Diversity of Morals." Monist 47(1962/63): 528-
       44.

McDowell, John. "Virtue and Reason." Monist 62(1979):331-50.

Meiland, Jack W. "Bernard Williams' Relativism." Mind 88
       (1979):258-62.

BIBLIOGRAPHY

A criticism of Williams' defense of relativism.
Meiland suggests a different way of rescuing relativism
from the charge of self-contradiction.

u   Monro, D.H. "Subjectivism versus Relativism in Ethics."
Analysis 11(1950/51):19-24.

u   Moore, G[eorge] E. Ethics. New York: H. Holt & Co., 1912.
An important criticism of subjectivism.   See chaps. 3,
4.

————. "A Reply to My Critics." Appears in S:PGEM,
pp. 533-627.

Nielsen, Kai. "Conventionalism in Morals and the Appeal to
Human Nature." Philosophy and Phenomenological Research
23(1962/63):217-31.

————. "Ethical Relativism and the Facts of Cultural
Relativity." Social Research 33(1966):531-51. Also in
R:UMP.

————. "Varieties of Ethical Subjectivism." Danish
Yearbook of Philosophy 7(1970):73-87.

Nissen, Ingjold. The Latest Forms of the Attitude Theories
in Ethics. Oslo: Kommisjon has J. Dybwad, 1951.

Parker, D[eWitt] H. "Value as any Object of any Interest."
Ethics 40(1929/30):465-73.

Perry, Ralph Barton. General Theory of Value: Its Meaning and

-247-

BIBLIOGRAPHY

Basic Principles Construed in Terms of Interest.
Cambridge: Harvard University Press, 1954. See esp.
chaps. 5, 12.

—————. "Real and Apparent Value." Philosophy 7(1932):62-67.

Protagaras of Abdera. Ancilla to the Pre-Socratic Philo-
sophers: Complete Translation of the Fragments in Diels,
Fragmante der Vorsokratiker. Translated by Kathleen
Freeman. Cambridge: Harvard University Press, 1971.
See pp. 125-27.

Roberts, George W. "Some Refutations of Private Subjectivism
in Ethics." Journal of Value Inquiry 5(1971):292-309.

Sartre, Jean-Paul. Existentialism and Human Emotions. Translated by Bernard Frechtman. New York: Philosophical
Library, 1957.

Schlick, Moritz. Problems of Ethics. Translated by David
Rynin. New York: Dover Publications, 1962.

Smith, J[ames] W[ard]. "Senses of Subjectivism in Value
Theory." Journal of Philosophy 45(1948):393-405.

u   Stevenson, C[harles] L. "Moore's Arguments against Certain
Forms of Ethical Naturalism." Appears in S:PGEM, pp. 71-90.

Taylor, Paul W. "The Ethnocentric Fallacy." Monist 47(1962/
63):563-84.

u   —————. Principles of Ethics. Belmont: Wadsworth Publishing

Co., 1975. See chap. 2.

Vlastos, Gregory. "Introduction: Protagaras," in Protagaras. Translated by Benjamin Jowett and extensively revised by Martin Ostwald. Edited by Gregory Vlastos. New York: Liberal Arts Press, 1956.

See pp. vii-xxiv. An excellent exposition of Protagaras' philosophy.

u Wellman, C[arl]. "The Ethical Implications of Cultural Relativity." Journal of Philosophy 60(1963):169-84. Also in T:PMP.

Westermarck, E[dvard] A. Ethical Relativity. New York: Harcourt, Brace, 1932.

————. The Origin and Development of the Moral Ideas. London: Macmillan & Co., 1906.

u Williams, Bernard A.O. Morality: An Introduction to Ethics. New York: Harper Torchbooks, 1972. See chap. 3, pp. 20-26.

u ————. "The Truth in Relativism." Proceedings of the Aristotelian Society 75(1974/75):215-28.

Wisdom, J[ohn] O. "Towards the Psychocentric Conception of Right." Proceedings of the Aristotelian Society 36(1935/36):61-78.

BIBLIOGRAPHY

The Golden Rule

    Gewirth, Alan. "The Golden Rule Rationalized." Appears in
        FUW:SET, pp. 133-47.

u   Hare, R[ichard] M. "Abortion and the Golden Rule." Philo-
        sophy and Public Affairs 4(1975):201-22.

    Hirst, E.W. "The Categorical Imperative and the Golden Rule."
        Philosophy 9(1934):328-35.

    Sher, G[eorge]. "Hare, Abortion, and the Golden Rule."
        Philosophy and Public Affairs 6(1976/77):185-90.

    Singer, Marcus G. "The Golden Rule." Appears in E:EP, vol.
        3, pp. 365-67.

Divine-Command Theory

    Adams, Robert Merrihew. "Autonomy and Theological Ethics."
        Religious Studies 15(1979)191-94.
        Replies to an objection to divine command theory.

    ————. "Divine Command Metaethics Modified Again."
        Journal of Religious Ethics 7(1979):66-79.
        Responds to Jeffrey Stout's 1978 article in the same
        journal on a 1973 paper by Adams.

    ————. "A Modified Divine Command Theory of Ethical
        Wrongness," in Religion and Morality: A Collection of
        Essays. Edited by Gene Outka and John P. Reeder, Jr.

BIBLIOGRAPHY

Garden City: Doubleday Anchor, 1973.

Adams defends the divine command theory. See pp. 318-47.

————. "Moral Arguments for Theistic Belief," in
Rationality and Religious Belief. Edited by C.F. Delaney.
Notre Dame: University of Notre Dame Press, 1979. See
pp. 116-40.

Augustine, St. The Enchiridion. Translated by J.F. Shaw.
Edinburgh: T & T Clark, 1873.

Barth, Karl. The Knowledge of God and the Service of God.
London: Hodder & Stoughton, 1938. See p. 146.

Brody, Baruch A. "Morality and Religion Reconsidered," in
Reading in the Philosophy of Religion: An Analytic
Approach. Edited by Baruch A. Brody. Englewood Cliffs:
Prentice-Hall, 1974.
Brody defends the theory against the Euthyphro objection.
See pp. 592-603.

Brown, Patterson. "God and the Good." Religious Studies
2(1966/67):269-76.

Burch, Robert. "Objective Values and the Divine Command
Theory of Morality." New Scholasticism 54(1980):
279-304.

Calvin, John. Institutes of the Christian Religion. Translated by Ford L. Battles. Edited by John T. McNeill.

BIBLIOGRAPHY

2 vols. Philadelphia: Westminster Press, 1960.

Geach, P[eter] T. Gives a negative review of Philip L. Quinn's
    book, Divine Commands and Moral Requirements. Philo-
    sophical Quarterly 30(1980):180-81.

Losonsky, Michael. "God, Property and Morality." Inter-
    national Journal for Philosophy of Religion 10(1979):131-39.
    He argues that Brody's recent defense of Euthyphro's claim
    fails.

Ockham, William of. Philosophical Writings. Translated and
    edited by Philotheus Boehner. Edinburgh: Nelson Philo-
    sophical Texts, 1957.

Plato. Euthyphro, Apology, Crito, and the Death Scene from
    Phaedo. Translated by F.J. Church. Indianapolis: Bobbs-
    Merrill, 1956. See esp. 9b - 11b in the Euthyphro.

Porter, Burton F. Deity and Morality: with regard to the
    Naturalistic Fallacy. London: George Allen & Unwin,
    1968.

Quinn, Philip L. Divine Commands and Moral Requirements.
    Oxford: Clarendon Press, 1978.
    Defends the theory against the Euthyphro objection. See
    esp. pp. 46-52, 64, 107.

Rowe, William L. A favorable review of Philip L. Quinn's
    book, Divine Commands and Moral Requirements. Philo-

sophical Review 89(1980):637-39.

Sharvy, Richard. "Euthyphro 9d - 11b: Analysis and Definition in Plato and Others." _Noûs_ 6(1972):119-37.

Stout, Jeffrey. "Metaethics and the Death of Meaning:
Adams' Tantalizing Closing." _Journal of Religious
Ethics_ 6(1978):1-18.

Discusses   a 1973 paper by Robert Merrihew Adams,
"A Modified Divine Command Theory of Ethical Wrongness."

Swinburne, Richard. _The Coherence of Theism._ Oxford:
Clarendon Press, 1977. See chap. 11, esp. pp. 203-9.

Wittgenstein, Ludwig. _Wittgenstein and the Vienna Circle:
Conversations recorded by Friedrich Waismann._
Translated by Joachim Schulte and Brian McGuinness.
Edited by Brian McGuinness. Oxford: Basil Blackwell,
1979. See p. 115 and contrast with Moritz Schlick's
view in _Problems of Ethics_ (New York: Dover Publications, 1962), p. 11.

The Intuitionism of Prichard, Moore, and Ross

Hudson, William D. _Ethical Intuitionism._ New York:
St. Martin's Press, 1967.

u   ————. _Modern Moral Philosophy._ Garden City: Doubleday
& Co., 1970. See chap. 3, secs. 2, 3.

BIBLIOGRAPHY

Karani, R.N. "Vindication of Ethical Intuitionism." Mind
     71(1962):535-38.

u   Nowell-Smith, Patrick H. Ethics. Baltimore: Pelican Books,
     1954. See chaps. 2-6.

u   Prichard, H[arold] A. "Does Moral Philosophy Rest on a
     Mistake?" Mind 21(1912):21-37. Also in M:CET, P:MO,
     PS:RCET, SH:RET.

     ——————. "Moral Obligation." Appears in P:MO, 87-163.

Rawls, John. A Theory of Justice. Cambridge: Harvard
     University Press, 1971. See pp. 34-41 on intuitionism.

Ross, Sir William D avid . The Foundations of Ethics.
     London: Oxford University Press, 1939. See esp. chaps. 3-8.

u   ——————. The Right and the Good. Oxford: Clarendon Press,
     1930. See esp. chaps. 1-3. Selections from this book
     also appear in B:MRPC, M:CET, PS:RCET, SH:RET.

u   Strawson, Peter F. "Ethical Intuitionism." Philosophy 24
     (1949):23-33. Also in B:VO, M:CET.

Urmson, J.O. "A Defence of Intuitionism." Proceedings of
     the Aristotelian Society 75(1974/75):111-19.

u   Warnock, G[eoffrey] J. Contemporary Moral Philosophy. New
     York: St. Martin's Press, 1967. See chap. 2 or
     H:NSE 2.

BIBLIOGRAPHY

Ethical Egoism

    Baier, Kurt. <u>The Moral Point of View: A Rational Basis of</u>
        <u>Ethics</u>. Ithaca: Cornell University Press, 1958. See
        chap. 8, sec. 1. Also appears in <u>SH:RET</u>(1970).

    Branden, Nathaniel. <u>The Psychology of Self-Esteem: A New</u>
        <u>Concept of Man's Psychological Nature</u>. Los Angeles:
        Nash Publishing Co., 1969.

u   Brunton, J.A. "Egoism and Morality." <u>Philosophical Quarterly</u>
        6(1956):289-303. Also in <u>M:CET</u>.

u   Falk, W[erner] D. "Morality, Self, and Others." Appears in
        <u>CN:MLC</u>, pp. 25-67; <u>PS:RCET</u>, pp. 360-90; <u>TD:E</u>, pp. 349-90.

    Glascow, W.D. "The Contradiction in Ethical Egoism." <u>Philo-</u>
        <u>sophical Studies</u> 19(1968):81-85.

u   Hospers, John. "Baier and Medlin on Ethical Egoism."
        <u>Philosophical Studies</u> 12(1961):10-16. Also in <u>R:UMP</u>, <u>T:PMP</u>.

    ————. "Rule-Egoism." <u>Personalist</u> 54(1973):391-95.

    Kalin, Jesse G. "In Defense of Egoism." Appears in <u>G:MRSI</u>,
        pp. 64-87.

u   ————. "On Ethical Egoism." Appears in <u>R:SMP</u>, pp. 26-41.

    ————. "Two Kinds of Moral Reasoning: Ethical Egoism as
        a Moral Theory." <u>Canadian Journal of Philosophy</u> 5(1975):
        323-56.

    Machan, Tibor R. "Recent Work in Ethical Egoism." <u>American</u>

BIBLIOGRAPHY

Philosophical Quarterly 16(1979):1-15.

——————. "Was Rachels's Doctor Practicing Egoism?"
Philosophia 8(1978):1-2.

Mack, Eric. "Egoism and Rights." *Personalist* 54(1973):5-33.

——————. "How to Derive Ethical Egoism." *Personalist* 52
(1971):735-43.

Mackie, J[ohn] L. "Sidgwick's Pessimism." *Philosophical
Quarterly* 26(1976):317-27.

Medlin, Brian. "Ultimate Principles and Ethical Egoism."
Australasian Journal of Philosophy 35(1957):111-18.
Also appears in B:VO, F:RR, G:MRSI, R:UMP, T:PMP.

Moore, G[eorge] E. *Principia Ethica.* London: Cambridge
University Press, 1903.

Tries to show that ethical egoism is self-contradictory.
See pp. 96-109.

Murphy, Frank J. "Moore on Ethical Egoism." *Personalist*
52(1971):744-49.

Tries to show that Moore's argument against ethical
egoism is inconclusive.

Nielsen, Kai. "On the Rationality of 'Rational Egoism.'"
Personalist 55(1974):398-400.

Rachels, James. "Morality and Self-Interest." Appears in
RT:PT, pp. 117-25.

BIBLIOGRAPHY

Rand, Ayn. Introduction to Objectivist Epistemology. New

York: Published by the Objectivist, 1967.

————. The Virtue of Selfishness: A New Concept of

Egoism. New York: New American Library, 1964.

Regis, Edward. "What is Ethical Egoism?" Ethics 91(1980/81):

50-62.

Sanders, S[teven] M. "A Credible Form of Egoism?" Personalist

57(1976):272-78.

Sidgwick, Henry. The Methods of Ethics. 7th ed. London:

Macmillan & Co., 1907.

See bk. 2 and "Concluding Chapter," and Mackie (1976) above.

Utilitarianism, General

Beccaria, Cesare B. Crimes and Punishments. Translated by

James Anson Farrer. London: Chatto & Windus, 1880.

Brock, Dan W. "Recent Work in Utilitarianism." American

Philosophical Quarterly 10(1973):241-69.

Hare, R[ichard] M. "Men of Ideas." Listener 99(1978):441.

Harrison, Jonathan. "Utilitarianism, Universalization, and

our Duty to be Just." Proceedings of the Aristotelian

Society 53(1952/53):105-34. Also in B:CU, O:JSP, TD:E.

Henson, R[ichard] G. "Utilitarianism and the Wrongness of

Killing." Philosophical Review 80(1971):320-37. Also in

R:UMP.

BIBLIOGRAPHY

Pickard-Cambridge, W.A. "Two Problems about Duty I - III."
Mind 41(1932):72-96, 145-72, 311-40.

u   Quinton, Anthony. Utilitarian Ethics. New York: St. Martin's
Press, 1973.

Talmage, R. S[tephen]. "Utilitarianism and the Morality of
Killing." Philosophy 47(1972):55-63.

"Ideal" Utilitarianism

Frankena, W[illiam] K. "The Naturalistic Fallacy." Mind 48
(1939):464-77. Reprinted in SH:RET.

Kerner, George C. The Revolution in Ethical Theory. Oxford:
Clarendon Press, 1966.

In chap. 1, he discusses Moore's ethics.

Moore, G[eorge] E. Ethics. London: Oxford University Press,
1912.

Argues for ideal utilitarianism. See chaps. 1 and 2, or
SH:RET, pp. 35-59.

————. Principia Ethica. London: Cambridge University
Press, 1903.

Argues for ideal utilitarianism. See esp. chap. 6, pp.
146-71.

Rashdall, Hastings. The Theory of Good and Evil; a Treatise
on Moral Philosophy. Oxford: Clarendon Press, 1907.

BIBLIOGRAPHY

See esp. bk. 1, chaps. 3-9, and bk. 2.

Russell, Bertrand. "The Elements of Ethics." Appears in
SH:RET, pp. 1-32.

Suter, Ronald. "Moore's Defense of the Rule 'Do No Murder.'"
Personalist 54(1973):361-75.

u   Urmson, J.O. "Moore's Utilitarianism." Appears in AL:GEMER,
pp. 343-49.

Hedonistic and Eudaemonistic Utilitarianism

u   Bentham, Jeremy. An Introduction to the Principles of Morals
and Legislation. London: Oxford University Press, 1879.
See esp. chaps. 1-4.

Bradley, F[rancis] H. Mr. Sidgwick's Hedonism: An Examination
of the Main Arguments of the Methods of Ethics. London:
H.S. King, 1877.

u   Ewing, Alfred C. Ethics. New York: Dover Publications, 1967.
See chap. 3 ("The Pursuit of the General Happiness").

Hutcheson, Francis. An Inquiry into the Original of our Ideas
of Beauty and Virtue: In Two Treatises. 3rd ed.
corrected. London: Printed for J. & J. Knapton, 1729.
See in this work his second treatise, Concerning Moral
Good and Evil. Hutcheson anticipates the utilitarianism
of Jeremy Bentham.

BIBLIOGRAPHY

Mill, James. _A Fragment on MacKintosh_. London: Longmans,
Green, Reader, & Dyer, 1870.

u   Mill, John Stuart. _Utilitarianism_. Edited by Oskar Piest.
Indianapolis: Bobbs — Merrill Co., 1957. See chaps.
1, 2, 4, 5.

Mitchell, Wesley C. "Bentham's Felicific Calculus." _Political
Science Quarterly_ 33(1918):161-83.

u   Rashdall, Hastings. "Can There be a Sum of Pleasures?"
Mind 8(1899):357-82. See also _The Theory of Good and
Evil: A Treatise on Moral Philosophy_. Oxford: Clarendon
Press, 1907. See bk. 2, chap. 1.

Shackelton, Robert. "The Greatest Happiness of the Greatest
Number: The History of Bentham's Phrase." _Studies on
Voltaire and the Eighteenth Century_ 90(1972):1461-82.

Sidgwick, Henry. _The Methods of Ethics_. 7th ed. London:
Macmillan & Co., 1907. See esp. bk. 1, chap. 9; bk. 2,
chap. 1; bk. 3, chaps. 11, 13, 14; bk. 4, chaps. 2-5.

Smart, J[ohn] C., and Williams, Bernard A.O. _Utilitarianism:
For and Against_. Cambridge: Cambridge University Press,
1973.

In the first half of this book, Smart argues for a eudaemonistic version of act utilitarianism. Williams offers a
critique of utilitarianism in the second half of this book.

BIBLIOGRAPHY

u   Sosa, Ernest. "Mill's Utilitarianism." Appears in SS:MU,
        pp. 154-72.

Viner, Jacob. "Bentham and J.S. Mill: The Utilitarian
        Background." American Economic Review 39(1949):360-82.
        Also in P:EJ.

Act and Rule Utilitarianism

u   Ezorsky, Gertrude. "A Defense of Rule-utilitarianism
        against David Lyons. . ." A review article of Lyons's
        book (below). Journal of Philosophy 65(1968):533-44.
        She contests Lyons's claim that rule utilitarianism
        collapses into act utilitarianism.

Kerner, George C. "The Immorality of Utilitarianism and the
        Escapism of Rule-Utilitarianism." Philosophical
        Quarterly 21(1971):36-50.

u   Lyons, David. The Forms and Limits of Utilitarianism.
        London: Oxford University Press, 1965.
        Argues that rule utilitarianism collapses into act
        utilitarianism. See chaps. 3,4.

u   McCloskey, H.J. "'Two Concepts of Rules' — a Note."
        Philosophical Quarterly 22(1972):344-48.
        Criticizes the article by Rawls.

u   Rawls, John. "Two Concepts of Rules." Philosophical

BIBLIOGRAPHY

<u>Review</u> 64(1955):3-32. Also in <u>A:PPUN</u>, <u>B:CU</u>, <u>B:VO</u>, <u>F:TE</u>,
<u>H:SU</u>, <u>M:CET</u>, <u>PS:RCET</u>, <u>R:UMP</u>, <u>T:PMP</u>, <u>TD:E</u>.
Rawls espouses rule utilitarianism in this article.
He rejects this doctrine in his book, <u>A Theory of</u>
<u>Justice</u>.

u   Smart, J[ohn] J.C. "Act-utilitarianism and Rule-utilitarianism." Appears in <u>Utilitarianism: For and Against</u>,
by J[ohn]J. C. Smart and Bernard A. O. Williams.
Cambridge: Cambridge University Press, 1973.
Argues that rule utilitarianism must become a "one-
rule" rule utilitarianism which is identical to
act utilitarianism. See pp. 9-12.

u   ————. "Extreme and Restricted Utilitarianism." Appears
in <u>B:CU</u>, pp. 99-115.
A defense of act against rule utilitarianism.

<u>Pleasure and Happiness</u>

Alston, William P. "Pleasure." Appears in <u>E:EP</u>, vol. 6,
pp. 341-47.

Anscombe, G.E.M. "On the Grammar of 'Enjoy'." <u>Journal of</u>
<u>Philosophy</u> 64(1967):607-14.

Aristotle. <u>Nicomachean Ethics</u>. Translated by H. Rackham.
Cambridge: Harvard University Press, 1975. See bks. 1, 10.

BIBLIOGRAPHY

u   Austin, Jean. "Pleasure and Happiness." Philosophy 43(1968):

   51-62. Also in S:M.

Barrow, Robin. Happiness. Oxford: Martin Robertson, 1980.

Benditt, Theodore. "Happiness." Philosophical Studies 25

   (1974):1-20.

Bertman, M. "Pleasure and the Two Happinesses in Aristotle."

   Apeiron 6(1972):30-36.

Brand, Gerd. The Essential Wittgenstein. Translated by

   Robert E. Innis. New York: Basic Books, 1979. See

   N ("Will, Religion, Ethics"), pp. 157-66.

Carson, Thomas. "Happiness and Contentment: A Reply to

   Benditt's 'Happiness.'" Personalist 59(1978):101-7.

Chardin, Pierre Teilhard de. On Happiness. London: William

   Collins Sons & Co., 1973.

Duncker, Karl. "On Pleasure, Emotion, and Striving."

   Philosophy and Phenomenological Research 1(1941):391-430.

Gauthier, David P. "Progress and Happiness: A Utilitarian

   Reconsideration." Ethics 78(1967/68):77-85.

Goldworth, Amnon. "Bentham's Concept of Pleasure: It's

   Relation to Fictitious Terms." Ethics 82(1972):

   334-43.

Hallett, Garth. "Happiness." Heythrop Journal 12(1971):301-3.

Hardie, W[illiam] F. R. Aristotle's Ethical Theory. Oxford:

BIBLIOGRAPHY

Clarendon Press, 1968. See chap. 2.

u   ————. "The Final Good in Aristotle's Ethics." Philosophy
40(1965):277-95.

Hare, R[ichard] M. Freedom and Reason. Oxford: Oxford
University Press, 1963. See pp. 125-29.

Jones, R.K. "The Ethological Fallacy: A Note in Reply to
Mr. Meynell." Philosophy 47(1972):71-73.

u   Kenny, A[nthony] J.P. "Happiness." Proceedings of the
Aristotelian Society 66(1965/66):93-102. Also in F:MC.

Lloyd—Thomas, D.A. "Happiness." Philosophical Quarterly
18(1968):97-111.

McGill, V.J. The Idea of Happiness. New York: Frederick
A. Praeger, 1967.

u   McNaughton, R[obert]. "A Metrical Concept of Happiness."
Philosophy and Phenomenological Research 14(1953):172-83.

Meynell, H[ugo]. "Ethology and Ethics." Philosophy 45(1970):
290-306.

Mill, John Stuart. Utilitarianism. Edited by Oskar Piest.
New York: Liberal Arts Press, 1957. See chap. 2.

u   Montague, Roger. "Happiness." Proceedings of the Aristotelian
Society 67(1966/67):87-102.

Perry, D[avid] L. The Concept of Pleasure. The Hague:
Mouton, 1967.

BIBLIOGRAPHY

Phelps, William Lyon. Happiness. New York: E.P. Dutton & Co., 1927.

Rawls, John. A Theory of Justice. Cambridge: Harvard University Press, 1971. See sections 15, pp. 90-95; 63, pp. 407-16; 83, pp. 548-54.

Reuning, Karl. Joy and Freude: A Comparative Study of the Linguistic Field of Pleasurable Emotions in English and German. Swarthmore: Distributed by the Swarthmore College Bookstore, 1941.

Ryle, Gilbert. "Pleasure." Proceedings of the Aristotelian Society, Supplementary Volume 28(1954):135-46. Reprinted in F:MC.

Scruton, Roger. "Reason and Happiness." Appears in P:NC, pp. 139-61.

Siegler, F[rederick] A. "Reason, Happiness and Goodness." Appears in WS:AE, pp. 30-46.

Simpson, R[obert] W. "Happiness." American Philosophical Quarterly 12(1975):169-76.

Solomon, Robert C. "Is there Happiness after Death?" Philosophy 51(1976):189-93.
Relevant to Aristotle's notion of 'happiness'.

Stace, W[alter] T. The Concept of Morals. New York: Macmillan & Co., 1937. See chap. 6.

BIBLIOGRAPHY

Tatarkiewicz, Wladyslaw. "Happiness and Time." Philosophy
and Phenomenological Research 27(1966/67):1-10.

Taylor, G[ordon] Rattray. Conditions of Happiness. Boston:
Houghton Mifflin Co., 1951.

Telfer, Elizabeth. Happiness: An Examination of a Hedonistic
and a Eudaemonistic Concept of Happiness and of the
Relations between them. New York: St. Martin's Press,
1980.

Tweyman, Stanley. "Truth, Happiness and Obligation: The
Moral Philosophy of William Wollaston." Philosophy
5(1976):35-46.

Watts, Alan W. Happiness and the Meaning of Happiness.
New York: Harper & Brothers, 1940.

Williams, Bernard A.O. "Aristotle on the Good: A Formal
Sketch." Philosophical Quarterly 12(1962):289-96.

Wilson, John. "Happiness." Analysis 29(1968/69):13-21.

Wittgenstein, Ludwig. Culture and Value. Translated by Peter
Winch. Edited by G.H. von Wright. Chicago: University
of Chicago Press, 1980. See pp. 1-5, 9, 11-14, 16, 22,
27, 29, 34-36, 38-41, 44-50, 52-64, 67, 71-74, 76-82, 85-87.

—————. Letters from Ludwig Wittgenstein, with a Memoir
by Paul Engelman. Oxford: Basil Blackwell, 1967. See
31·3·17, 30·5·20, 21·6·20, 19·7·20, 2.1·21, 7.2·21,

BIBLIOGRAPHY

pp. 78-81, 92-93, 96-99, 142-145.

─────. Notebooks 1914-1916. 2d ed. Translated by
G.E.M. Anscombe. Edited by G.H. von Wright and G.E.M.
Anscombe. Chicago: University of Chicago Press, 1979.
See 25·5·15, 26·5·15, 27·5·15, 6·5·16, 11·6·16, 5·7·16,
6·7·16, 7·7·16, 8·7·16, 14·7·16, 21·7·16, 24·7·16,
29·7·16, 30·7·16, 1·8·16, 2·8·16, 4·8·16, 5·8·16,
7·8·16, 11·8·16, 12·8·16, 13·8·16, 16·8·16, 2·9·16,
11·9·16, 12·9·16, 9·10·16, 12·10·16, 15·10·16, 17·10·16,
20·10·16, 21·10·16, 29·10·16, 4·11·16, 7·1·17, 8·1·17,
10·1·17.

─────. Tractatus Logico-Philosophicus. Translated by
D.F. Pears and B[rian] F. McGuinness. London: Routledge
& Kegan Paul, 1974. See Preface and pp. 5, 56-59, 66-67,
70-74.

─────. Wittgenstein and the Vienna Circle: Conversations
Recorded by Friedgrich Waismann. Translated by Joachim
Schulte and Brian McGuinness. Edited by Brian McGuinness.
Oxford: Basil Blackwell, 1979. See pp. 68-69, 92-93,
115-18.

─────. Wittgenstein's Lectures, Cambridge, 1932-1935.
Edited by Alice Ambrose. Totowa: Rowman & Littlefield,
1979, See pp. 36-40.

BIBLIOGRAPHY

—————. "Wittgenstein's Lecture on Ethics." Philosophical
Review 74(1965):3-26.

u   Wright, George Henrik von. The Varieties of Goodness. New
York: Humanities Press, 1963. See chap. 5 or TW:TW.

The Appeal to Nature for Moral Guidance

Aquinas, St. Thomas. Summa Theologica, in Selected Political
Writings. Translated by J.G. Dawson. Edited by
Alessandro Passerin d' Entrieve. Totowa: Barnes &
Noble Books, 1981.

Aristotle. Eudemian Ethics. Translated by Michael Woods.
Oxford: Clarendon Press, 1982. See bks. 1, 2, 8.

—————. Nicomachean Ethics. Translated by H. Rackham.
Cambridge: Harvard University Press, 1975.

Bambrough, Renford. "Essay on Man." Appears in P:NC, pp. 1-13.

Black, Max. "The Gap between 'is' and 'should'." Philosophical Review 73(1964):165-81. Also in H:IOQ.

Broad, C[harlie] D. "Review of Julian S. Huxley's Evolutionary
Ethics." Mind 53(1944):344-67.

Cronin, Michael. The Science of Ethics. 2 vols. 2d ed.
New York: Benziger, 1939.

Crowe, Michael B. The Changing Profile of the Natural Law.
The Hague: Nijhoff, 1977.

BIBLIOGRAPHY

Dawkins, Richard. The Selfish Gene. New York: Oxford
    University Press, 1976.

Dilman, Ilham. Morality and the Inner Life: A Study in
    Plato's Gorgias. Totowa: Barnes & Noble Books, 1979.
    See chap. 6 ("Callicles on Morality and Nature"),
    pp. 83-104.

Epictetus. The Works of Epictetus. Translated by E. Carter.
    Boston: Little Brown, 1865.

Flew, Antony G.N. Evolutionary Ethics. New York: St. Martin's
    Press, 1967.

u   Franklin, R[ichard] L. "Recent Work on Ethical Naturalism."
    Appears in R:SE, pp. 55-95.

Geach, P[eter]T. God and the Soul. New York: Schocken
    Books, 1969.

u   Harrison, Jonathan. "Ethical Naturalism." Appears in
    E:EP, vol. 3, pp. 69-71.

Hofstadter, Richard. Social Darwinism in American Thought,
    1860-1915. Philadelphia: University of Pennsylvania
    Press, 1944.

Huxley, Julian. Evolutionary Ethics. London: Oxford University
    Press, 1943.

Huxley, Thomas, and Huxley, Julian. Evolution and Ethics.
    London: Pilot Press, 1947.

BIBLIOGRAPHY

Lao Tzu. The Way of Life according to Laotzu. Translated
   by Witter Bynner. New York: Capricorn Books, 1962.

Lecomte de Noüy, Pierre. Human Destiny. New York: Longmans,
   Green & Co., 1947. See chap. 16 ("The Telefinalist
   Hypothesis" (Summary)), esp. pp. 223-27.

Locke, John. Essays on the Law of Nature. Edited by W.
   von Leyden. Oxford: Clarendon Press, 1954.

Marcus Aurelius Antoninus. The Meditations of the Emperor
   Marcus Aurelius. Translated by George Long. New York:
   A.L. Burt, 1864.

McInerny, Ralph. "Naturalism and Thomistic Ethics." Thomist
   40(1976):222-42.

Mill, John Stuart. "Nature." Appears in his Nature and
   Utility of Religion. New York: The Liberal Arts Press,
   1958. See pp. 3-44.

Nielsen, Kai. "Conventionalism in Morals and the Appeal
   to Human Nature." Philosophy and Phenomenological Research
   23(1962/63):217-31.

————. "On Taking Human Nature as the Basis of Morality."
   Social Research 29(1962):157-76.

Passerin d'Entrèves, Alessandro. Natural Law. London:
   Hutchinson's University Library, 1951.

Passmore, John. "Attitudes to Nature." Appears in P:NC,

BIBLIOGRAPHY

pp. 251-64.

Phillips, D[ewi] Z. "The Possibilities of Moral Advice."

Analysis 25(1964/65):37-41. Also reprinted in Moral

Practices, by D[ewi] Z. Phillips and H.O. Mounce.

New York: Schocken Books, 1970. Also in H:IOQ.

Phillips discusses Black's article mentioned above.

Quinton, Anthony M. "Ethics and the Theory of Evolution."

Appears in Biology and Personality: Frontier Problems

in Science, Philosophy, and Religion. Edited by Ian T.

Ramsey. Oxford: Basil Blackwell, 1965.

He considers critically the views of Herbert Spencer,

W.K. Clifford, T.H. Huxley, C.H. Waddington, and

J.S. Huxley, and he finds all of them wanting. See

pp. 107-31.

————. "Has Man an Essence?" Appears in P:NC, pp. 14-35.

Seneca. Letters from a Stoic. Translated by Robin Campbell.

Baltimore: Penguin Books, 1969.

Spencer, Herbert. The Principles of Ethics. New York:

D. Appleton & Co., 1895.

Thoreau, Henry David. The Annotated Walden. Edited by

Philip van Doren Stern. New York: Clarkson N. Potter,

1970.

Veatch, Henry B. For an Ontology of Morals: A Critique of

BIBLIOGRAPHY

Contemporary Ethical Theory. Evanston: Northwestern
University Press, 1971.
Gives an overview of analytic ethics.

————. "Natural Law: Dead or Alive." Literature of
Liberty 1(1978):7-31.
His answer: "It's very much alive!"

————. Rational Man: A Modern Interpretation of Aristotelian Ethics. Bloomington: Indiana University Press,
1962.

Waddington, C.H. "Naturalism in Ethics and Biology."
Philosophy 37(1962):357-61.

Williams, Cora M. A Review of the Systems of Ethics Founded
on the Theory of Evolution. New York: Macmillan & Co.,
1893.

Wilson, Edward O. Sociobiology: A New Synthesis. Cambridge:
Harvard University Press, 1975.

Wollheim, Richard. "Natural Law." Appears in E:EP, vol. 5,
pp. 450-54.

Kant's Ethics: First Version

Acton, H[arry] B. Kant's Moral Philosophy. New York: St.
Martin's Press, 1970.

Aune, Bruce. Kant's Theory of Morals. Princeton: Princeton

BIBLIOGRAPHY

University Press, 1979.

Aune takes into account all of Kant's principal writings
on morality and presents them in a contemporary idiom.

Beck, Lewis W. A Commentary on Kant's Critique of Practical
Reason. Chicago: University of Chicago Press, 1960.

Carritt, E.F. "Moral Positivism and Moral Aestheticism,"
an excerpt of which is reprinted in SH:RET(1952), pp.
405-14.

Dietrichson, P[aul]. "What Does Kant Mean by 'Acting from
Duty'?" Kant Studien 53(1961/62):277-88. Also in
W:K.

Frankena, William K. Ethics. Englewood Cliffs: Prentice-Hall,
1963.

On Kant's ethics. See esp. pp. 16-18, 25-29, 51, 53, 55, 96.

Gewirth, Alan. "Categorial Consistency in Ethics."
Philosophical Quarterly 17(1967):289-99.

Glass, Ronald. "The Contradictions in Kant's Examples."
Philosophical Studies 22(1971):65-70.

Haezrahi, Pepita. "The Concept of Man as an End-in-Himself."
Kant Studien 53(1961/62):209-24.

Hare, R[ichard] M. "Universalisability." Proceedings of the
Aristotelian Society 55(1954/55):295-312.

Harrison, J[onathan]. "Kant's Examples of the First Formulation

BIBLIOGRAPHY

of the Categorical Imperative." With comments by John Kemp and reply. Philosophical Quarterly 7,8(1957/58): 228-58. Also in W:K.

Hochberg, Gary M. "A Re-Examination of the Contradictions in Kant's Examples." Philosophical Studies 24(1973): 264-67.

Kalin, Jesse. "A Note on Singer and Kant." Ethics 78(1967/68):234-36.

Kant, Immanuel. Critique of Practical Reason. Translated by Lewis White Beck. New York: The Bobbs-Merrill Co., 1956.

u   ————. Lectures on Ethics. Translated by Lewis Infield. New York: Harper & Row, 1963.

u   ————. The Moral Law: Or, Kant's Groundwork of the Metaphysic of Morals. Translated by H.J. Paton. New York: Harper & Row, 1964.

————. "On a Supposed Right to Tell Lies from Benevolent Motives." Reprinted as an appendix in Kant's Critique of Practical Reason and Other Works on the Theory of Ethics. Translated by Thomas K. Abbott. London: Longmans, Green & Co., 1898. See pp. 361-65.

Kemp, John. Reason, Action and Morality. New York: Humanities Press, 1964. See chap. 5.

Körner, Stephan. Kant. Baltimore: Penguin Books, 1955.

BIBLIOGRAPHY

See chaps. 5, 6.

Lo, Ping-cheung. "A Critical Reevaluation of the Alleged
'Empty Formalism' of Kantian Ethics." Ethics 91(1981):
181-201.

Murphy, Jeffrie G. Kant: The Philosophy of Right. New York:
St. Martin's Press, 1970.

Paton, Herbert J. "An Alleged Right to Lie: A Problem in
Kantian Ethics." Kant Studien 45(1953/54):190-203.

—————. The Categorical Imperative: A Study in Kant's
Moral Philosophy. New York: Harper & Row, 1967.

Ross, Sir William D. Kant's Ethical Theory: A Commentary on
the Grundlegung zur Metaphysik der Sitten. Oxford:
Clarendon Press, 1954.

Singer, Marcus G. "The Categorical Imperative." Philosophical
Review 63(1954):577-91.
This also forms a part of his Generalization in Ethics.
New York: Atheneum, 1971.

Williams, Terence C. The Concept of the Categorical Imperative:
A Study of the Place of the Categorical Imperative in
Kant's Ethical Theory. Oxford: Clarendon Press, 1968.

Wolff, R[obert] P. The Autonomy of Reason: A Commentary on
Kant's Groundwork of the Metaphysic of Morals. New York:
Harper & Row, 1973.

BIBLIOGRAPHY

Agapism and the Second Version of Kant's Ethics

Barth, Karl. Church Dogmatics: A Selection. Translated by
G.W. Bromiley. New York: Harper & Brothers, 1962.

Beehler, Rodger. Moral Life. Totowa: Rowman & Littlefield,
1978.

Donagan, Alan. The Theory of Morality. Chicago: University
of Chicago Press, 1977.

Downie, R[obert] S., and Telfer, E[lizabeth]. Respect for
Persons. New York: Schocken Books, 1970.

Ebreo, Leone. The Philosophy of Love. Translated by
F. Friedeberg-Seeley and Jean H. Barnes. London:
Soncino Press, 1937.

Frankena, William K. "Love and Principle in Christian Ethics,"
in Faith and Philosophy. Edited by Alvin Plantinga.
Grand Rapids: William B. Eerdmans Publishing Co., 1964.
See pp. 203-25. Also reprinted in F:PM.

Freud, Sigmund. Civilization and Its Discontents. Translated
by James Strachey. New York: W.W. Norton & Co., 1961.
See pp. 48-62.

Fromm, Erich. The Art of Loving. New York: Harper & Row,
1962.

Geach, P[eter] T. God and the Soul. New York: Schocken Books,
1969.

BIBLIOGRAPHY

Gilleman, Gérard, S.J. The Primacy of Charity in Moral Theology.
    Translated by William F. Ryan, S.J., and André Vachon, S.J.
    Westminster: Newman Press, 1961.

Harris, E.E. "Respect for Persons," in Ethics and Society.
    Edited by Richard T. De George. Garden City: Anchor
    Books, 1966.

Kant, Immanuel. See references given under previous heading,
    Kantian Ethics: First Version.

Kierkegaard, Søren. Works of Love. Translated by Howard and
    Edna Hong. New York: Harper & Brothers, 1962.

Maclagan, W.G. "Respect for Persons as a Moral Principle."
    Philosophy 35(July & October, 1960):193-217, 289-305.

Montefiore, Alan. "Self-Reality, Self-Respect, and Respect
    for Others." Appears in FUW:SET, pp. 195-208.

Mo Tzu. Mo Tzu; Basic Writings. Translated by Burton Watson.
    New York: Columbia University Press, 1963.

Niebuhr, Reinhold. The Nature and Destiny of Man. 2 vols.
    New York: Charles Scribner's Sons, 1949.

Nygren, Anders. Agape and Eros. Translated by Philip S.
    Watson. Philadelphia: The Westminster Press, 1953.

Outka, Gene. Agape: An Ethical Analysis. New Haven: Yale
    University Press, 1972.

    A comprehensive account of modern treatments of the love

commandment.

Ramsey, Paul. <u>Basic Christian Ethics</u>. New York: Charles
Scribner's Sons, 1950. See esp. pp. 165-84, 326-66.

Rollin, Bernard E. <u>Animal Rights and Human Morality</u>. Buffalo:
Prometheus Books, 1981.
See esp. pp. 9, 15-19, 51, 73, 78, 93, 116, and 147 for
criticisms of Kantian ethics and agapism.

Singer, Irving. <u>The Nature of Love: Plato to Luther</u>. New
York: Random House, 1966.

Stob, Henry. "The Concept of Love: Eros and Agape," in
<u>Ethical Reflections: Essays on Moral Themes</u>. Grand
Rapids: Eerdmans Publishing, 1978. See pp. 113-22.

Zemach, Eddy M. "Love thy Neighbor as Thyself or Egoism and
Altruism." Appears in <u>FUW:SET</u>, pp. 148-58.

<u>Source and Justification of Morality and Moral Codes</u>

Balfour, James. "On the Idea of a Philosophy of Ethics."
Appears in <u>SH:RET</u>, pp. 645-55.
Deals with the problem of proving or justifying the
propositions which lie at the root of any system of
morals.

Bhattacharyya, N.C. "Mr. Taylor on Justifying a Way of Life."
<u>Indian Journal of Philosophy</u> 3(1961/62):204-206.

BIBLIOGRAPHY

Tries to show that Taylor's method of "Justifying a
Way of Life" (same journal, 1961) is inadequate.

Daniels, Norman. "Wide Reflective Equilibrium." Journal of
Philosophy 76(1977):256-82.

Downie, R[obert] S., and Telfer, E[lizabeth]. "Autonomy."
Philosophy 46(1971):293-301.

Ewing, Alfred C. "The Autonomy of Ethics." Appears in
Prospects for Metaphysics: Essays of Metaphysical
Exploration. Edited by Ian T. Ramsey. New York:
Greenwood Press, 1969.
Tries to show that it is impossible to construct a
natural theology which leads deductively to ethical
conclusions. See pp. 33-49.

Frankena, William K. "Three Questions about Morality."
With comments by Alan Gewirth, G.J. Warnock, and Harald
Ofstad. Monist 63(1980):3-68.
See esp. Lecture I ("Must Morality Have an Object?"), and
Lecture III("Has Morality an Independent Bottom?").

Gewirth, Alan. Reason and Morality. Chicago: University of
Chicago Press, 1978.
Tries to provide a rational basis for morality.

u   Hare, R[ichard] M. "The Argument from Received Opinion."
Appears in H:EPM, pp. 117-35.

BIBLIOGRAPHY

Harkness, Georgia E. The Sources of Western Morality from
   Primitive Society through the Beginnings of Christianity.
   New York: Charle's Scribners Sons, 1958.
   An exploration of the ancient origins of modern ethics.
Holland, R.F. "The Autonomy of Ethics." Proceedings of the
   Aristotelian Society, Supplementary Volume 32(1958):25-
   48.
   Part of a symposium. See H.D. Lewis on the same topic.
Kropotkin, Prince [Petr] A. Ethics, Origin and Development.
   Translated by Louis S. Friedland and Joseph R. Piroshnikoff.
   New York: Dial Press, 1924.
   A Marxist account of the development of ethics from
   primitive to modern Western society.
Kurtzman, D[avid] R. "'Is', 'Ought' and the Autonomy of
   Ethics." Philosophical Review 79(1970):493-509.
Lecky, William E.H. History of European Morals, from Augustus
   to Charlemagne. 3d ed. 2 vols. New York: D.
   Appleton & Co., 1929.
Lewis, H.D. "The Autonomy of Ethics." Proceedings of the
   Aristotelian Society, Supplementary Volume 32(1958):
   49-74.
   Part of a symposium. See R.F. Holland on the same topic.
Mardiros, A[nthony] M. "A Circular Procedure in Ethics."

BIBLIOGRAPHY

Philosophical Review 61(1952):223-25.

Nielsen, Kai. "Can a Way of Life Be Justified?" Indian
Journal of Philosophy 1 (1960):164-74.

—————. Ethics without God. Buffalo: Prometheus Books,
1973.
An effort to show that ethics is an autonomous field
without need of a theological foundation.

—————. "Is 'Why Should I Be Moral?' an Absurdity?"
Australasian Journal of Philosophy 36(1958):25-32.

—————. "Why Should I Be Moral?" Methodos 15(1963):275-306.

Peach, Bernard. "C.I. Lewis and the Foundations of Ethics."
Noûs 9(1975):211-25.

Pepper, Stephen C. The Sources of Value. Berkeley: University
of California Press, 1958.

Perry, T[homas] D. "Moral Autonomy and Reasonableness."
Journal of Philosophy 65(1968):383-401.

Phillips, D[ewi] Z. "Does It Pay to be Good?" Proceedings
of the Aristotelian Society 65(1964/65):45-60.   Also in
TD:E.

Phillips, D[ewi] Z., and Mounce, H.O. "On Morality's Having
a Point." Philosophy 40(1965):308-19. Also in H:IOQ,
T:PMP. A revised version appears in D[ewi] Phillips
and H.O. Mounce, Moral Practices. New York: Schocken

BIBLIOGRAPHY

Books, 1970.

Prior, Arthur N. "The Autonomy of Ethics." Australasian
Journal of Philosophy 38(1960):199-206.

Remnant, Peter. "Professor Rynin on the Autonomy of Morals."
Mind 68(1959):252-55.

Rhees, Rush. "Some Developments in Wittgenstein's View of
Ethics." Philosophical Review 74(1965):17-26. Also
reprinted in Discussions of Wittgenstein. New York:
Schocken Books, 1970.

Rynin, D[avid]. "The Autonomy of Morals." Mind 66(1957):
308-17.

u   Schneewind, J[erome] B. "First Principles and Common Sense
Morality in Sidgwick's Ethics." Archiv für Geschichte
der Philosophie 45(1963):137-56.

Shorter, J.M. "Prof. Prior on the Autonomy of Ethics."
Australasian Journal of Philosophy 39(1961):286-87.

Sidgwick, Henry. The Method of Ethics. 7th ed. London:
Macmillan & Co., 1907. See pp. 363 ff.

Singer, Peter. "Sidgwick and Reflective Equilibrium."
Monist 58(1974):490-517.

Smart, J[ohn] J.C. "The Methods of Ethics and the Methods
of Science." Journal of Philosophy 62(1965):344-49.

Stern, K[enneth]. "Testing Ethical Theories." Journal of

BIBLIOGRAPHY

Philosophy 63(1966):234-38.

Stocks, John Leofric. Morality and Purpose. Edited by

D[ewi] Z. Phillips. London: Routledge & Kegan Paul,

1969.

Taylor, Paul W. "On Justifying a Way of Life." Indian

Journal of Philosophy 2(1961):163-75.

Thornton, J.C. "Can the Moral Point of View Be Justified?"

Australasian Journal of Philosophy 42(1964):22-34.

Veatch, Henry B. "The Rational Justification of Moral

Principles: Can There Be Such a Thing?" Review of

Metaphysics 29(1975/76):217-38.

Walsh, W[illiam] H. "The Autonomy of Ethics." Philosophical

Quarterly 7(1957):1-14.

Warnock, G[eoffrey] J. The Object of Morality. London:

Methuen & Co., 1971.

Westermarck, Edward. The Origin and Development of the Moral

Ideas. New York: Macmillan & Co., 1906.

Wiggins, David. "Truth, Invention, and the Meaning of Life."

Proceedings of the British Academy 62(1976):331-78.

Suggests that Wittgenstein's philosophy of mathematics

yields a model for a satisfactory conception of the

metaphysics of value.

BIBLIOGRAPHY

Moral Skepticism and Objectivity in Morals

u   Aiken, Henry D. "The Concept of Moral Objectivity."

        Appears in A:RC, pp. 134-70; CN:MLC, pp. 69-105.

Bambrough, Renford. Moral Scepticism and Moral Knowledge.

        Atlantic Highlands: Humanities Press, 1979.

        A defense of the objectivity of moral judgment.

————. "A Proof of the Objectivity of Morals." American

        Journal of Jurisprudence 14(1969):37-53. Also in R:UMP.

u   Blackburn, S[imon] W. "Moral Realism." Appears in C:MMR,

        pp. 101-24.

————. "Rule-following and Moral Realism." Appears in

        HL:WFR, pp. 163-87.

        Defends a projective, Humean picture of morality against

        moral realism. Part of a colloquium with John McDowell.

Britton, Karl. "On Knowing the Difference between Right

        and Wrong." Proceedings of the Aristotelian Society,

        Supplementary Volume 37(1963):1-10.

Cavell, Stanley, and Sesonske, Alexander. "Moral Theory,

        Ethical Judgments and Empiricism." Mind 61(1952):543-63.

Cherry, Christopher. "Agreement, Objectivity and the Sentiment

        of Humanity in Morals." Appears in P:NC, pp. 83-98.

Cohen, F.M. "Knowledge and Moral Belief." Australasian

        Journal of Philosophy 43(1965):168-88.

BIBLIOGRAPHY

u   Cooper, N[eil]. "Rules and Morality." <u>Proceedings of the</u>
       <u>Aristotelian Society, Supplementary Volume</u> 33(1959):
       159-72.

u   Edwards, Paul. <u>The Logic of Moral Discourse</u>. Glencoe:
       Free Press, 1955. See pp. 66-75, and chap. 5.

Ehman, Robert R. "Moral Objectivity." <u>Philosophy and</u>
       <u>Phenomenological Research</u> 28(1967):175-87.

Flew, A[ntony]. "Must Morality Pay? or What Socrates Should
       Have Said to Thrasymachus." Appears in <u>C:SMP</u>, pp. 109-33.

Foot, P[hilippa] R. "The Philosopher's Defence of Morality."
       <u>Philosophy</u> 27(1952):311-28.

Gass, William. "The Case of the Obliging Stranger."
       <u>Philosophical Review</u> 66(1957):193-204.

u   Gewirth, Alan. "Must One Play the Moral Language Game?"
       <u>American Philosophical Quarterly</u> 7(1970):107-18.

Harrison, Jonathan. "Ethical Objectivism." Appears in
       <u>E:EP</u>, vol. 3, pp. 71-75.

————. "Moral Scepticism." <u>Proceedings of the Aristotelian</u>
       <u>Society, Supplementary Volume</u> 41(1967):199-214.
       Part of a symposium. See also R.F. Holland on the same
       topic.

Holland, R.F. "Moral Scepticism." <u>Proceedings of the</u>
       <u>Aristotelian Society, Supplementary Volume</u> 41(1967):185-98.

Part of a symposium. See also Jonathan Harrison on the
same topic.

Hudson, W[illiam] D. "On the Alleged Objectivity of Moral
Judgments." Mind 71(1962):530-34.

Hume, David. Treatise of Human Nature. Edited by L.A. Selby-
Bigge. Oxford: Clarendon Press, 1955.
Bk. 3, part 1, is a classic criticism of objectivism.

Kneale, William. "Objectivity in Morals." Philosophy 25
(1950):149-66. Also in SH:RET (1952).

Kupperman, Joel J. Ethical Knowledge. New York: Humanities
Press, 1970. See part 2.

Mabbott, J.D. "True and False in Morals." Proceedings of the
Aristotelian Society 49(1948/49):133-50.

u   Mackie, J[ohn] L. "A Refutation of Morals." Australasian
Journal of Philosophy 24(1946):77-90.

Mayo, B[ernard]. "A Correspondence Theory of Value."
Proceedings of the Aristotelian Society 73(1972/73):181-
92.

————. "Objectivity in Morals." Philosophy 26(1951):85-88.

u   McClosky, H.J. "A Difficulty for Some Nonobjectivist Metaethics." Philosophical Studies 14(1963):81-82.

McDowell, John. "Non-cognitivism and Rule-following."
Appears in HL:WFR, pp. 141-62.

BIBLIOGRAPHY

Argues against both non-cognitivism and a full-blown
moral platonism and in favor of some sort of intermediate
position. Part of a colloquium with Simon Blackburn.

Meynell, H[ugo]. "The Objectivity of Value Judgments."
Philosophical Quarterly 21(1971):118-31.

u   Nielsen, Kai. "On Moral Truth." Appears in R:SMP, pp. 9-25.

Pettit, Philip. "Evaluative 'Realism' and Interpretation."
Appears in HL:WFR, pp. 211-45.
Offers an account of realism and anti-realism and a
limited defense of Taylor's position. Part of a
colloquium with Charles Taylor.

Phillips, D[ewi] Z., and Mounce, H.O. Moral Practices.
New York: Schocken Books, 1970.

Pincoffs, E[dmund] L. "Objectivity and Henry Aiken."
Journal of Philosophy 61(1964):192-97.

Price, Richard. A Review of the Principal Questions in Morals.
Edited by D. Daiches Raphael. Oxford: Clarendon Press,
1948.
This is a classical and influential defense of one form
of objectivism.

Rhees, Rush. "Some Developments in Wittgenstein's View of
Ethics." Philosophical Review 74(1965):17-26. Also in
Rhees's Discussions of Wittgenstein. New York: Schocken

BIBLIOGRAPHY

Books, 1970.

Ryle, Gilbert. "On Forgetting the Difference between Right
and Wrong." Appears in M:EMP, pp. 147-59.

Sartre, Jean-Paul. Existentialism and Human Emotions.
Translated by Bernard Frechtman and Hazel B. Barnes.
New York: Philosophical Library, 1957.

Sellars, Roy W. "In What Sense Do Value Judgments and Moral
Judgments Have Objective Import?" Philosophy and
Phenomenological Research 28(1967):1-16.

Sidgwick, Henry. "Symposium——Is the Distinction between
'Is' and 'Ought' Ultimate and Irreducible?" Proceedings
of the Aristotelian Society 2(1892):88-92.

u   Singer, M[arcus] G. "Moral Scepticism." Appears in C:SMP,
pp. 77-108.

u   Swinburne, R[ichard] G. "The Objectivity of Morality."
Philosophy 51(1976):5-20.
Argues for objectivism.

Taylor, Charles. "Understanding and Explanation in the
Geisteswissenschaften." Appears in HL:WFR, pp. 191-210.
Defends a realist position on value. Part of a colloquium
with Philip Pettit.

Jarvis [Thomson], Judith. "In Defense of Moral Absolutes."
Journal of Philosophy 55(1958):1043-53.

BIBLIOGRAPHY

Walsh, W[illiam] H. "Scepticism about Morals and Scepticism
about Knowledge." Philosophy 35(1960):218-33.

Wellman, Carl. "Ethical Disagreement and Objective Truth."
American Philosophical Quarterly 12(1975):211-21.

Wittgenstein, Ludwig. "A Lecture on Ethics." Philosophical
Review 74(1965):3-12.

Psychological Egoism

Butler, Joseph. "A Dissertation upon the Nature of Virtue."
Added to The Analogy of Religion, Natural and Revealed.
New York: E.P. Dutton & Co., 1906.

————. Fifteen Sermons Preached at the Rolls Chapel.
London: G. Bell & Sons, 1964. See esp. his Preface and
Sermons 1 and 11.

Feinberg, Joel. Reason and Responsibility: Readings in Some
Basic Problems of Philosophy. 3rd ed. Encino: Dickenson
Publishing Co., 1974. See pp. 501-12.

Frankena, William K. Ethics. Englewood Cliffs: Prentice-Hall,
1963. See pp. 19-21.

Hume, David. Appendix 2 of his Enquiry Concerning the Principles
of Morals. 2d ed. Edited by L.A. Selby-Bigge. Oxford:
Clarendon Press, 1951.

MacIntyre, Alasdair. "Egoism and Altruism." Appears in E:EP, vol. 2, pp. 462-66.

Sartre, Jean-Paul. The Transcendence of the Ego: An Existentialist Theory of Consciousness. Translated by Forrest William and Robert Kirkpatrick. New York: The Noonday Press, 1957. See chap. 1, sec., c.

Schlick, Moritz. Problems of Ethics. Translated by David Rynin. New York: Dover Publications, 1962. See pp. 56-78.

"Ordinary Language" Philosophy

Austin, J.L. "A Plea for Excuses." Proceedings of the Aristotelian Society 57(1956/57):1-29. Reprinted in C:OL, L:PL.

An excellent account of his way of doing philosophy.

Cavell, Stanley. "The Availability of Wittgenstein's Later Philosophy." Philosophical Review 71(1962):67-93.

Also in L:PL.

Explains the relevance of Wittgenstein's appeal to every-day language.

──────. "Must We Mean What We Say?" Inquiry 1(1958):172-212.

Also in C:OL, L:PL.

Tries to show that some of the arguments Benson Mates brings against Ryle and Austin are irrelevant to their

BIBLIOGRAPHY

main concerns. An excellent defense and clarification
of so-called ordinary-language philosophy.

Fodor, Jerry A., and Katz, J.J. "The Availability of What
We Say." Philosophical Review 72(1963):57-71. Also in
L:PL.
An attempt to refute Cavell's position and to discredit
ordinary-language philosophy.

Hare, R[ichard] M. "Philosophical Discoveries." Mind 69(1960):
145-62. Also in L:PL.
An important article on ordinary-language methodology.
Makes many of the same points Cavell makes in defense
of it.

Henson, Richard G. "What We Say." American Philosophical
Quarterly 2(1965):52-62. Also in L:PL.
A reply to Fodor and Katz's attack on Cavell and ordinary-
language philosophy.

Mates, Benson. "On the Verification of Statements about
Ordinary Language." Inquiry 1(1958):161-71. Also
appears in C:OL, L:PL.
A criticism of the work of so-called ordinary-language
philosophers, for example, Ryle and Austin.

Ryle, Gilbert. "Ordinary Language." Proceedings of the
Aristotelian Society, Supplementary Volume 28(1954):77-94.

BIBLIOGRAPHY

Also reprinted in C:OL, L:PL.

Tries to correct some misunderstandings of ordinary-
language philosophy and of what is meant by 'ordinary
language'.

Weitz, Morris. "Oxford Philosophy." Philosophical Review
62(1953):187-233.

A clear and useful account of Oxford and so-called
ordinary-language philosophy.

Wittgenstein, Ludwig. Philosophical Investigations. 3rd ed.
Translated by G.E.M. Anscombe. New York: Macmillan &
Co., 1958.

Probably the most important work in the "later" philosophy
of Wittgenstein.

Glossary of Relevant Philosophical Terms

The following guide is not comprehensive. It is simple a glossary of common terms you have been introduced to in this book, and will probably encounter reading other philosophical works, especially in ethics. Any term underlined is defined separately.

aesthetic — of, relating to, or dealing with aesthetics or the beautiful (aesthetic theory). Artistic (a work of aesthetic value).

aesthetics — a branch of philosophy dealing with the nature of art, beauty, the sublime, the pretty, meaning in art, artistic criticism, the form-content distinction, etc.

agape — love expressed freely and without calculation of cost or gain to the giver or the merit of the loved one. The love of God for man is held to be its highest manifestation. Christian brotherly love strives to be like this. Distinguished from eros and philia.

agapism — the ethics of love. It maintains that what is morally right is to love your neighbor—that is, everyone—equally and as much as yourself, with agape love.

agnostic — one who doubts the knowability of God or who is noncommittal about His existence and nonexistence.

amoral — nonmoral. An amoral person, or amoralist, is one without moral values.

appeal to nature (in ethics) — the view that the morally right thing to do is what is natural or in harmony with nature. Sin, or wrongdoing, is to go against nature. It may be interpreted as either an approbative or an objectivist theory.

approbative theory — one that determines what is morally right or wrong, good or bad, solely on the basis of someone's, or a group's, approving, or disapproving, or having a pro, or con, attitude towards it. Not to be confused with either emotivism or a noncognitive theory.

argument	the <u>reasons</u> (<u>proof</u>, <u>evidence</u>) offered in support or denial of something. In logic, a series of statements called <u>premises</u> logically related to a further statement called the <u>conclusion</u>. Arguments are divided into two general categories: <u>deductive</u> and <u>inductive</u>.

axiological theory
a theory that makes obligations dependent on <u>values</u>.

axiology
the study of <u>values</u> in general (in <u>aesthetics</u>, economics, and the like, as well as in <u>ethics</u>).

begging the question
the fallacy of assuming the <u>conclusion</u> of an <u>argument</u> by using the conclusion as a <u>premise</u>. It is called begging the question because a person who does this assumes the truth of the very point raised in the question. Example: responding to a question about <u>psychological egoism</u>, I try to show that people always acts selfishly by giving an argument that assumes that people always act selfishly.

Categorical Imperative
see <u>Imperative, Categorical</u>.

circularity
circular reasoning or arguing in a circle. Applied as a criticism to views, <u>arguments</u>, reasoning, definitions, that repeat themselves. Thus it would be circular to define what is morally right, or wrong, in terms of itself.

cognition
knowing or being aware of something.

cognitive
of, relating to, or involving <u>cognition</u>. Thus a cognitive judgment has a <u>truth-value</u> and is meaningful, and a sentence that has <u>cognitive significance</u> can be used to express a thought.

cognitivist, ethical
someone who contends that <u>moral judgments</u> or statements are meaningful and can be true or false.

cognitive meaning or significance
a sentence or judgment has <u>cognitive</u> meaning or significance if it can be used to express a thought or to say something true or false.

conclusion   a statement that has been or can be inferred from other statements. It is often introduced with words like 'therefore', 'consequently', 'hence', etc.

condition, necessary
   a necessary condition for something is one without which the thing would not exist or occur. Example: being a male is a necessary condition for being a bachelor, since if there were no males, there would be no bachelors.

condition, sufficient
   a sufficient condition for something is one given which the thing does exist or occur. Example: being a wife is a sufficient condition for being a female, since if there is a wife, there is a female.

consequentialism (in ethics)
   the view that the moral rightness or obligatoriness of an act can be determined solely by the goodness or badness of its consequences. Deontologists reject this view.

contradiction something that is false no matter what state the world is in. Example: "The ball has exactly a three inch diameter and it does not have exactly a three inch diameter, at one and the same time."

conventionalism (in ethics)
   an approbative theory that makes what is morally right (or wrong) rest on its being approved (or disapproved) of by a group of people. Closely related to subjectivism.

deductive argument
   an argument whose conclusion should be logically implied by its premises. It is a valid deductive argument whenever its conclusion necessarily follows from, or is implied by, its premises. In such a case, if the premises of the argument are true, the conclusion must also be true.

definist mistake or fallacy (in ethics)
   the alleged mistake or fallacy of attempting to define moral or ethical terms by terms which are not themselves moral or ethical. This is also called the naturalistic fallacy.

definite description

a referring expression of the form 'the such and such', for example, 'the President of the United States in 1985' or 'the greatest phoney ever'. It is typically used to pick out one unique individual or thing. Cf. and contrast proper names.

deontologist

someone who holds a deontological view.

deontological view

one that denies that the moral rightness (or wrongnes) of an act is entirely dependent on the goodness, or badness, of its consequences. Contrasted with consequentialism. See deontologist, moderate and extreme.

deontologist, extreme

someone who holds that the goodness or badness of an act's consequences never has anything to do with its moral rightness or wrongness. Cf. and contrast deontologist, moderate. Contrast consequentialism.

deontologist, moderate

someone who denies that you can determine the moral rightness or wrongness of an act solely on the basis of the goodness or badness of its consequences, but who nevertheless grants that an act's good or bad consequences are relevant to the question whether it is morally right or wrong. Hence more moderate than a deontologist, extreme variety. Cf. and contrast consequentialism.

dissolution of a moral disagreement

the vanishing of a moral disagreement, but not by the parties' agreeing to perform one of the disputed actions.

dissolution of a moral problem

the vanishing of a moral problem, but not by the agent's choosing one of the actions he or she is torn between on the basis of moral or other deeply cherished values and beliefs.

divine-command theory

an approbative theory. It makes the moral rightness (or wrongness) of an act depend on God's approval (or disapproval).

egoism, ethical   an <u>objectivist theory</u>. It determines the moral rightness or wrongness of an action solely on the basis of the goodness or badness of its actual or probable long-range consequences for the self. Personal (individual or specific) ethical egoism is different from impersonal (universal or general) ethical egoism. See <u>egoism, impersonal ethical</u> and <u>egoism, personal ethical</u>.

egoism, impersonal ethical
the view that an action is morally right if and only if it is actually or probably in the overall self-interest of the agent performing it.

egoism, personal ethical
the view that an action is morally right if and only if it is actually or probably in my overall self-interest, that is, it actually or probably benefits me in the long run, where 'me' is to be replaced in all its occurrences by a proper name or a <u>definite description</u> (something of the form 'the such and such').

egoism, psychological
the doctrine that every voluntary act is determined solely by a desire of the agent to maximize his or her own welfare.

emotivism   the doctrine that <u>moral</u> and other value judgments lack <u>cognitive meaning</u> and <u>truth-value</u> and only function to express the judger's feelings and/or to arouse similar feelings in others. They are held not to be judgments in the strict sense, but to be emotive. A noncognitive, nonapprobative view that also rejects objectivism.

empirical   derived from, or related to, experience, especially observation.

enthymeme   a <u>syllogism</u> in which one of the <u>premises</u> is implicit.

epistemological   having to do with knowledge.

epistemology   theory of knowledge. That branch of philosophy that investigates the nature, origin, and limits of knowledge, belief, and <u>evidence</u>.

eros	possessive desire or love, commonly sensual, sexual, or erotic. Distinguished from <u>agape</u> (brotherly love) and <u>philia</u> (personal affection or fondness).
ethical definism	the view that ethical terms can be defined exclusively by the use of nonethical, or empirical and logical, terms. Some philosophers think this view is fallacious or a mistake. See <u>definist mistake or fallacy</u> and the <u>naturalistic fallacy</u>.
ethics	moral philosophy or philosophical thinking about <u>morality</u>, <u>moral problems</u>, <u>moral reasons</u>, and <u>moral judgments</u>. That branch of philosophy that inquires into what it is to be a moral person and how people ought to act morally. Some of the primary concepts it is concerned with are ought, obligation, duty, right, wrong, the desirable, the good, and the bad.
eudaemonia	happiness or well-being, acclaimed by Aristotle as the universally recognized chief good for human beings.

eudaemonistic theory
one that defines or explains moral obligation by reference to happiness or personal well-being, where happiness and personal well-being are distinguished from mere pleasure. Contrasted with <u>hedonistic theory</u> or <u>hedonism</u>.

Euthyphro objection (to the <u>divine-command theory</u>)
the objection that things are commanded by God for the reason that they are morally right; they are not morally right for the reason that they are commanded by God.

evidence	that which tends, or is used, to prove or to support some <u>conclusion</u> or claim.
extension	all the things to which a term truly applies. Thus the extension of the term 'human being' is all the human beings. Contrasted with <u>intension</u>.

extensional equivalence
two terms or expressions are extensionally equivalent if and only if they apply truly to the same things.

golden rule	do unto others as you would want others to do unto you (positive formulation). Do not do to others what you would not want done to you (negative

formulation). If interpreted literally, it is an approbative view.

good, extrinsic or instrumental
    that which is desired or valued as a means to something else that is valued in and for itself. See value, extrinsic or instrumental.

good, intrinsic or ultimate
    that which is desired or valued in and for itself. Example: pleasure. See value, intrinsic or ultimate.

hedonism, ethical
    the doctrine that pleasure and the absence of pain are the only intrinsic goods.

hedonism, psychological
    the doctrine that all human actions are motivated solely by the desire to secure pleasure for the agent and to avoid pain. A form of psychological egoism.

hedonistic calculus
    Jeremy Bentham's method of determining which actions produce the greatest amount of pleasure over pain. It takes into account the pleasure's (and the pain's) intensity, duration, extent, propinquity (nearness), certainty, fecundity (fruitfulness or fertility), and purity (the degree to which it is mixed with its opposite, which in the case of pleasure is pain, and in the case of pain is pleasure).

hedonistic theory (in ethics)
    one which considers pleasure and the absence of pain to be the only intrinsic goods.

immoral
    not moral, in the sense of being wicked or morally wrong. Immoral conduct is unvirtuous conduct.

immoral conduct
    acting contrary to morality; unvirtuous conduct.

imperative, hypothetical
    an imperative that is conditional on a wish or a desire. Example: "If you want to fight alcoholism, then you must (or ought) to support Alcoholics Anonymous." Distinguished from Imperative, Categorical or from unconditional imperatives.

Imperative, Categorical (in the philosophy of Kant)
the unconditional <u>moral</u> law for all rational beings. Kant's formulation of it: "Act only according to a <u>maxim</u> by which you can at the same time will that it shall become a universal law." His other formulations of it are all supposed to be formulations of one and the same imperative. Distinguished from <u>imperative, hypothetical</u>.

inductive argument
an <u>argument</u> in which the <u>conclusion</u> expresses something that does not follow with logical necessity from the <u>premises</u>. Example: the weather forecaster's reasons for thinking it will rain do not logically imply that it will but constitute an inductive argument in support of that conclusion. This kind of argument is contrasted with a <u>deductive argument</u>.

infinite-regress objection
objection that a certain view or <u>argument</u> leads to an infinite regress, that is, is a never-ending act of reasoning backward.

intension
meaning, sense, or connotation of a word or expression. For example, the intension of 'triangle' includes that of 'plane figure'. Contrasted with <u>extension</u>.

intensionality
a characteristic of certain concepts (belief, hunting, wanting, looking for, desiring, etc.), but not of others (shooting, wounding, hitting, touching, etc.). Belief (and desire) are intensional relations because something believed (or desired) under one description might not be believed (or desired) under another description of one and the same thing. In contrast, shooting is a nonintensional relation because something shot under one description must be shot under another description of one and the same thing.

intuitionism (mathematical)
the name given to the school of mathematics founded by L. E. Brouwer (1881-1966). Its insistence on intuitively understandable construction as the only method for mathematical existence proofs leads to a rejection of certain methods and assumptions of classical mathematics. For example, it denies the universal validity of the <u>law of excluded middle</u>.

This carries with it the rejection of the <u>law of double negation</u>, and hence the method of indirect proof (<u>proof, indirect</u>).

intuitionism (in ethics)
the traditional <u>objectivist</u> doctrine that there is an immediate awareness that is neither deductive nor inductive of the moral rightness or wrongness of particular actions (Prichard); of kinds of actions (Ross); or of the intrinsic goodness or badness of things (Moore). Suter's modified form of Rawlsian intuitionism is also an objectivist view that denies that there is either a single moral principle, or priority rules for a plurality of such principles, to determine what is morally right.

justificatory
tending or serving to justify; justificatory reasons are contrasted with mere causes.

Kant's ethics
an <u>objectivist</u> view. There seem to be at least two versions of it, one based on the first and the other on the second basic formulation of the <u>Categorical Imperative</u>.

Kantian (in ethics)
someone whose ethical views closely resemble those of Kant.

law of double negation
the view that the negation of a negative <u>proposition</u> or statement is equivalent to the proposition or statement in its positive form.

law of excluded middle
the view that either a <u>proposition</u> or statement is true or that it is false—one or the other but not both—at the same time and in the same respect.

law of nature
scientific law or general statement describing an invariable regularity among phenomena under certain conditions. Example: the law of gravity. The requirement or precept that we should act in certain ways (and refrain from acting in certain others), because these accord with (or go against) our nature or essence. Example: it is sometimes said that husband and wife should use the "rhythm" method if they fear pregnancy and they cannot abstain from sex.

maxim (in <u>Kant's ethics</u>)

a particular principle of action adopted by an individual, such as "Always keep your promises."

metaethical   of or relating to <u>metaethics</u>.

metaethics   that part of <u>ethics</u> dealing with the meaning of ethical terms, the nature of <u>morality</u>, moral language, discourse, and reasoning.

moral   of or relating to <u>morality</u>. Moral may be opposed to <u>immoral</u> or it may be contrasted with <u>nonmoral</u>.

moral action   in one sense, it is an action motivated at least in part by <u>moral reasons</u>. It is then contrasted with a <u>nonmoral action</u>, or one not motivated by any moral reasons. In another sense of the expression, a moral act is a morally right act. It is then contrasted with <u>immoral conduct</u>.

moral disagreement

a disagreement between two or more people, typically about what to do. At least one of the disputants must support his or her position with <u>moral reasons</u>.

moral judgment   judgment about actions, people, their character traits, intentions, motives, etc., resting on <u>moral reasons</u>.

moral principle   a principle that tells us what we may, should, must, or must not, do, morally speaking. Example: "You should always repay your loans."

moral problem   a <u>moral</u> dilemma, in which a person has one or more moral objections to at least one of the alternatives, which are usually actions. The objections are either objections to the action in itself or because it rules out another morally compelling alternative.

moral reason   a statement or judgment used in support of a <u>moral conclusion</u>. A value that motivates us to act morally.

moral value   see <u>moral reason</u>.

morality   a <u>moral</u> code or moral guide to life and conduct. Not every guide to life and conduct is a moral one.

morality has an external object
>the view that <u>morality</u> is simply an instrument for achieving some end, object, or purpose beyond itself. That is, <u>moral actions</u> and discourse are mere means to the bringing about of some state of affairs (the external object) that is only contingently connected to them. Contrasted with the view that <u>morality has only an internal object</u>.

morality has only an internal object
>moral actions and discourse are not mere means to some external object. Contrasted with the view that <u>morality has an external object</u>.

naturalistic fallacy
>the alleged fallacy or mistake of defining ethical terms by nonethical ones. G. E. Moore coined the expression. It would be less misleading to call this alleged fallacy the <u>definist mistake</u>. The notion of a naturalistic fallacy is also connected with the notion of a bifurcation between 'ought' and 'is', between value and fact, and between the normative and the descriptive. Thus it is said that you commit the naturalistic fallacy if you attempt to derive the Ought from the Is.

noncognitive theory
>one that maintains that <u>moral judgments</u> lack both <u>cognitive significance</u> and <u>truth-value</u> (they are noncognitive). Note that this does not make 'noncognitivism' synonymous with 'emotivism', for emotivism also contains the doctrine that value judgments function to express the judger's feelings and/or to arouse similar feelings in others. See <u>emotivism</u>.

noneudaemonistic theory
>one that denies that a person's greatest good is happiness or that happiness is the only thing that is good in itself.

nonmoral
>amoral. Not moral, in the sense of pertaining to or relating to <u>morality</u>.

nonmoral action
>an action motivated only by nonmoral considerations, not moral ones. Hence, in one sense, not a <u>moral action</u>.

nonsequitur   any <u>conclusion</u> (inference) that does not follow from
                its <u>premises</u>. Hence a fallacy or invalid <u>argument</u>.

normative   regulative, guiding; thus normative principles purport
                to offer guidance. Normative relates especially to
                what should or ought to be done.

normative judgments
                value judgments of all sorts, including <u>moral</u> ones.

normative systems of conduct
                any action-guide. It may or may not be <u>moral</u>.

objectivist theory
                a nonapprobative view that <u>moral judgments</u> have a
                <u>truth-value</u> and that it is possible to have a correct
                (or a mistaken) belief about what is morally right or
                wrong or good or bad.

ought-statement, categorical
                a statement or judgment of the form "We ought (or
                ought not) do so and so," for example, "We ought
                not to neglect our children," "You ought to have
                gone to your appointment." Distinguished from
                <u>ought-statement, hypothetical</u>.

ought-statement, hypothetical
                a   qualified   or   conditional   ought-statement.
                Examples: "If it hurts her feelings, you shouldn't do
                it." "You ought to take Michigan Avenue if you
                want   to   go   to   the   Capitol."   Cf. <u>imperative,</u>
                <u>hypothetical</u>.

philia   personal affection, fondness. Contrasted with <u>eros,</u>
                which is possessive love, and with <u>agape</u>, which in
                human beings is brotherly love when its object is
                other human beings.

philosopher, ordinary-language
                one who appeals to accepted linguistic practices or
                the way fluent, competent, and able users of the
                language use words and sentences, in order to
                describe their meaning and to dissolve traditional
                philosophical problems. Sometimes called "Oxford
                philosophy." Not to be confused with commonsense
                philosophy (see <u>philosopher, commonsense</u>).

philosopher, commonsense
                one who appeals to opinions or beliefs accepted by

people of "plain common sense," generally to refute philosophical views thought to be erroneous. Not to be confused with an ordinary-language philosopher (see philosopher, ordinary-language).

postulate   an assumption, presuppostion, or hypothesis asserted without proof but accepted as true.

premise   a statement assumed to be true, employed (usually together with at least one other such statement) to argue toward a conclusion.

premise major   in a categorical syllogism, the premise that contains the term that is the predicate of the conclusion. Thus "All men are mortal" is the major premise in the syllogism "All men are mortal. Socrates is a man. Therefore, Socrates is mortal."

premise, minor   in a categorical syllogism, the premise that contains the term that is the subject of the conclusion. Thus, in the above syllogism, "Socrates is a man" is the minor premise.

prescriptivism (in ethics)
the view that moral terms are used, not for persuading, but for commending and prescribing, functions which are not to be confused either with describing or persuading. Moral terms are used to tell people to do or to prefer something.

prescriptivist   someone who views moral utterances as a species of prescriptive discourse. Hare is a prescriptivist. He finds it illuminating to compare and contrast moral utterances with another form of prescriptive discourse, namely, imperatives. He thinks moral judgments (as well as all value judgments) are universalizable, unlike singular imperatives.

prima facie   at first sight. Contrasted with 'actual'.

prima facie duty (Ross)
a duty regarded as self-evident and that is your actual duty if no other prima facie duty conflicts with it and that may sometimes be your actual duty even if other prima facie duties do conflict with it. Example: we have a prima facie duty to relieve distress.

proof	demonstration. In logic and math, the series of <u>arguments</u> based on the rules of inference of logic and math that are used to derive the <u>conclusion</u> from the <u>premises</u>.
proof, indirect	a <u>proof</u> which supposes the negation of what it sets out to prove; it shows that a <u>contradiction</u> can be derived from this supposition and what is known; hence it concludes that the supposed statement must be false and its negation, or the positive statement, true. Cf. <u>reductio ad absurdum</u>.
proposition	a sentence or statement that asserts or denies something, or what is asserted or denied. It is usually thought to have two possible <u>truth-values</u>, true or false.

psychological egoism
      see <u>egoism, psychological</u>.

qua	in the capacity or character of; as.
reason	statement or judgment used in support of a <u>conclusion</u> or to explain or to justify purposive actions.

reductio ad absurdum
      an <u>argument</u> that demonstrates (indirectly) that a statement is true by showing that its negation leads to an absurd, unacceptable, or a contradictory <u>conclusion</u>. An indirect proof (see <u>proof, indirect</u>).

rule-deontologist
      a "<u>deontologist</u>" with regard to rules rather than acts; that is, one who holds that the validity of a moral rule, <u>maxim</u>, or principle, is not determined solely by whether following it promotes the good. Cf. and contrast <u>deontologist</u>.

skepticism (moral)
      the philosophical position of one who maintains that knowledge about what is morally right (or wrong) is not possible.

solution to a moral problem
      the decision to do one of the things that is unacceptable to someone. Or the decision to do something acceptable to someone but incompatible with some other thing he or she approves of. And

the decision is made on the basis of <u>moral</u> or other deeply cherished values and beliefs.

Sophists   Itinerant educators who toured the cities of Greece in the fifth century B.C. Protagoras was the most famous of the Sophists.

statement, analytic

a statement true or false because of the meanings given the words in the statement. Hence it needs no verification in experience. Example: "A bachelor is an adult unmarried male."

statement, factual

a statement that attempts to say something true about "the world," about the way things are. It can be true or false but it is neither a <u>tautology</u>, an analytic statement (see <u>statement, analytic</u>), nor a mathematical statement.

statement, identity

a statement of the form "$\underline{a} = \underline{b}$," where '$\underline{a}$' and '$\underline{b}$' are either proper names or <u>definite descriptions</u> (something of the form "the such and such"). Example: "Marilyn Monroe is the woman who married Jim Dougherty, Joe DiMaggio, and Arthur Miller."

subjectivism   the view that a particular action is morally right (or wrong) if and only if some individual thinks or believes that it is morally right (or wrong). Individual or specific variants of subjectivism suppose that 'some individual' can be replaced by a proper name or <u>definite description</u>. General or universal variants of subjectivism take 'some individual' to means any individual.

syllogism   a valid <u>deductive argument</u> that consists of a major <u>premise</u>, a minor premise, and a <u>conclusion</u>, often used to prove a conclusion by showing that it follows from known premises. The word is often restricted to the case where both premises and the conclusion are categorical <u>propositions</u> which have between them three, and only three, terms. Example: "Every virtue is laudable. Kindness is a virtue. Therefore kindness is laudable." See <u>premise, major</u> and <u>premise, minor</u>.

tautology   something true no matter what state the world is in. Example: "All white swans are white." Cf. and

and only if of all the actions open to us it is likely
to maximize, or in fact maximizes, the happiness of
all sentient beings.

utilitarianism, hedonistic (in its act–utilitarian form)
the view that a particular action is morally right if
and only if it actually or probably produces at least
as great a balance of pleasure over pain as any
alternative action open to the agent.

utilitarian, "ideal" (in its act–utilitarian form)
a nonhedonistic and noneudaemonistic form of act
utilitarianism. This view typically stresses that
there are many things that are intrinsically good
besides pleasure, happiness, and avoiding pain—for
example, knowledge, friendship, beauty, and
appreciation of beauty. You should consider all the
things that are intrinsically good (bad and
indifferent) when determining what is the morally
right (wrong) thing to do.

utilitarianism, restricted
see utilitarianism, rule.

utilitarianism, rule
the view that a particular act is morally right if and
only if it is required by a rule that, if adopted,
would produce, or probably produce, at least as much
good as the adoption of some alternative rule. The
rule need not be hedonistic or eudaemonistic, though
it may be either. Sometimes called restricted
utilitarianism.

value, extrinsic or instrumental
the value that something has because it is a means
to something intrinsically good. Things of
instrumental value need not be of intrinsic or
ultimate value, but they may be. Contrast value,
intrinsic or ultimate.

value, intrinsic or ultimate
the value of something worthwhile on its own
account and not merely as a means. Contrasted
with instrumental and extrinsic value (value, extrinsic
and instrumental) and good, extrinsic and
instrumental.

value, taking a consideration to be of ultimate or intrinsic
people take a consideration to be of ultimate or

intrinsic value if they regard it as a fundamental and terminating consideration; they see it as something important, valuable, or desirable in itself or for its own sake, and not merely as being good as a means, or as merely having extrinsic or instrumental value; finally, their not being able to justify their claim that the consideration is important in itself does not make them have any doubts about its importance.

INDEX

Abortions, 107, 127-28
Act utilitarianism, xii, 60, 89-100
  eudaemonistic, 90, 91, 94-100
  hedonistic, 89-100
  ideal, 89, 91-100
  objection that it is immoral, 96-99
  objection that it involves a double standard, 99-100
  problem about what is good, 91-93
  problem of knowing what is morally right, 94-96
  rule utilitarianism reducible to it, 101-102
Acting morally, 73, 88, 114
  contrasted with acting as if moral, 135
Acting on God's will, whether it is acting morally, 135. See also Divine-command theory
Agape, human. See Agapism; Love
Agapism, xii, 60, 117-26
  Confucianism, 117
  contrasted with utilitarianism, 118
  focuses on the motives of the act, 118
  Mohism, 117
  objection that agape is not our only moral value, 122-23
  objection that it disregards morally relevant considerations, 121-22
  objection that it condones unjust acts, 118
  objection that it provides no moral guidance, 115-16, 118-19
  objection that it violates the dictum that 'ought' implies 'can', 123-25
  problem about animals, 120-21
  question whether all people deserve to be loved, 119-20
Agapist. See Agapism
Allen, Woody, 24
American Civil Liberties Union, 68
Amoralist. See Amoral or Nonmoral person
Amoral or nonmoral person, 20-21, 37-40, 141-42
Analytic statement. See Statement, analytic
Anderson, Robert, 4
Animals, whether morality applies to them, 10, 90, 120-22
Anscombe, G. E. M., 42
Appeal-to-nature doctrine, xii, 7, 60, 102-108
  interpreted as an approbative theory, 103-105
    Euthyphro objection, 104
    objection that it is nonsensical or anthropomorphic, 103-104
    objection that it gives no guidance, 104-105
  interpreted as a nonapprobative theory, 105-108
    objection that it gives no guidance, 107-108

Du Nouy, Lecomte. See Lecomte du Nouy
Duration of pleasures and pains, 94.
  See also Hedonistic calculus
Durocher, Leo, 139

Edwards, Paul, 106
Egoism. See Ethical egoism; Psychological egoism
Eliot, T. S., 26
Emerson, Ralph Waldo, 4, 40, 124, 138
Emotive theory of ethics. See Emotivism
Emotivism, 25, 65, 127.
  See also Ayer, A. J.; Stevenson, Charles
Empirical claims, 50.
  See also Sciences, reasoning in
Empirical sciences, 49
  reasoning in, 49-52
End in itself. See Values, intrinsic;
  Values, ultimate
Enthymeme, 33. See also Syllogism
Epictetus, 102-103
Ethical conventionalism. See Conventionalism
Ethical egoism, xii, 60, 82-88
  objection that it is not an ethical doctrine, 39, 87-88
  objection that it is morally and psychologically
    unacceptable, 84-87
  problem about benefit and self-interest, 84
    eudaemonistic answer, 84
    hedonistic answer, 84
    Rand's answer, 84
    self-realization answer, 84
  two forms of
    impersonal, 83
    personal, 82-83
      problem of who is to be the key individual, 84
Ethical subjectivism. See Subjectivism
Ethical theories, 61-125
  approbative, 63-80
    golden rule, 71-74
    conventionalism, 64-71
    divine-command theory, 74-80
    subjectivism, 64-71
  axiological theories, 97-98
  deontological theories, 98, 108-125, 129-31
  emotivism, 25, 28
  objectivist theories, 81-125, 128-29, 129-31
    appeal to nature for moral guidance, 102-108
    agapism, 114-25
    ethical egoism, 82-88
    intuitionism, 25, 81-82, 127-31
    Kant's ethics, 108-125
    utilitarianism, 89-102

I Chih, 117
Ideal utilitarianism. See Act utilitarianism, ideal;
    Act utilitarianism, rule utilitarianism reducible to it
Identity, statements of. See Statements, identity
Impersonal ethical egoism. See Ethical egoism,
    two forms of, impersonal
Indirect duties to animals, 120-21. See also
    Animals; Kant's ethics, second version; Agapism
Individual ethical conventionalism. See
    Conventionalism, individual variants of
Individual ethical egoism. See Ethical egoism,
    two forms of, personal
Individual ethical subjectivism. See
    Subjectivism, individual variants of
Indefinability of good
    Moore's argument from simplicity, 92
    Moore's "open question" argument, 92-93
"Inner-directed" people, 64
Instrumental values. See Values, instrumental;
    Values, means to an end; Values, extrinsic
Intensional equivalence, 75-78
Intensionality of belief. See Beliefs,
    intensionality of
Intensionality of desire. See Desires,
    intensionality of
Intension, 75-76
Intensity of pleasures and pains, 94.
    See also Hedonistic calculus
Interest theories, 63. See also
    Approbative theories
Intrinsic goods. See Values, intrinsic;
    Values, ultimate
Intrinsic values. See Values, intrinsic;
    Values, ultimate
Intuition, knowing what is right or wrong by, 130
Intuitionism, 25, 50, 81-82, 127-31
    in mathematics, 50-51
    Moore's. See Moore, G. E.
    objectivist form author defends, xii, 127-31, 136-37
    Prichard's. See Prichard, H. A.
    Rawls's conception of, 127
    Ross's. See Ross, Sir David
Intuitions of ends that intrinsically good, 89, 93-94
Intuitive faculty, 130

James, Henry, 57
James, William, 63, 119
Jehovah's Witnesses, 8-9, 13, 15, 16, 23
Jesus Christ, 47, 121
Jones, James H., 38-39

Noncognitive theory of ethics, 25. <u>See also</u>
    Emotivism

Objectivist theories and views, xii, 81–125
    agapism, 117–25. <u>See also</u> Kant's ethics,
        second version
    appeal-to-nature doctrine, 105–108
    assume truth in morals, 81
    emotivism not an objectivist view, 81
    ethical egoism, 82–88
    how they view moral disputes, 81
    intuitionism usually objectivist, 81–82, 127–28
    Kant's ethics, 108–125
    nonapprobative, 81
    presupposes no theory of truth, 81
    utilitarianism, 89–102
Oedipus, 69–70. <u>See also</u> Subjectivism;
    Belief, intensionality of
Ordinary-language philosophers, 130–31
Original sin
    one sense of that doctrine that is true, 20
"Other-directed" people, 64
'Ought' implies 'can', 108, 123–25
Ought statements. <u>See</u> Statements, ought
Outka, Gene, 122

Pain, avoidance of, 90.
    <u>See also</u> Act utilitarianism, hedonistic;
    Moral reasons
Pascal, Blaise, 106
Paton, H. J., 109
Peacock, 115
Pegis, Anton, 76
Peirce, Benjamin, 50
Peirce, Charles Sanders, 50
Pennock, J. Roland, 23
Percy, Walker, 106
Perelman, S. J., 118
Perry, Ralph Barton, 63
Personal ethical egoism. <u>See</u> Ethical egoism,
    personal
Persons, 121
Phillips, D. Z., 134
Philosophical accounts
    when descriptively adequate, 44–47
Picasso, Pablo, 38
"Plain man," the, 130–31
Plato, 74–76, 139
Pleasure, 89–96. <u>See also</u> Hedonistic calculus
Plurality of principles, priority rules for, 127
Polyandry, 107

Respect for human life, 8, 27; for the dead, 26;
for persons, 26-27, 115-16, 118-119, 122-23, 125, 139
two senses of 'respect for people', 119-20.
See also Moral reasons
Restricted utilitarianism. See Rule utilitarianism
Restriction on ultimate values, 41, 43-45. See also
Moral reasons, author's account of
Revolutions in science, 51-52. See also
Sciences, reasoning in
Rhees, Rush, 59, 134
Riesman, David, 64
Rooney, Mickey, 36
Ross, Sir David, 81, 109, 127-31. See also
Intuitionism; Deontology, moderate
Rule utilitarianism, xii, 91, 101-102
reduces to act utilitarianism, 101-102
Russell, Bertrand, 89, 94

Sandburg, Carl, 124
Sanders, S. M., 82
Sartre, Jean-Paul, 3-4, 85
Schurz, Carl, 125
Schwarzkogler, 72, 129
Sciences
controversies in, 49-52
criteria for doing good or bad science, 51-52
empirical, 49
formal or nonempirical, 49
mistakes in, contrasted with moral mistakes, 136
"normal" as opposed to "revolutionary," 51-52
questions in, contrasted with everyday
empirical questions, 50
reasoning in, 49—52
contrasted with moral reasoning, 51-52
reasons in, 49-52, 137. See Nonmoral reasons
Self-evidence, 25, 129-30
Self-interest, 84. See also Ethical egoism,
problem about benefit
Sellars, W., 89, 93, 113
Seneca, 102
Shackelton, Robert, 90
Shakespeare, William, 5-7, 14, 17, 22, 24, 30, 51,
56, 63, 84, 131-32, 136
Shaw, George Bernard, 72, 120,
Shelley, Percy, 119
Sidgwick, Henry, 67, 86, 90, 96, 100, 128
Singer, Peter, 121, 140
Skepticism about morality, 132-33
Smart, John J. C., 90
Smith, Logan Pearsall, 111
Smith, S. A., 82

Sociobiologists, 140
Socrates, 74-76, 139
Sophists, 63
Sophocles, 47, 69-70, 122
Spencer, Herbert, 103, 138
Stalin, 58, 67
Statements
  analytic, 31, 34, 40, 113
  categorical, 31
    ought, 31, 35-37
  empirical. See Statements, factual
  factual, 29, 31, 35-37, 45-46
  hypothetical, 31-32
  identity, 69-70
  mathematical, 31, 40
  ought, 31-32
  tautological, 31, 34, 40
Steinem, Gloria, 107
Stevenson, Charles L., 24, 28-31, 35, 40, 81, 127
  his analysis of moral reasons, 28-31
Stevenson, Robert Louis, 59
Stoics, contrasted with Christians, 123-24
Strachey, James, 119
Subjectivism, xii, 63-71
  objection that it is circular if definitional, 64-65
  general variant of, 67-68
    objection that it leads to the conclusion
      that anything goes, 67
    objection that it leads to a contradiction
      given the facts, 67-68
  individual form of, 66-67
    objection that it is counterintuitive, 66
    objection that it could be used to
      justify immoral acts, 66-67
  relativistic variants of, 68-71
    problem about agreements and disagreements, 70-71
    reductio ad absurdum of, based on the
      intensionality of belief, 68-70
Suicide, Kant on, 112
Sutherland, James, 115
Syllogism, 31-37
  enthymeme, 33

Taoism, 102. See also Appeal-to-nature doctrine
Tautology, 31, 32. See also Statements,
  tautological; Statements, analytic
Tefler, Elizabeth, 121
Theresa of Calcutta, Mother, 67, 124
Thomas Aquinas, Saint, 76, 103, 107, 120
Thoreau, Henry David, 67, 102, 107
Tolstoy, Leo, 48, 105, 136